ADVANCE PRAISE FOR *THE GANG'S ALL QUEER*

"With deep understanding and brash wit—Vanessa Panfil's own and that of the gay gang members whose voices pop from these pages—*The Gang's All Queer* cuts through all sorts of false assumptions about gangs, gay men, masculinities, and sexualities. Panfil's account is complex, vibrant, surprising, and moving."
 —Joshua Gamson, author of *Modern Families: Stories of Extraordinary Journeys to Kinship*

"Panfil's work is a well-researched new and innovative contribution to the gang literature that fills an important gap in both criminological and sociological treatments of transgression. This book deserves to be read widely and used as an antidote to the hackneyed stereotypes that still constitute much of the discourse in this sub-field."
 —David Brotherton, author of *Youth Street Gangs: A Critical Appraisal*

"There is so much that is fascinating, original, and important about this book. . . . It rejuvenates and invigorates our thinking about masculinity and queer theory, and it is a breath of fresh air for gang scholarship. This revolutionary and honest work is sure to enliven most courses in criminology or sociology, stir surprise and debates in students, and endure in their memory for years to come."
 —Robert Garot, author of *Who You Claim: Performing Gang Identity in School and on the Streets*

"Offering powerful ethnographic evidence that homosexual sex practices and queer subjectivities extend to all realms of social life, *The Gang's All Queer* poses a much-needed challenge to criminologists' inattention to the complexities of gender and sexuality within gangs. Panfil's analysis raises timely and provocative questions about the social construction of crime and the very definition of gangs themselves."
 —Jane Ward, author of *Not Gay: Sex between Straight White Men*

ALTERNATIVE CRIMINOLOGY SERIES

General Editor: Jeff Ferrell

Pissing on Demand: Workplace Drug Testing and the Rise of the Detox Industry
Ken Tunnell

Empire of Scrounge: Inside the Urban Underground of Dumpster Diving, Trash Picking, and Street Scavenging
Jeff Ferrell

Prison, Inc.: A Convict Exposes Life inside a Private Prison
by K.C. Carceral, edited by Thomas J. Bernard

The Terrorist Identity: Explaining the Terrorist Threat
Michael P. Arena and Bruce A. Arrigo

Terrorism as Crime: From Oklahoma City to Al-Qaeda and Beyond
Mark S. Hamm

Our Bodies, Our Crimes: The Policing of Women's Reproduction in America
Jeanne Flavin

Graffiti Lives: Beyond the Tag in New York's Urban Underground
Gregory J. Snyder

Crimes of Dissent: Civil Disobedience, Criminal Justice, and the Politics of Conscience
Jarret S. Lovell

The Culture of Punishment: Prison, Society, and Spectacle
Michelle Brown

Who You Claim: Performing Gang Identity in School and on the Streets
Robert Garot

5 Grams: Crack Cocaine, Rap Music, and the War on Drugs
Dimitri A. Bogazianos

Judging Addicts: Drug Courts and Coercion in the Justice System
Rebecca Tiger

Courting Kids: Inside an Experimental Youth Court
Carla J. Barrett

The Spectacular Few: Prisoner Radicalization and the Evolving Terrorist Threat
Mark S. Hamm

Comic Book Crime: Truth, Justice, and the American Way
Nickie D. Phillips and Staci Strobl

The Securitization of Society: Crime, Risk, and Social Order
Marc Schuilenburg

Covered in Ink: Tattoos, Women, and the Politics of the Body
Beverly Yuen Thompson

Narrative Criminology: Understanding Stories of Crime
Edited by Lois Presser and Sveinung Sandberg

Progressive Punishment: Job Loss, Jail Growth and the Neoliberal Logic of Carceral Expansion
Judah Schept

Meth Wars: Police, Media, Power
Travis Linneman

Hacked: A Radical Approach to Hacker Culture and Crime
Kevin F. Steinmetz

The Gang's All Queer: The Lives of Gay Gang Members
Vanessa R. Panfil

The Gang's All Queer

The Lives of Gay Gang Members

Vanessa R. Panfil

NEW YORK UNIVERSITY PRESS
New York

NEW YORK UNIVERSITY PRESS
New York
www.nyupress.org

References to Internet websites (URLs) were accurate at the time of writing. Neither the author nor New York University Press is responsible for URLs that may have expired or changed since the manuscript was prepared.

ISBN: 978-1-4798-0520-4 (hardback)
ISBN: 978-1-4798-7002-8 (paperback)

For Library of Congress Cataloging-in-Publication data, please contact the Library of Congress.

New York University Press books are printed on acid-free paper, and their binding materials are chosen for strength and durability. We strive to use environmentally responsible suppliers and materials to the greatest extent possible in publishing our books.

Manufactured in the United States of America

10 9 8 7 6 5 4 3 2 1

Also available as an ebook

For the victims and survivors of the Pulse Orlando shooting, and everyone who dares to live out loud.

CONTENTS

ACKNOWLEDGMENTS

Data collection for this study was supported in part by two financial awards from the University at Albany's Initiatives for Women, specifically the Karen R. Hitchcock New Frontiers Fund. This book was completed because I received support from the School of Criminal Justice at the University at Albany, the School of Criminal Justice at Rutgers University-Newark, and the Department of Sociology and Criminal Justice at Old Dominion University. I especially thank my colleagues and the doctoral students at ODU for their encouragement as I revised and finished this book. Cheers also go to the professional development/writing groups I've been a part of: Academic Pursuit at UAlbany and the "J-Team" at Rutgers.

I have been fortunate to have stellar mentorship. Jody Miller deserves much praise for reading many drafts (probably too many to count) of this manuscript, providing valuable comments, and helping me find my voice as a queer and feminist scholar. I am always in awe of Jody's critical and constructive eye. Dana Peterson advocated for me as I conducted this research and writing, and had faith in my ability to complete this project even when my own was wavering. I am inspired by her "onward and upward" spirit. Jamie Fader was influential in the design of my study and instrument, and helped me problem-solve often. Frankie Bailey helped me think through popular culture and historical representations.

I also consider myself very lucky to be part of a vibrant community of queer criminology scholars committed to social change. I am particularly appreciative for my dear friends Allyson Walker, Aimee Wodda, and Jordan Blair Woods, who read drafts and talked through difficult decisions with me. They have been excellent compasses in my scholarship and my life, and I treasure them. For needed breaks from or tireless encouragement for book writing, I thank my good friends Heidi Grundetjern, Chris Smith, Rose Bellandi, Raquel Derrick, Amy Hayter,

Michelle Hand-Lang, Alison Reed, Elizabeth Groeneveld, Topher Lawton, and Seigo Nishijima. It is truly a gift to be surrounded by positive, caring people.

In Columbus, my siblings, nieces, and nephews always warmly welcomed me home. They bring me so much joy! I miss them daily. I am especially grateful to my parents, Peter and Rachel Panfil, for being infinitely supportive of my queer activism and scholarship. I am beyond thrilled when they talk about my work with such pride.

At NYU Press, editor Ilene Kalish has my sincere gratitude for all of her work on this book, and her boundless enthusiasm for it. Thanks also go to Caelyn Cobb for editorial assistance. The manuscript was improved by reviews from Valerie Jenness, Wesley Crichlow, Robert Garot, and two other, anonymous reviewers. I also thank Jeff Ferrell for including me in the Alternative Criminology series, and for his and Clinton Sanders's call for a queered cultural criminology over 20 years ago.

Finally, I am eternally grateful to the 53 men who participated in my study, and to others who helped connect us. Thank you for sharing not only your words and experiences, but your fears, dreams, humor, and wisdom with me. I learned just as much about myself during this process as I learned about you. I will express my gratitude to you by always working to improve the lives of queer young people.

Portions of this book appear in these previous works of mine: "Better Left Unsaid? The Role of Agency in Queer Criminological Research," *Critical Criminology* 22(1): 99–111; "Gay Gang- and Crime-Involved Men's Experiences with Homophobic Bullying and Harassment in Schools," *Journal of Crime and Justice* 37(1): 79–103; "'I Will Fight You Like I'm Straight': Gay Gang- and Crime-Involved Men's Participation in Violence," in *Handbook of LGBT Communities, Crime, and Justice*, edited by Dana Peterson and Vanessa R. Panfil, 121–145, New York: Springer; "Queer Anomalies? Overcoming Assumptions in Criminological Research with Gay Men," in *Qualitative Research in Criminology (Advances in Criminological Theory, Vol. 20)*, edited by Jody Miller and Wilson R. Palacios, 169–189, New Brunswick, NJ: Transaction Publishers; *Socially Situated Identities of Gay Gang- and Crime-Involved Men*, University at Albany; (with Jody Miller), "Feminist and Queer Perspectives on Qualitative Methods," in *Routledge Handbook of Qualitative Criminology*, edited by Heith Copes and J. Mitchell Miller, 32–48, New York: Routledge.

Seeking "Homo Thugs"

A defining moment in my life occurred near the end of my college career. After several years of frequent LGBTQ activism, I began to be invited to speak at community workshops and in schools regarding the challenges facing LGBTQ youth, as well as their resilience. One afternoon, several of us spoke to a college class of future teachers and school counselors. I mentioned that neighborhood concerns could also affect school performance, such as in the case of young gay men who are involved in crime or gangs.

"A homo thug!" one of the students called out. "They're called homo thugs now," he declared with certainty and a smile. A sly, knowing smile. The class snickered, but I met his eyes.

I looked at his basketball jersey, his doo rag, his close-shaven goatee.

"Homo thugs," I repeated. "I'll remember that," and smiled back.

By the end of that year, I sent in my graduate school applications and made it clear that I wanted to study gay gang members. My path was set.

This book is just one bend in a long and winding road. At the beginning of my senior year of high school, I became involved with several LGBTQ advocacy groups in Columbus, Ohio. Just a few months prior, the U.S. Supreme Court had struck down all remaining domestic sodomy laws with *Lawrence v. Texas*, but many states, including my home state of Ohio, had few, if any, protections for LGBTQ people in the realms of employment, housing, adoption, child custody, healthcare, marriage, or school-based bullying.

My civic participation impressed upon me the realities that many young queer people face with regard to homophobic school climates, families who react negatively to their identities, street harassment, and other harmful experiences that can lead to increased substance abuse, mental health concerns, and suicide. Adolescence is already a difficult time for many, featuring tumultuous romantic relationships, schoolyard trials, and growing pains. I was certainly going through those myself. For urban queer youth, these can be complicated by struggling school districts and neighborhood disorder, which can make our identities feel like another liability; a source of uncertainty instead of a source of pride. Luckily, Columbus youth could access a visible, vocal, and vibrant urban queer community, which included bars and cafes as well as community outreach organizations. We'd stay as late as we could until they closed, carded us, or kicked us out for being too rowdy.

One of the organizations I became involved with was a drop-in center for gay, lesbian, bisexual, questioning, and transgender youth and allies ages 12–20; it also offered opportunities to get involved with LGBTQ advocacy. During my years with the center, their demographic was primarily urban, non-white kids who received additional services from other community agencies or the state. Many were also in the process of questioning their sexuality and/or gender identity, and coming out as gay, lesbian, bisexual, transgender, or another "queer-spectrum" sexual or gender identity. There were some who we would not see for weeks or months at a time, only to later find out that one had been detained for assaulting a staff member at a group home; another had been removed from the only foster parent he had ever lived with who had acknowledged his gay identity. As a member of the center's Youth Advisory Board, I was part of the first discussions the center had ever had about youth who came to it with knives or guns. While we wanted to maintain a safe space for everyone, we knew some youth felt they needed these implements for protection against the world outside the center, and had to create policies to deal with this reality. In light of these situations, I started to think about how the class, race, and sexuality of young people combined to shape their lives, specifically regarding their choices to join gangs, fight, sell drugs, and sometimes even sell sex. Their life experiences were vastly different than my own as a white, middle-class, queer woman, and I needed to learn more.

My research was borne of my efforts to do just that. Shortly after I began graduate school, I reached out to people I knew when I lived in Columbus to see if they'd be interested in talking to me about being a gay gang member. Although I did have some trouble with my initial recruitment, I didn't seem to have much difficulty establishing rapport with participants, despite some concern I would. Because my sex, race, or education level could have discouraged them from sharing certain details of their lives with me, our shared knowledge as young queer people helped participants to feel that the social differences between us were not so great because I, in a way, spoke their language (both literally and figuratively). I understood their narratives of feeling "different" from a very young age. I understood the process of coming out as a seemingly neverending series of personal disclosures (with varying levels of risk associated with each, though many are fairly innocuous and without negative consequences). And I understood the struggle to live as an openly gay person while steering clear of pitfalls such as drugs, "drama," and even death. When participants didn't feel the need to elaborate on a gay-related concept, they would sometimes say, "You're gay, you understand." Of course I still always pressed for detail, because I could not presume that I did know what they meant in light of our social differences on dimensions such as biological sex, race, and class, but indeed, I often did understand.

There were also many moments of nostalgia during my data collection, especially related to Columbus's queer scene. Depending on who was working that night, some of the gay establishments would allow underage patrons to stay until 11 p.m. or midnight; others would let them stay at all hours as long as they didn't cause trouble. These places were an oasis where LGBTQ youth could get a taste of the nightlife before coming of age, since no other bars/clubs in Columbus carved out space for them. There were teen clubs, but I can hardly imagine it being easy for young queer people to dance with and show affection to same-sex romantic partners there. The "gay scene" provided opportunities for queer kids from all over the city to connect, as did the LGBTQ community agencies. Many of the men in this study named specific establishments or organizations in their interviews, and we had moments of longing for our teen years, an establishment or organization that had come under new management or leadership, or one that had closed. Or, alternatively, we'd make a plan to go to one of the places that was still open and thriving, and sometimes, we did actually go together.

Despite that piece of friendly advice years ago, most of my participants don't actually use the term "homo thug," partially because they resist claiming identities as "thugs," and some are not out to their gangs, limiting their public usage of self-identifiers such as "homo." I hope that even this nugget about the men I spoke with helps illustrate what this book is about: highlighting the identities and experiences of gay gang- and crime-involved young men, both challenging and providing further nuance to what we think we know about urban gay men and the ways they form close bonds and negotiate complex lives.

These days, it may seem like the necessary quest for respectable identity and acceptance for LGBTQ people has come to an end. I have met plenty of people who have never heard of the Stonewall Riots, but have definitely heard of Neil Patrick Harris. Gays and lesbians can serve openly in the military, and the Supreme Court has ruled that same-sex marriage is legal throughout the United States. However, these victo- ries largely represent assimilationist ideals, and benefit some groups' interests or desires far more than others. Our fight is far from over. We should be concerned with the lived realities of LGBTQ young people, many of whom already experience marginalization on the basis of their race or ethnicity, their refusal to fit within society's expectations for their gender presentation, the acts they commit in order to feed and clothe themselves, or the ways they literally fight back against violence. What of these young people, who still experience harassment, assault, and exclusion of many forms? How are we to understand how they both respond to and resist this exclusion, especially if we don't ask? We cer- tainly had better start trying.

Introduction

Real Men, Real Gangs

Before our interview, I had been told that 28-year-old James[1] was "a real thug." I had also heard he was "a gangbanger," "a Blood," "in and out of jail," "tatted up," and "a drug dealer," but I still wasn't quite sure what to expect. True to form, he had several visible tattoos of his gang's symbols and colors, as well as a version of its name. To further show his loyalty, he was dressed almost head-to-toe in red: red shirt, red leather sports jacket, red shoes, but dark gray jeans. He wore his hair in dreads, but they had grown out from his scalp somewhat. I started by asking him about his family growing up, to which he exclaimed, "Family, fuck that." He proceeded to tell me about a difficult childhood that included his father's absence and his own physical and sexual abuse. I then asked about his neighborhood, which he described as "rough," violent, and riddled with drug activity. He went so far as to suggest, "somebody can die right in front of you, and like, it's just another day." Fatalistically, he described his negative experiences growing up as "typical Black male shit."

With 12 years of gang involvement under his belt, James had one of the longest gang histories of all my research participants; three of those years were spent in prison. During the interview, he pulled out a palm-sized bag of weed and began to roll blunts (marijuana cigars) and smoke them, his speech sometimes becoming muffled because he was trying to speak without exhaling. I learned that he also sold weed, and he described it as the job he used to support his son, though he mentioned that he wanted to stop spending money on "stupid shit" and become an "entrepreneur" by starting his own small business.

This scene isn't unique for gang researchers. Stories of neighborhood conflict, participation in violence, drug selling, and incarceration are common in our work. However, James and I also spent time discussing how he came to realize that he was attracted to other men, his long-term relationship with his boyfriend, and his desire to come out as bisexual to his family of origin and his fellow gang members, all of whom were heterosexual. It would seem that this wrinkle *does* make James's story unique, as there is virtually no research that has documented the lived experiences of gay gang members. On the contrary, however, James wasn't the first of my research participants to share these revelations: he was referred to my study by his boyfriend, who was also involved with another straight street gang, and I had already interviewed dozens of other gay or bisexual gang members. In fact, there were a few other gay gang members in the apartment waiting for us to finish up the interview, and several more who would join us later that evening to attend a hip hop–themed night at a local gay club.

I should note that this is not a case of queer[2] Columbus exceptionalism: "homo thugs" and gay gang- and crime-involved men have been referenced and depicted in documentaries, television series, reality shows, music, and print media over the last several decades, probably the most well-known being Omar Little from *The Wire*. It's just that they have received little to no attention in scholarly works, and thus are poorly understood and incompletely portrayed.

After the interview, we joined the rest of the guys in the living room. James went to the fridge and cracked open a Budweiser. I couldn't help wondering if this was his drink of choice because of the red label. He slowly paced between the kitchen and the living room, beer in one hand, his other hand near his low waistband, and still never took off his coat. This all made me think he wasn't completely at ease with this crowd, or was on his way out the door. Despite this, he participated in the conversation somewhat, though his contributions were less animated than those offered by the other speakers. His boyfriend, Spiderman, walked by and quietly said something to him. They went into the hallway, out of view of almost everyone else, presumably to talk privately. I happened to see them sneak a quick kiss so I immediately looked away, feeling as though I saw something intimate that I was not meant to see. They joined us in the living room shortly afterward.

Later that evening, several members of the Royal Family, an all-gay gang with at least 15 members, came over to eat the dinner Ricky cooked before we headed to the club. James had left by that point. One of the Royal Family's members is Imani, a 21-year-old African American man

I've known since he was 15 or 16. We had met in 2006 at the LGBTQ drop-in youth center. Although I am several years older than he is, at the time we met, we were both seeking services and opportunities for gay activism; this is also true for the other members of the initial group of participants in my study. This youth center is located in Columbus, Ohio, the city where I grew up and where I recruited these young men to participate in this study.

One of my earliest memories of Imani was when he came to the center and told us about a confrontation with several young men on his way home from school. After two instances of their harassing him for being gay, following him, and attempting to jump him, he felt compelled to fight back. During this fight, Imani ended up cutting one of the assailants. I had not thought about this incident in several years, until he recounted the story in detail during his interview a couple of months prior to this particular evening. Imani had recently joined the Royal Family after a chance physical encounter with a group of college-aged men who harassed him and his friends, calling them "faggots" and following them on a public street in a gay-friendly part of town. Several of his relatives were deeply immersed in street gangs, but he had never joined these groups. He supported himself financially with small-time hustles and help from his parents, with whom he lived and who were fully aware of his sexual orientation. On the weekends, Imani competed in a semi-underground dance scene, referred to by different people as "vogue," "ballroom," or just "balls," where he typically wore gender-bending outfits. He had even "dressed up" in women's clothes to sell sex. He always has been talkative, boisterous, and flamboyant, which belies his willingness to fiercely defend himself and his friends.

James and Imani—and their gangs—clearly are very different from each other, but on the whole, they each share many similar experiences with other young men in gangs. However, their gay sexual identities complicate criminology's portraits of gangs, gang members, and gang life. Although gay gang- and crime-involved men have entered the broader consciousness thanks to popular culture, criminology scholars remain stuck in a "heterosexual imaginary"[3] where assumed heterosexuality is not questioned, where queer folks don't exist, and the possibility of men such as James, Imani, and Omar seems at best unlikely and at worst, impossible.

This book is a response to two specific assumptions that pervade much of the existing criminological research: first, that male gang members and active offenders are exclusively heterosexual; and second, that gang membership and violence are ways to construct stereotypical masculine and heterosexual identities only, typically at the expense of women/girls, gay men, and folks who don't seem to follow society's gender "rules." These assumptions likely have resulted from the association of violence and other criminal behavior with traditional scripts of masculinity.[4] In many ways, illegal pursuits such as street robbery and violence are described, by criminologists and many perpetrators themselves, as essentially "masculine games."[5] More specifically, street gangs are regarded as hypermasculine groups,[6] and may even have prohibitions against same-sex sexual activity.[7] Indeed, some of the early and influential works in criminology, such as Walter Miller's articulation of his "focal concerns" theory,[8] outline how gay bashing, using "fag" and "queer" as epithets, and an expressed disdain for effeminacy (often associated with gayness) are components of the masculine toughness valued by delinquent peer groups. These scholarly works exist alongside cultural stereotypes of gay men as effeminate pacifists, which have also influenced where they *do* appear in criminological texts: as victims of anti-gay bias crimes, homophobic bullying in schools, and intimate partner violence. Additionally, historian Allen Bérubé argues that the political strategies used by the mainstream gay rights movement perpetuate stereotypes of gay men as white and middle class to win "credibility, acceptance, and integration."[9] All of these influences have kept the gang and crime lives of young gay men largely unexplored by scholars.[10]

I seek to critically interrogate these assumptions by investigating the experiences of 53 gay gang- and crime-involved men. I will provide an in-depth understanding of how these men construct and negotiate both masculine and gay identities through gang membership and criminal involvement. In order to produce such an understanding, I explore the neighborhood, peer, and familial contexts of these young men's lives, but especially as they relate to forming, disclosing, and negotiating gay identities. I combine qualitative data generated by in-depth interviews and ethnographic fieldwork with gay gang- and crime-involved men with threads of criminological scholarship, such as research on masculinity construction through gang membership and crime commission[11] and the impact of organizational characteristics (in this case, gang sexual orientation composition) on gang members' experiences.[12] I also frame these analyses with concepts from other academic disciplines, as criminology and criminal justice scholarship alone lacks some of the tools necessary to understand these men's lives.

Performances of Masculine Identity

This study is guided by symbolic interactionism, a social science theoretical framework which argues that actions and the meanings we assign to them are socially situated and are performed for real or presumed audiences.[13] Gender is one such performance, where we are held accountable for our displays of masculinity or femininity and whether it conforms to society's expectations. Transgressing these boundaries can get you stigmatized, laughed at, ostracized, or worse.[14] The ways we are expected to "do gender" can be affected by other social statuses, such as our race, class, and sexual orientation.[15] Men are especially bound to rigid standards of masculinity, where they are expected to exert power over women and achieve prestige within institutions—for example, "climbing the corporate ladder"—which might include using aggressive behavior or force. This concept is often referred to as "hegemonic masculinity," and is perpetuated most often by white men in power.[16] Normative masculinity, including heterosexuality, is what is considered standard, idealized, and expected, and becomes the yardstick by which men are measured. Within this meaning system, men who do not follow these standards are given less status and respect than men who do. Much of this book deals with how gay men make sense of, respond to, and resist this imposed masculinity and heteronormativity.

Some scholars argue that members of less powerful groups, such as non-white and/or poor men, perform masculinity that places a higher value on violence or on gaining respect through ways of making money that might not be fully legal, because they are often excluded from legitimate employment. Masculine performances could include the "cool pose," in which Black males exaggerate heterosexuality to gain status and prestige when other avenues are blocked or absent.[17] Markers of masculinity include respect, violence, independence, sexual prowess, and the exclusion of gay males. Furthermore, urban sociologist Elijah

Anderson notes that when symbols of success such as employment are difficult to acquire in poor, urban areas, respect becomes the currency of the street. In the extreme, a violent death may be preferential to being "dissed."[18] In these contexts, young men may perceive that the potential of "being labeled a punk" exists "every time you walk up that street,"[19] which produces the motivation to project aggressive attitudes. Men who enact these forms of masculinity may view themselves as resistant to the dominant cultural system (even when their behavior looks pretty close to the "mainstream" version),[20] but such options need more exploration. Criminologist Jody Miller notes that the emphasis on typical gendered actions prevents an understanding of how these acts are responses to exclusion of varied forms.[21] Nearly all forms of masculinity contain many of the same basic "masculine norms," which include dominance, power over women, physical toughness, pursuit of status, and "disdain for homosexuals."[22]

The tension should be clear: race- and class-based differences have been theorized, but what about the masculinity of gay men? Gay men may value the honor-based masculinity valued by heterosexual men, but they may have to do additional "identity work" because their sexuality is in opposition to the traditional masculine ideal. Gay men arguably have fewer resources with which to perform traditional masculinity (such as a lack of sexual relationships with women), though they may *not* value this masculinity over other forms. They also may be the target of violence committed by other men in search of masculine status. Gay men's claims to masculinity are therefore more tenuous, and the risk for status challenges is ever present. This risk is heightened when their mannerisms are inconsistent with what is expected of men, and perhaps even more so for non-normatively gendered gay men of color. By appropriating the aggressive masculinity implicit in the "cool pose," gay men can attempt to protect themselves from those who may wish to challenge feminine men. Of this identity work, one New York City club goer commented to a *Village Voice* reporter: "A lot of people don't like faggots. There are all these myths about faggots being soft and feminine, like you're lacy and wear chiffon and listen to Barbra Streisand. Straight-up homies, niggaz, and thugz can do what they want. You can walk through projects and be gay. But you can't walk through the project and be a faggot, because that's when they'll mock and harass."[23] Acutely aware of what is culturally expected of him as an urban Black male, a man can avoid harassment with this performance of "thug" masculinity.

Of course, the literature on masculine performance is in no way limited to criminology. Indeed, most of the scholarly work on gay men's constructions of masculinity and gay identity appears elsewhere. Diverse sources evaluate important topics such as gay men's experiences and challenges as fathers,[24] their negotiations of race, culture, and sexuality,[25] reconciling religion with gayness,[26] and their resistance strategies via avenues such as mainstream LGBTQ political movements.[27] I argue that, in order to be seen as fully realized individuals, analyses of gay gang- and crime-involved men should focus on the methods they use to construct masculine and gay identities, including but in no way limited to gang membership and crime commission. To draw from the examples above, how does James reconcile being a gang member, a drug dealer, and a bisexual (though mostly closeted) man? How does Imani marshal masculine resources to prove his fortitude, in light of negative assumptions about him as an openly gay man? In terms of criminological or other social science work, there is little from which to draw, which makes prioritizing participants' own meanings to be of central importance.

Gay Men Becoming Visible

Why are gay men mostly absent in criminology and criminal justice research? First, the literature focuses on gay men's victimization and thus implies that gay men have little agency. That is, many scholars assume gay men have little *choice* or *power* to control interpersonal interactions, and are fairly silent on whether or not gay men engage in serious crime, including violent street crimes, for comparable reasons as other similarly situated men. Second, this coverage provides an incomplete picture regarding their involvement in gangs, violence, and crime, not only by a lack of attention to these issues, but partially by obscuring factors relating to identity construction. For example, existing research is of little help in assessing whether gay identity plays any role in a young person's decision to join a gang, or in considering what type of gang to join. And, further, it provides very little insight into how urban gay men perceive their own criminality in light of expectations within criminal subcultures about hypermasculinity. How do marginalization and exclusion shape attitudes toward femininity and gayness, which could be either downplayed or celebrated in the course of young men's daily lives and their gang/criminal involvement? These are but a few of the unanswered questions that hold promise for better understanding the meanings, identities, and social worlds of gay gang- and crime-involved urban young men.

To be clear: it is commendable that scholars have given attention to the victimization of LGBTQ people, and I am indebted to the pioneers who came before me and blazed new paths regarding research on anti-LGBTQ victimization, same-sex intimate partner abuse, and the experiences of LGBTQ youth in schools.[28] However, I encourage moving beyond victimization's patterns, characteristics, and effects,[29] and seeking understanding about responses and resistance to victimization. For example, the literature includes little information on whether or not gay men "fight back" against their attackers,[30] despite a cultural context where men are encouraged to defend themselves aggressively and to correct emasculating scenarios. Some research has discussed LGBTQ young people who physically retaliate when they are homophobically bullied in schools,[31] but it's much more common for research to focus on bullying's consequences, like negative school outcomes and increased depression, suicide attempts, and substance use.[32] Although these are fundamentally important issues to consider, these experiences have largely been disconnected from other findings regarding LGBTQ youths' avenues for resiliency and agency, or even their defensive strategies. For example, research suggests sexual minority youth are more likely to engage in fighting and weapons carrying than their peers,[33] but the extent to which these acts are defensive in nature is unclear. Although I am fully aware that blurring the lines between victims and perpetrators can be less than savory from a sociopolitical standpoint,[34] investigating responses to structural or situational exclusion, with attention to intersecting social statuses, is necessary to provide a more dynamic portrait of how people are actually responding to or participating in violent encounters.[35]

Finally, there is virtually no academic research on gay gang-involved men; the research that can shed any light on gay-identified gang members suggests they participate in gay-bashing incidents to construct masculine personas and to conceal their sexual identities from their gangs.[36] The research on gang-involved young lesbians suggests the opposite— gang involvement to fight back against school-based, anti-lesbian harassment.[37] In light of the fact that so few sources exist to give us insight into queer people's gang membership and how heterosexism contextualizes those experiences, nuanced analyses are critically important.

Such heteronormative and victim-focused scholarly coverage of gay men in particular has likely resulted not only from a decoupling of gay identity and hegemonic masculinity, but the subsequent assumption that all hypermasculine men must be heterosexual. Even the sources that flirt with queer people's agency and involvement in violence focus on their school-based experiences, without similar investigation into the experiences of queer young people in their neighborhoods and communities. This is especially true for urban queer people of color.[38] Having seen firsthand how resilient and strong LGBTQ people can be, I am particularly struck by such static depictions. By being represented solely as passive victims of bias crimes, intimate partner violence, or homophobic bullying, they are regarded as lacking the ability to respond to and resist their victimization. I and other scholars centrally involved in the development of queer criminology refute these assumptions and argue that LGBTQ persons should be seen as fully realized citizens with the same capabilities as others—including those for gang and crime involvement.[39] In my days as a young queer activist, I couldn't have predicted that I'd now be repeating, "We CAN be gang members and we CAN commit crimes!" Radical gay liberation groups such as Queer Nation have encouraged LGBTQ people to fight back, both literally and figuratively, against society's devaluing of their lives and in scenarios where they might be actual victims of violence.[40] Resistance can take many forms, and this book explores some that have been vastly underrepresented or unexplored. I draw from the sensibilities that characterize queer criminology: providing a deep and nuanced investigation into LGBTQ people's experiences with crime, victimization, and the criminal justice system; critiquing mainstream criminology's assumptions, which are reproduced in its theories and studies; and working toward reducing invisibility, inequality, and injustice.[41]

Experiences with victimization, discrimination, or marginalization likely play important roles in decisions to enact violence, join gangs, participate in illicit economies, and/or commit other crimes. However, without exploration into individuals' *responses or resistance to* their exclusion, these experiences remain unclear, and our understanding partial, continuing to render LGBTQ people's lives as less than whole.

Voices That Matter

The guiding framework for this book is that identity construction is an interactive process, sometimes called "identity work." Sociologist Amy Best notes that much of the scholarship on young people's identity work views identities not just as "interactional work" but as "projects," which are "formed out of the discursive repertoires youth use to make sense of, interpret and narrate their worlds."[42] Repertoires can include symbols and sites, as well as practices and ritual enactments. In this case, symbols might be manners of dress or tattoos; sites might be gay bars, homes, public streets, or vogue balls; and practices and ritual enactments might be gang involvement, selling drugs or sex, dancing, dating, and fighting back. I was able to see some of these symbols and practices and be present in these sites, but I draw extensively from young men's narratives to understand repertoires more thoroughly.

Performances of identity include narratives as a way to "create, present, and sustain personal identities that are congruent with and supportive of the self-concept."[43] Also known as "personal myths," narratives are acts of imagination that integrate the past, present, and future to make a "compelling aesthetic statement"[44] or an evaluative point about the self.[45] Self-narratives also provide a way for us to make sense of our lives.[46] In our self-stories, we aim to present ourselves as individuals who are consistent, competent, and moral;[47] to do so, we must justify any untoward behavior with a socially situated account that seeks to assert the positive value of the act despite evidence to the contrary. By using speech to create accounts, our words have the "ability to throw bridges between the promised and the performed."[48] Accounts, or motives, reflect awareness of the possible consequences.[49] Justifications, then, are meant to cognitively transform conceptions of the harmful behavior from "culpable" to "righteous" by arguing its social or moral value.[50]

Common in narrative "identity work" is boundary maintenance, an impression management technique. Boundary maintenance is a way for us to present ourselves the way we'd truly like to be seen. We might stress the social distance between ourselves and other groups, especially those whom we personally deem less worthy of respect.[51] Enforcing social distance may be especially important for individuals who already have little social status, and find it necessary to distance themselves from individuals or groups with whom an association would taint their claim to decency. For example, a drug user may characterize himself as a "hustler" but not a "crackhead";[52] a drug dealer may refer to himself as a "broker" or a "middleman" as opposed to a "real dealer."[53] The semantic boundaries narrators construct represent symbolic boundaries, or conceptual distinctions made by people to acquire status and claim group membership.[54] In part, we define who we are by defining who we are not. The construction of identity is a constant interactive process.

The men in my study often considered the ways they would be perceived by others as a guiding concern in their performances of identity. Were they acting too gay or too feminine? Too weak or too inexperienced? The list of considerations was long. They endeavored to negotiate identity within a complex meaning system that in some ways necessitated forays into unfamiliar cultural territory. They wanted to lay claims to authentic, or "real" identities, by showing to what extent they were "real men," members of "real gangs," and whether their "realness" as gay men allowed them entitlement to masculine and gay respectability.

Men's identity work that is present in the data includes a series of seemingly contradictory propositions. Although gay men are perceived as weak and passive in popular culture, my participants were willing to advocate for themselves violently. Some joined straight gangs even though they knew they were gay, and many actually found a same-sex-oriented underground world, even within these primarily heterosexual gangs. However, they still presented traditional masculine personas to their gangs. The young men who joined gay gangs may have danced competitively, "dressed up" in women's clothes to sell sex, and voiced deeply held affection for their fellow gang members, but still brawled with, cut, and shot at their enemies, many of whom were in rival gay gangs. Moreover, for all of my research participants, their behavior went against several salient aspects of the masculine ideal, but they simultaneously endorsed many of the same elements of it and attempted to patrol the femininely gendered behavior of other gay men. They fought to defend members of the gay community, even those who they deemed to be "fags," despite an apprehension and distaste for these flamboyant men. They resisted stereotypes of gay and Black men as deadbeats and offenders, but in order to not be financial deadbeats themselves, they sometimes offended. Their social worlds and constructed meanings were contested, fluid, and context-dependent. These are the major themes that will be traced throughout this book.

Gay Gangsters in Columbus, Ohio

The men who will be described in this book ranged in age from 18 to 28, with an average age of 21.5. The sample was racially diverse, but the majority were men of color (77 percent Black or African American, 11 percent white, 2 percent Latino, and 9 percent biracial). Over three-quarters had been arrested and over half had been incarcerated (77 percent and 55 percent, respectively), with a wide range of two days to eight years of total incarceration. Forty-eight (91 percent) identified as a member or an affiliate of a gang, crew, clique, set, posse, or organization at some point in their lives. The remaining five men had also engaged in repeated criminal activity as part of a group, but denied that their groups were gangs. The eligibility requirements for the study included being 18 or older, male, gay or bisexual,[55] and either a gang member or involved in illegal activity. Participants selected their own "code names" for use in the study, some of which are quite stylized. Gang pseudonyms were also selected with participants' help.

I met these men in a variety of ways, but primarily by getting in touch with people I used to know in Columbus—like Imani—and first interviewing them. I conducted face-to-face, in-depth, semi-structured interviews with each of the 53 participants, and spent additional time with about half of them to better understand their lives. This study is primarily interview-based, but also partially ethnographic. I also asked the initial sample to refer other men who fit the criteria and might be interested in talking to me. The Methods Appendix explains my data collection in fuller detail, including the sampling strategy, interviews, fieldwork, and sample.

During the interview, I asked each participant about his life history, his relationships and sexual identity, his gang and/or criminal experiences, his experience with the criminal and juvenile justice systems, and what it meant for him to "be a man," among other topics. I spent considerable time with participants discussing their identity construction as gay men, including their masculinity. For example, I talked with each about how old he was when he first considered himself to be a man, what made him a man, and what words he would use to describe himself as a man. I also asked what qualities make someone a "real" man, whether they knew people who were not real men, and what qualities those men lacked or possessed. Even prior to my asking these questions directly, participants made many comments about "real men." They also wanted to discuss other dimensions of realness: "real gangs," men who were gay but who were not out, and which openly gay men were worthy of respect based on their behavior. In the analyses that follow, I try to capture the nuances of participants' narratives.

Though I focus on identity construction and negotiation in this book, this focus is set within the context of most participants being gang members, many of whom were still actively involved. Participants represented 38 different gangs, with some belonging to multiple gangs over time. In order to evaluate differences in gang structures and their effects on the gang experience, I sought to compare gangs based on their sexual orientation composition, or their ratio of straight to gay, lesbian, or bisexual members. So, I asked participants to estimate what percentage of their gang's members were gay, lesbian, or bisexual.[56] Much variation existed among gangs with a majority of heterosexual members, ranging from "0 percent besides me" to nearly 50 percent. Several majority-heterosexual gangs had a substantial proportion of GLB members (one-quarter to nearly one-half), though most had a smaller proportion of GLB people (or at least identifiably or known gay members).[57] Among the gangs with a majority of GLB members, they made up 100 percent or nearly 100 percent of the gang. Of the 48 current or former gang members in my study, 26 participants were or had previously been members of gangs with 100 percent or nearly 100 percent GLB members. I refer to these gangs as "gay gangs," to the gangs with a critical mass of GLB people as "hybrid gangs,"[58] and to the gangs with a small percentage of GLB members as "straight gangs." This book is partially structured by these direct gang comparisons.

All of my participants lived in central Ohio, all but one in Columbus's metropolitan statistical area. Columbus is Ohio's capital and a very large city—the 15th largest in the U.S.,[59] to most people's surprise. Columbus is sometimes referred to as the "GLBT mecca of the Midwest," as its gay pride parade draws 200,000 spectators and is one of the largest Pride festivals in both the Midwest and the country.[60] Since 2010, the parades have regularly lasted two hours or longer, with a mixed bag of participants, including local community agencies, gay-owned or gay-friendly establishments, LGBTQ groups from large corporations, elected officials, and candidates for public office. There are many places to go that welcome and celebrate the LGBTQ crowd, typically evidenced by rainbow flags or other visible LGBTQ symbols.

However, despite the existence of vibrant and enduring gay communities in several Ohio cities, as recently as 2007, Ohio as a whole ranked 51 out of the 50 states and the District of Columbia "in affirmation and protection of LGBT individuals."[61] In 2004, Ohio voters passed Issue 1, an amendment to the Ohio constitution that defined marriage as a union between one man and one woman. This measure banned performing same-sex marriages *and* recognizing such marriages performed in other states. Sixty-two percent of all Ohio voters supported Issue 1; 52 percent of voters in Franklin County (which encompasses Columbus) supported it. The percentage of voters who supported Issue 1 in Franklin County was smaller than in any other county in Ohio.[62] Although Ohio passed a version of the Comprehensive Safe Schools Act in 2012, it did not specifically enumerate protections based on sexual orientation and gender identity.[63] Nearly all (98 percent) of sexual minority students surveyed in Ohio have heard "gay" used in a negative way.[64] And it was a plaintiff from Ohio whose marriage equality case made it all the way to the Supreme Court of the United States as the history-making *Obergefell v. Hodges* (2015). All of this suggests that Ohio has some distance to travel to be a safer and more welcoming place for queer and gender non-conforming people.

What about gangs in Columbus? As it is a major city, Columbus is not immune to gang problems. Larger cities are more likely to report long-standing gang problems than smaller ones,[65] but Columbus is not classified as a "chronic" gang city. Instead, it is classified as an "emergent" gang city because its gang problem arose after 1985.[66] Criminologist Ronald Huff argues that, by 1985, Columbus's political leaders could no longer deny the gang problem after several highly publicized incidents, including gang-related assaults on both the governor's daughter and the mayor's son.[67]

Today, political leaders no longer deny the problem; they use it as a platform. In a 2011 interview with *The Columbus Dispatch* where he announced his intent to run for a fourth term as mayor, incumbent Michael B. Coleman identified "the gang problem" as an area of focus in his upcoming campaign and possible continued tenure as mayor.[68] Attempts to suppress gang activity in Columbus include "sweeps" of public areas where gangs are believed to sell drugs, such as downtown parks.[69] While Columbus gangs might call themselves Bloods, Crips, or Gangster Disciples, research in Columbus has revealed most gangs to be "homegrown" and not "chapters" of gangs from chronic gang cities (such as Los Angeles or Chicago) or connected to a nationwide network of gang members.[70]

Despite media coverage of gangs in Columbus, the gay gangs have not garnered any media attention that I am aware of. An issue that I consistently grapple with when talking to other people about this research is whether the groups represented in my sample (especially the all-gay ones) are "real" gangs, and whether my participants are actually gang members. I have lamented this issue elsewhere—multiple times, in fact[71]—and it is no doubt related not only to stereotypical expectations about gang members but also to the thriving debate in the gang literature about what constitutes a "gang," and a recognition that members' self-descriptions of "gangs" may differ between and among different groups. I should specify that no matter which definition of gang is used, nearly all gangs and gang members in my sample fit with the dominant criminological definitions of gangs, such as the Eurogang Program of Research definition: they are durable, street-oriented youth groups whose identity includes involvement in illegal activity.[72] They even square with many law enforcement definitions of gangs. For example, each is also an "ongoing formal or informal organization, association, or group of three or more persons" that has common identifiers, a pattern of criminal activity, and the commission of criminal offenses as one of its primary activities.[73] I note instances where participants' gangs depart from some attribute of these two definitions in later chapters, but I reiterate that such instances were extremely rare.

Beyond this, my research participants *self-identify* as gang members, though many prefer to use an alternate term for their group, such as "posse" or "clique." According to criminologist Finn Esbensen and colleagues, the self-nomination technique has been found to be "a particularly robust measure of gang membership capable of distinguishing gang from nongang youth."[74] And still other definitions situate gangs within the social structure. In their definition of a gang, David Brotherton and Luis Barrios propose characteristics such as providing "a resistant identity, an opportunity to be individually and collectively empowered, [and] a voice to speak back to and challenge the dominant culture."[75] My analyses also include reflection on these elements.

Resistance in Action

In the chapters that follow, I explore these men's identities and social worlds. Though I do discuss their gang activities and behavior, I focus more on what life is like for gay men who are gang involved: their experiences, how they see themselves, and their relationships with others, all through the lenses of being male, gay, and gang affiliated. Part I focuses on constructing and understanding gay identity, with chapters 1 and 2 exploring the cultural messages participants have been exposed to and internalized regarding gay men and "fags," framing these analyses within the context of men's early life experiences, coming out stories, and personal opinions about such matters. Part II presents a comparative portrait of the experiences of men in gay, straight, and hybrid gangs, evaluated in chapters 3, 4, and 5, respectively. Such experiences are largely determined by the sexual orientation compositions of their gangs. I investigate dimensions such as getting into gangs, activities engaged in with gang members, and how being either "out" or closeted structures the gang experience, particularly as it relates to negotiating gay identity. In keeping with the theme of negotiating acceptable and unacceptable gay male identity and resistance, Part III explores two possible forms of resistance. Chapter 6 details participants' violent responses to anti-gay harassment and threats of violence, which I call fighting back, and these responses' role in identity construction. I round out the analyses with an exploration of participants' involvement in underground economies in chapter 7. I discuss how these men balanced stereotypes and participation in illegal money-making activities to construct respectable masculine and gay identity in the face of structural constraints. I end the book by reflecting on boundaries in the Conclusion, both as they relate to academic work and to the tensions and contradictions present in participants' narratives. Throughout, I contextualize participants' narratives as responses and resistance to exclusion.

With this book, my hope is to talk about gay gang members not in ways that exoticize them, but in nuanced ways that provide a better understanding of their daily lives and social worlds. My goal is to complicate what we think we know about gang members and gay men, because it is quite easy to believe that gang members behave one way and gay men behave another, with little overlap between the two. Indeed, James and Spiderman can't share that kiss just anywhere, and not all urban young gay men are as self-assured as Imani. However, these three men and dozens more wanted to speak to me about their lives, suggesting a desire to bring their experiences out of fuzzy shadows and rumors and instead into focus, to confront stereotypes and claims made about them, and for us to instead take seriously the claims made *by* them. This isn't just a book about gay gang members in Columbus, Ohio, but an attempt to provide some insight into what it means to be gay in contexts that seem like they provide little opportunity to do so. The men in my study make their own way when a path doesn't seem to be available. This book is a story of these paths toward empowerment.

PART I

Understanding Gay Identity

1

"Why Do I Have to Hide It?"

Forming a Gay Identity

It's a warm day in early fall, and I am sitting with Imani in the living room of the house he shares with his parents. His cousin Rose is also there, as is the toddler of another one of their cousins who needed a babysitter while she ran some errands. Imani is telling me about his gender presentation, and how he modifies it when necessary, especially to avoid trouble in public. He says, "Hold on, I'm finna[1] [gonna] show you a real masculine picture of me." He finds a picture of him in dark pants, a leather jacket, and a baseball hat, leaning away from the camera, face emotionless. I actually don't recognize him at first, but the man in the picture does look stereotypically masculine: reserved, tough, and confident. I ask, "That's you?" He replies, "See? You wouldn't even know." He turns to Rose. He asks her the same thing.

"Rose, does this look like me?"

"What?"

"Guess who that is."

"You."

"Don't I look so hood?"

"No."

Rose denies Imani's request that she authenticate his realness and hoodness with a totally straight face, but he doesn't take it very seriously. I chuckle.

Imani continues by talking to the baby who is visiting. "They're mean. They cain't take my manliness!" He turns back to me. "I'm mad you asked me was that me, oh my God! That don't look like me, or somethin'?"

I offer that since we were talking about a number of people today, I wasn't sure if it was his boyfriend or him. That is the truth. But I confirm that it does look like him, just that I thought he was trying to show me a really masculine picture of the boyfriend. Imani is delighted.

"She thought I was masculine! Oh! Come on! Come on. My picture serves realness. I cain't wait to call my momma and talk to her. Like, 'Gurl, my friend thought I was a MAN!'" He shows me several more pictures, asking me to confirm that he looks masculine in each one. He pokes fun at himself by flipping his long, dreaded hair behind his shoulders and saying, "I am a whole lady." He has clarified to me several times that he doesn't actually want to be a woman, though he claims he sometimes can be "fishier" (more feminine) than women; he describes this as being "real cunt." He also maintains, "Cunt is cute." However, he explains that he can't be feminine most of the time or he'll run into problems with his family, his neighbors, and his clique. Sometimes, he says, he has to be "a whole man."

I think back to being in King's bedroom over a year ago. He had pictures of Prada and Gucci purses and shoes taped to the wall above his bed, as if their location there would produce nothing but luxurious dreams. Even his pets were named after famous designers. King lamented that neither his financial situation nor his living arrangements would permit him to explore his passion for high-end fashion, typically marketed to affluent female customers: "It's mostly only models and rich white ladies who *really* get to wear that stuff." He went through his closet and gave me a fashion show of sorts, demonstrating how he wears solid colored or patterned scarves around his head in his neighborhood or when his gang would meet, but draped around his neck in downtown Columbus when he went to gay clubs; or a flashy leather jacket that was made by one of his "client's peoples" that doubled as a status piece on the streets and garnered positive attention in gay circles—flexible pieces for the multifaceted urban gay man who described himself as "fashion forward."

King added, "Now, I like the Gucci scarves too, but I will *not* do the man purse."

* * *

Both Imani and King suggested that despite a preference for gender fluidity in their daily lives, their public gender presentation was more on the masculine end of the spectrum, sometimes out of necessity or in response to expectations imposed on them. There is an expressed contempt in modern society for "feminine" behavior.[2] Misogynistic and homophobic cultural messages provide motivation for gender patrolling of boys and men, where members of society seek to change the behaviors of gender non-conforming males through informal social sanctions such as name-calling and physical harassment. Such actions are intended to punish transgression in an attempt to ensure males' conformity to traditional masculinity and sexuality. Men who refuse to fight or otherwise assert their dominance in aggressive ways may be scolded with epithets that allude to femininity or gayness, such as "punk," "sissy," and "fag."[3] Unsurprisingly, homophobic epithets are more often used by males[4] in an attempt to control or challenge another male's masculinity. They might even call other males "fags" preemptively—to reduce the likelihood that they themselves will be insulted in that way.[5] Political organizer Suzanne Pharr argues that homophobia and heterosexism are "weapons" of sexism. Gay men, especially visible gay men, are seen as a threat to male dominance and control because they are perceived as "traitors" to their sex.[6]

Cultural messages that glorify masculinity and heterosexuality pervade many young people's lives, starting long before they have formed or disclosed their sexual and gender identities. These messages can also be affected by salient social characteristics like gender, race, and religious affiliation. Expectations imposed onto participants influenced how they understood their sexual identities, but also affected how they disclosed those identities to others and the reactions of other people. Imani was delighted to be read as masculine, and King found it necessary to present as a typical urban Black male when going out in public, all because not being masculine enough would attract negative attention from family, peers, and strangers.

This chapter explores how identifying as a gay man has been understood by participants and by others in their lives. Following a mostly chronological progression, I begin by discussing early perceptions of participants' gender presentations as expressed by their families, peers, and themselves, followed by their behavior to conceal (at least strategically) their same-sex attractions. In addition to their experiences of gay identity formation, I also describe their coming out processes, including when and how they revealed their sexual identities to valued others in their lives, the reactions to these disclosures, and the social statuses that might explain such reactions. I focus primarily on familial and community dynamics here, and discuss peer interactions more in depth in subsequent chapters.

Early Experiences

As noted, the use of homophobic and misogynistic epithets can be used to "patrol" the behaviors of other males, especially gender atypical ones, in an attempt to ensure their conformity to masculinity and heterosexuality.[7] Nearly two-thirds of my participants had been teased in school because of their sexuality or perceived sexuality, sometimes leading to fights. Their perceived gayness was usually linked with gender-atypical behavior, though often, participants couldn't quite put their finger on what other children sensed. Those with gender-atypical behaviors or "feminine sides" identified these as the reasons they were targeted for homophobic teasing, even before they began to identify as gay.[8] Oz remembered, "I really didn't realize that [I] was gay until I was around 12 or 13, and people were sayin', I was really really feminine when I was in schoo[l]. And they was like, 'Oh, Oz, you're gonna be gay, you're gay,' and I'm like, 'No, I'm not gonna be gay.' . . . But I always had a feeling, like, 'Maybe I am!'" Ricky recalled that he was called "gay-gay" growing up, because "they said I had a switch, I never knew what a switch was." Participants typically used the word "switch" to mean swishing their hips while walking. Similarly, people asked JD if he was gay because of "the way I carried myself," and Hurricane stated, "I was always picked with, growin' up through school because people saw my feminine side." Joe explained that while he was questioning his sexuality, everyone had assumptions about him because of the way he dressed; his frustration with constant teasing even led him to bring an aerosol can and lighter to school and start spraying it at classmates.

Casper, Raphael, Jordan, and Kevin all specifically mentioned that their hanging around with girls more than guys resulted in problems in school with classmates or suspicions from their parents. DJ explicitly stated, "Some people say if you have a lot of girls in your life, then you tend to turn feminine, and that's what makes you turn gay." Imani joked that maybe he was supposed to have been "born a woman" since he bonds with his girl cousins more than his boy cousins. He said this to me in front of his cousin Rose, who thought it was quite entertaining.

Jordan articulated a number of reasons why participants were teased for being gay, nearly all of which hinged on societal expectations for boys, laced with moral meanings:

> I didn't really like high school, cuz it was a really awkward time for me, because I didn't really identify as gay, even though I knew I was, and I was still pretty religious, and just, a lot of conflict, and I felt like a freak, and I didn't really fit in with people. . . . I think [I knew I was gay] way back, when I was in, like, kindergarten, because I feel like I was always very influenced by females growing up, I always liked, like I guess, like, girl things, and I always hung out with girls, all the time. And then whenever we'd play something, I'd want to be, like, the girl in it. . . . I got teased a lot, because I was pretty feminine, and into really girly things, so they'd be like, "Oh, you're gay," and I'd just be like, "Oh, shut up, no I'm not," or something.

This excerpt illustrates the tension in conceptualizing gender-atypical behavior: Jordan hesitates to call such activities "girl things" or "being the girl," since he identifies as male and is not ashamed to engage in such behaviors. All of the pressure he felt to conform was external. By contrast, because his gender presentation was normative for a boy, King thought his high school classmates perceived him to be "weird," "odd," or "just young" because of his "sorta feminine" behavior, but not necessarily gay. For boys whose feminine behaviors or styles were visible, assumptions were made about their sexual orientation, and they were teased as a result.

Despite the fact that the majority of participants knew before their teen years that they were attracted to males, they felt pressure to conceal their sexual interests from schoolmates for a period of time. Otherwise, they thought they would face ridicule or actual physical violence. Rashad remembered, "I thought it was bad to be gay, cuz that's how everybody was where I was living, if you were gay, you either had to be quiet about it, or it'd be problems." Rocc explained, "Growin' up, it was always, 'This fag that,' and 'Faggot this' and 'Faggot that,' so, I guess that's kinda the attitude I carried, like, 'Shit, I can't do this, this shit is wrong, bein' a fag.'" Max said he spent time with "straight people" in high school because he did not want to be "known" as gay, or for his mother to find out. In a striking comment on his behavior despite saying he was "born gay," he stated, "before I knew what it was, I knew how to hide it." That comment resonated particularly strongly with me on a personal level, since I had the exact same feeling as early as first grade. Tony remembered,

> I always been like this since I was little. I remember in fourth grade, I used to look at lil boys, I used to think they was cute and stuff. I never said that out loud, and I would always hang with the girls, and I already knew somethin' wasn't right. . . . I didn't figure [being gay] out 'til 10th grade. I knew, okay, this is set in stone. I was just like, this is what it is. But earlier, I used to just fight it like, "I gotta get over this lil thing," I used to always try to look at girls, females, in the way I'm (wiggles fingers in air as air quotes) "supposed to," I guess. Quotations! So, it just didn't work out.

Participants knew precisely what was expected of them and that they were "different," sometimes using precisely that word to categorize themselves before they knew what "gay" meant: when I asked Reese when he started to think of himself as gay, he answered back, "As different?" before telling me about his same-sex attractions dating back to kindergarten. Eric remembered, "I've obviously had these feelings since I was a kid, I was always different, and my mom, she'll tell you that now, she likes to go through pictures of me when I was a kid, like, 'Oh, look at you! You were so gay! Why didn't I know?'" Interestingly, some research on sexual identity formation actually utilizes this framework in its data collection instruments, first asking when someone "felt different" and why.[9] Narratives about feeling "different" further underscore a push for participants to eventually construct respectable gay identities to reduce ostracism, but explain why they first felt it necessary to obscure their gay identity.

Cover-Ups and "Holdin' In That Big Secret"

In order to counteract assumptions about their sexuality that they knew might be difficult for them to deal with, participants enacted a number of strategies. One such strategy was attempting to "pass"[10] as straight by using girls as "cover-ups," which some people might call "beards." Kevin started off by saying, "I've always been the princess of the girls, which is so stupid, because I'm a boy, but I've always been very princess-y." Before he came out, Kevin dated a girl as a "cover-up," even though he didn't like her romantically: "I knew that I only wanted to be with dudes, but so people would not say, 'Oh, you're a fag,' or, 'Oh, you're gay,' or, 'You like guys,' or you know, shit like that. I said, 'Okay, I'm straight. I have a girlfriend. Do you see her? She's right here.'" Dollars dated a "cover-up" because he feared more than name-calling once his classmates "started to suspect" his gayness; he claimed that at "the school I went to, the kids there didn't believe in homosexuality. . . . You get beat up, and that's it, every day after school." Jordan also suggested that in his school career, the only time he heard about gay people was when he was admonished, "Don't be gay," and "Don't be a fag or you'll get your ass kicked." Ricky articulated that having crushes on girls was a way to hide being gay from "regular society." And Max said, "When I was hidin' it, I felt horrible, because there was girls that liked me and stuff, and I had to act like I liked them back."

These efforts extended beyond school and into the family. Commenting on a multi-year relationship he had with a young woman which made him unhappy, Steve said, "It was pretty much a cover-up with my family, to get them to shut up, and quit asking me if I was gay." Tony also admitted to having girlfriends just to avoid the subject with his older brothers, despite declaring, "I already knew all along what I liked"; the same went for Jeremy, who knew he "never liked females" but dated one to get his brothers off his back. Tony also explained that once his dad got custody of him, he intentionally acted like he was straight so that his dad wouldn't suspect he was gay and be disappointed in him. Such efforts reiterate the expectation of heterosexuality that young people face, particularly young men.

There also was the option of outright denial if one was asked directly. Darius's mother asked him several times if he was gay, and he denied it each time until he finally told her. When JD was confronted about being gay and denied it, people claimed that he must at least be bisexual, which he also denied until he became an adult. Other participants denied being gay to their classmates; some like Reese waited until completing school to come out. Strategies for obfuscation also existed, such as Javier and Josh telling their moms that the boys they brought around were friends when they were really boyfriends, or D.C. and Dollars letting parents think that the boyfriends they were going to see were male friends from sports or school. Though lying did take its toll. JD said, "Holdin' in that big secret, like, 'Oh, I'm not gay,' I feel like that turned me into a big liar, you know, just holdin' back that one lie, you start lyin' about everything else!"

These suppressions of the self had negative psychic consequences for many. Reese stated that from ages 13 to 18, "I was always real angry because I wanted to come out but I was afraid to, because I didn't know how people would react," and because he didn't know many gay people, he didn't want to be "the oddball." Although Steve wasn't technically out to his family, he felt like the "outcast" because he believed his family already knew about him. Max recounted, "I was so uncomfortable with the fact that I was gay myself, so I couldn't be [around my family], because I felt like I had to lie to them, so I didn't wanna be around them." Greg suggested that the fear of negative reaction is what stops many people from coming out, primarily because "a lot of people will look down on it."

Most of the participants who were not out to their parents stayed hidden not because they knew definitively that their families would react negatively; instead, they simply were *unsure* of how their families would react. For example, Bob thought his family "wouldn't really care," DJ thought his mother would ultimately "accept me for who I am," and Rocc thought his mom would eventually "get over it" after her initial "shock," but all three were nervous about the disclosure and were not ready to make it. Regarding telling his friends, Rocc also said he didn't want to be "the outcast." Internalized cultural messages regarding appropriate gender presentation and sexuality presented a dilemma to participants: they could be themselves, with negative social consequences, or hide their identities, with undesirable personal consequences. In light of these choices, several men waited until they left school or became adults to come out to friends and family, precisely due to the homophobic harassment they faced or expected to face.

Importantly, not all participants who were out to their families came out on their own accord or timeline—they tried to prevent the disclosure, but it happened anyway. Several participants' families found letters they had written to love interests, or they were caught engaging in same-sex affection. Others were outed to at least some members of their family by their interactions through technology that were discovered by others: instant messages for Silas, Internet pornography for Dollars, Rocc's Facebook messages, Max's hacked Facebook where someone posted a sexually explicit status update ("Max is sucking on some dick"), and more.

In some ways, the negative emotions caused by either refusing to acknowledge one's sexuality or staying closeted to friends or family were the catalyst for coming out, especially when participants were exposed to circumstances where they *could* be out. Dollars commented, "I just had this feelin' like I was gay, and me tryna be straight was makin' me uncomfortable. I would be really sad, and depressed and all of this, but then when I was gay, it felt like I could be free, and be whoever I wanted to be. I wouldn't have to hide behind this shadow guy, I wouldn't have to hide behind this confused dude, I would just be me." Using a similar metaphor for being hidden, Brad relayed, "I'm tired of standin' in the shadows wonderin' what it would always be like, if I'd ever be as happy with [a man] as I could be with anybody else." The image of the closet itself evokes a sense of darkness and isolation. Josh recounted, "I just had to come out [of] the closet. I couldn't hold it in no more." They first had to come to the realization that any negative perspectives they had heard did not suit them. Boss remembered, "As long as I've been able to understand it, I've been gay, [and] I just feel like society and my family has made it to be a bad thing, so until I started makin' my own decisions, till I started thinkin' for myself, it was a bad thing." Because Jordan had only been told that being gay was wrong, he had to learn about gay people on his own and come to his own conclusion, and didn't come out until age 18. Rocc suggested, "I guess after high school, you really just don't care what people think. I guess that comes with growin' up and knowin' who you are."

Similarly, Bird knew he was gay from a young age, but had to reframe his thinking: "I knew it wasn't right, but I always had this thing in my mind like, I'm going to make it right without them judging that I'm gay. . . . I knew I was gay when I was like six, and then I didn't come out until I was in the 10th grade, because as I got older I started learning different things and I'm like, being gay is not that bad. Why do I have to hide it?" Bird's idea of "making it right" is telling in that he wants to be seen as a person who is worthy of respect, even if he is gay. Because sexual identity formation is set within a context of heterosexist stigma, identity confusion is common among young people who are questioning and forming their sexual identities.[11]

For some participants, the hoped-for change in their interactions with others came to fruition. Greg said, "It seemed like after I came out, people was more acceptin', like, accepted me more. So after that, I can say life got a little bit better, wit social life out there." Toby was tired of hiding his sexuality, especially after going to a gay club. He remembered, "Why be in the closet, when I have so much fun bein' myself?" He then posted pictures he took with his boyfriend on Facebook, and when he didn't get any negative feedback, he realized that it was "okay to say I'm gay." Max astutely stated, "When you get grown and you're gay, you realize, I can't do nothin' but be me." He added, if people didn't like it, they could choose to not be around him, but it was their loss; this was a sentiment echoed by other participants who had lost contact with family or friends because of their decision to come out. However, this ability to slough off the "haters" was counterbalanced against whom they chose to come out to; for the traditionally masculine men still not out to their straight gangs, concerns about loss of status and physical safety prevented a cavalier attitude about the consequences of coming out.

"It Does Hurt to Have a Gay Son"

There was substantial variation regarding when participants came out to valued others in their lives, who they came out to first, and the reactions they received. The reactions to such disclosures basically provide a digest of cultural messages regarding gay people. Importantly, neither the men nor I found it easy to classify these reactions into categories such as positive, neutral, or negative, since they changed over time and regularly had elements of each. Thus, the cultural messages that participants were exposed to were dissonant and complex, and not always easy to negotiate.

Despite concerns about being accepted in schools and communities, the majority of participants came out to similar-age peers before coming out to family. Importantly, all participants encountered welcoming or accepting reactions from at least some in their lives. In general, similar-age peers were most likely to express accepting attitudes regarding participants' sexual identities, even being willing to defend them from harassment, but parents and family members also expressed these sentiments. Raphael's family told him, "If you the same person as you was before you told us, then we cool wit it," and he added that they have indeed been cool with it; it was only his mother who was initially mad about it but then "got over that real quick." Even Jayden, who thought his family was going to "disown" him because "they don't play" and "don't like it," said his parents responded to him with, "We gon' love you for you, cuz you my son." Toby stated his sister likes the fact that he's gay, because "every sister wants a gay brother." Josh's sister even tried to encourage him to come out at a young age by telling him, "It doesn't matter what mommy thinks, or what other people think, just be true to yourself."

The list of people who told participants that they "already knew" these young men were gay and in some cases were "just waiting to be told" is long: Baby's grandparents; Reese's friends; "a lot of people" in Greg's life; Batman's cousins; Tony's sister and brothers; Nate's family; Jeremiah's sister; Ali's, ATL's, JD's, Jeremy's, and Raphael's respective moms; Josh's sister; and more. For the most part, the fact that these folks "already knew" meant that participants faced little to no negativity from those individuals when they came out. Some participants even made light of such disclosures. Adidas came out to his parents but joked, "As far as family, it was a known thing, kinda. I think they kinda knew at birth. It's one of those things, I came out holdin' the rainbow flag." Mini noted, "I knew I was gay, but they knew I was gay before I even knew what the word 'gay' was, what the word 'gay' mean." And Jeremy said that his mother told him about how little boys used to say that he pinched them on the butt.

In this way, coming out was sometimes a bit anticlimactic for participants, but they were relieved to not have to navigate difficult interactions. I chuckled during Adidas's interview since we had similar coming out stories regarding our moms. He recounted:

I was nervous. It was freshman year when I decided to tell, cuz I don't like being sneaky, and I'm like, oh my God. My best friends were with me, and I walked in the kitchen, and I'm like, something bad's gonna happen after I tell my mom. So, I'm like, "Mom, I think I'm bi." And she's just like, "Okay," and continues washing the dishes. And I'm like, "That's all?" She's like, "What do you want me to say? There's a lot of people in our family like that." I'm like, "Really?" She's like, "Yeah." And I'm like, "Oh, okay. Alright, bye!"

Prevalent cultural messages made participants expect the worst in such scenarios; comments participants made off-handedly such as, "All moms get mad when you first come out to them," evidence this expectation. And, although Batman thought his mom didn't really care too much because she told him it was who he was and his decision, he isn't sure if she is supportive per se, though believes that she is. Such ambiguities likely occur because the neutral or positive reaction exists within a context of innumerable negative cultural messages.

In addition to positive or neutral reactions, family members offered useful education. Tony, JD, and Jeremy all stated that their family members advised them to use a condom when they had sex with men. Tony's brothers went a step further and told him, "You can be gay, but chu ain't gonna be no bitch ass nigga. . . . You ain't 'bout to let no nigga call you no fag, or nuttin' like that." These reactions illustrate a number of important messages for young gay men, such as that their identities are normal, they are worthy of love and respect, and they should advocate for themselves.

Unfortunately, many reactions from other figures in their lives were not as uniformly positive, or were extremely negative. Disbelief was common, with suggestions that their gayness was temporary. For example, Oz's father told him, "It's just a phase, you're gonna get through it," while Brad's family argued that they "didn't raise no fag" and that the reason he thought he was gay was because he had "been locked up [in prison] so long" and not gotten any female attention. Of course, Oz and Brad roundly denied these claims, as did others who were pestered by such questions. Tony noted that his dad repeatedly (and still) asked him why he is gay. King's aunt asked him, "Are you sure you want to live this lifestyle?" and assured him, "You can always come back," to which he responded that he was only sexually attracted to men and their physical attributes. Toby resented the fact that his mother wished he would "come to my senses." Aga explained,

> I don't like the boys in my family, because they be tryna tell me that I can get a girl. I know I can get a girl, but that's not what I'm attracted to. Like, my

mom, she teases me about being gay, but it really doesn't hurt me, because I know what I want, I'm not confused in what I want. I'm homosexual, I know I want to be wit a man, that's it. They keep on sayin', why don't I try it, and stuff like that. I don't wanna try it, at all. That's not what I wanna do.

Similarly, Kevin also stated that his grandmothers say to him, "I want you to be straight, I want you to be with a woman." He said his mother also thought this, but she knew it would never happen. Concerns about heterosexuality manifested in family members who not only wished that participants would have female partners, but that they'd have children. Silas said that his family accepts him, but as for his father, "He would rather that I be straight, obviously, that's just how dads are, I guess, he'd rather me be straight and have a kid and a girlfriend, or wife, but he accepts me, and he's okay with it." Even Joe, whose mother warmly accepted him upon coming out, lamented that his mom did want grand-kids, and he wasn't sure how that was going to happen now. Of course, it is important to mention that 10 men in my sample were fathers, and those who wanted children in the future expressed knowledge of options such as adoption and surrogacy, but these were not conversations they tried to engage in with their families. Furthermore, some participants identified as bisexual at the time of the interview, but sometimes down-played their attraction to women so that their families would take their disclosures seriously. When Batman's mother asked him, "Are you sure this isn't just a phase?" he tried to convince her that he was attracted solely to guys so that she wouldn't doubt him.

The questioning was particularly acute when participants were open, such as bringing boyfriends around or dressing in clothes stereotypi-cally attributed to women's fashions. Aga said that his mom asks him "every day" about his "lifestyle," perhaps because she had already seen so much: "I'm really open wit my mom. Like, she done seen me dress up [in women's clothes], and have boyfriends, and relationships, stuff like that. Yeah, she see a lot!" Derrick's family also questioned him often by asking why he did the things he did. He explained, "I used to dress like a girl around them too, and they're like, 'Why do you do that?' And all this and that. I just do it for the fun of it, that's all." That is, participants were challenged not only on their sexual identities, but also on their gender presentations.

All of this brings me to an important point regarding language and identity: although some participants identified as bisexual and not as gay (exclusively male-attracted), all participants at one point or another reflexively referred to cultural messages about "gay" men or people, which is in a way a linguistic shorthand for a cultural concept. That is, because heterosexuality is the cultural ideal, participants' peers or families judge them to be "gay" (thus embodying a host of negative social meanings regarding gender and sexuality) as a result of their identifying as anything other than strictly heterosexual. I reproduce the shorthand here not to erase any participant's bisexual identity, but to reflect their speech patterns and cultural referents.

In general, such interactions illustrate the murky waters that participants wade into when having any discussion of their sexual identities with their families. Participants were confused when their loved ones gave them negative messages about themselves, but attempted to frame those messages constructively. Toby said of his mother, "She feels like me being gay, I'm not gonna have a lot of opportunities in life [and] like I'm gonna be judged in life, so, it's gonna make me miss an opportunity to get a job, or be able to live in the world as a normal person. I don't understand, I don't know why she thinks like that, but that's what she thinks." Even for those whose families were initially fairly supportive or have become more supportive over time, heteronormative messages still persist. On his relationship with his mother, Marcus noted, "It's unconditional love cuz she is my mom, but she was like, 'It does hurt to have a gay son.'"

Some participants also reported that their families have called them "fags," which I detail shortly. Although less common, several were even threatened with or subjected to physical violence by their families for their sexual identities. Upon finding a letter he wrote to a boyfriend, Eric's mom punched him in the face, threatened him with a butcher knife, and told him, "I raised you better than this!" Bird's cousin told Bird's brother to talk to him, because he "found that fag shit" on his Facebook; his advice to Bird's brother was, "You need to straighten him out, you need to rough him up." These destructive interactions were not limited to verbal and physical abuse. For example, Juan's family cut off his contact with friends by grounding him, taking away electronic access to other people, and also sent him to a therapist to "fix" him, while Dollars's stepfather tried to place him in military school because he was gay. Such instances even resulted in homelessness or child welfare involvement. Dollars left home as a teenager to live with his sister due to his family's disapproval; Brian's adoptive family refused to allow him back into their home after he came out to them during his juvenile incarceration; Ricky got "put out" at 16 because his mom "didn't wanna accept it"; Hurricane says that he and his brother were treated differently because his brother was straight and he was gay, resulting in conflicts with his mother and his placement in group homes and foster care. These incidents reiterate the serious consequences young people can face after coming out to unsupportive parents, particularly for young men who face other forms of social marginalization.

"Not Here, Not Right Now": Negotiating Gay Identity within Families

Families were often very concerned with how "gay" participants appeared. Being "too gay" meant different things for different families. Dancing, tight clothing, and talking openly about boyfriends and sex were the most common complaints from participants' families. ATL said that his brother didn't like gay people: "If I bring a gay person around, he got somethin' to say, or if I'm around dancin', he'll have somethin' to say." D.C. was very active in performing arts, but his mom would tell him that his ballet tights or dance leggings looked "too gay" on him, that she didn't approve of him bringing his boyfriend into her home, and even that she didn't want D.C. going over to a boyfriend's house because she wasn't sure how other people would react to him being gay. In order to have a good relationship with his extended family, Bird said he "would have to dress completely different so they won't judge me." Brad thinks that his family accepted his boyfriend Reese so readily because he is outgoing and would never wear women's clothes. Some objections were more obscure; for example, ATL's family did not approve of his tongue piercing because they thought, for a man, it communicated gayness and promiscuity.

The objections were also sometimes amorphous, because family members objected fundamentally to participants' gayness, but attributed it indirectly to their behavior. Derrick said of his father, "He try to say I do gay stuff around him, like, that he don't be around that type of stuff. I don't pay no attention to him. I be cussin' him out, if he call me out my name [insults me by calling me a derogatory term instead of my name]. . . . He's like, 'Don't do that faggot shit, cuz I don't be around gay people.' . . . And I don't understand, but I be tryin' to talk to him about it sometimes, and sometimes he listen, sometimes he won't." It is likely that Derrick was frustrated not only by his father's denigration of his identity, but with his unwillingness to try to resolve the problem between them. Brandon said that although he didn't act differently around his family, he couldn't really be himself because "they just don't like the fact" that he's gay; "they don't like hearin' about it, or seein' it." Such conflicts prevent close and trusting familial relationships. In a striking case, Dollars wanted to set his family off: "When I'm around my family, sometimes I do stuff on purpose just to piss them off for how they treated me. So, I'll wear super tight, ultra-skinny jeans from Wet Seal, and some designer underwear, and a really tight shirt over at their house. And my Coogi boots, I'll have them on, and they'll just be like, 'No, take it off.'" Just as Derrick stood up to his father when he called him names, Dollars is now grown and didn't want to tolerate attempts to control his personal style. He already owned each of those garments, but wearing them all at the same time at his family's house was a way for him not only to annoy them, but to resist their proscriptions regarding his gender presentation.

With the exception of Dollars, most participants wanted to avoid conflict. One of the easiest ways to do so was to simply avoid the subject. Javier said that his mom knew about him being gay, but they never talked about it, because she had said in the past that being gay was an "abomination." Greg also noted that he and his mother don't argue about his gayness solely because they do not talk about it and he doesn't bring it up, "because it's just not somethin' she's comfortable with." Dollars said, "I keep my business separate from my family cuz how they talk. I don't tell them anything that goes on with me." Their contact was mostly limited to Facebook. And Joe explained the two reasons why he didn't talk much about boyfriends with his family: "One, it's none of their business. It never was and it never will be. And two, why even bother? They probably don't wanna hear stuff like that, anyway."

In other cases, the family themselves avoided the subject on their behalf. Of his family, Rashad said, "They know I'm gay, but they don't speak on it. They never talk about sex as in lover, partner, mate, no." Johnny explained that although his family doesn't "down-talk" (insult) his sexuality, whenever he brings a boyfriend around, they will acknowledge him with brief greetings, but not accept him into the family. And Oz's mom said that although she wouldn't want to talk about his boyfriends or be excited about it, she "could deal with it." Completely staying away from family was another option, though it was typically segments of their families they had to avoid, not everyone.

Another strategy was similar to the earlier "cover-ups" and strategic presentation discussed, by intentionally acting straight or masculine. Toby gets along with his sister and cousin, but said that he can't be himself around his parents or extended family. When I asked how he feels he has to act around them, he replied, "I won't act no feminine, like, you couldn't tell [I was gay] or nothin'. I would act real masculine around them. Talk about girls, and stuff like that. I don't like that, though, but it is what it is."

Another strategy was knowing when and where their families would be more comfortable with them being recognized as gay. Kevin had a rich description of the circumstances where he could be visibly gay, at least according to his mother:

My mom doesn't want me to be overly flamboyant out in public, like, if I'm with her, in some instances, she'll be like, "Oh hahaha, you're so gay," and be kidding around with me, but I'll do something in a different situation, and she's like, "No, don't do that, not here, not right now." I'm like, "Okay." So, it's very time-and-a-place for everything, kind of situation. Like, I could be kickin' it with my mom when we're at the house, she knows I vogue, she knows I walk runway, she knows how gay I am. But, if I take that out in a public setting, it has to be the right setting for that situation. It can't be in downtown Columbus while traffic is rolling around and everybody is there. . . . She doesn't mind if it's in the house. I'm a very religious person, so she doesn't want it there [at church], even though most, I mean, if you don't know that I'm gay, by just looking at me, you're an idiot. She doesn't mind it out in public, like, we'll go to an amusement park, and I'll just be me. . . . I can't walk into her job with a pair of straight-legged jeans on and some ruffly shirt and, you know, a rainbow tattooed across my forehead, and she'd be like, umm (makes lip-smacking sound, points finger in air) "Too gay." . . . My mom has seen me in booty shorts, but she's like, "Okay, you're going to the club, that's fine. Just as long as you're not going somewhere corporate with that on."

Jeremy recounted a parallel scenario:

I went and I dressed up. And he [my brother] was in the house. That was this year, it was this past Pride. And I was in the bathroom, and I looked at myself, I said, "Oh my God, my brother's out there, what the fuck is he gonna say?" And I came out, he was like, "Eee! Look at chu! Look at chu!" I was like, "Aww." He kept touchin' my hair, like, "Oooh, you got that lil silky—" I'm like, "Boy!" But everything went good. And when I'm dressed up like a girl, he call me by my girl name, he's very respectful, and he dares somebody to say somethin'.

In these ways, some family members decided that the "time and place" acceptable for gay or flamboyant behavior was precisely when they were in their own homes or surrounded by other gay people, such as at Pride or clubs. It is also telling that Kevin's mother had no problem with him being "so gay" in public as long as it was at an amusement park, where the crowd provides some anonymity, but not in downtown Columbus (where people might know them) and certainly not where her professional or social reputation was on the line ("her job" or at their church). "Too gay" guidelines likely have practical applications, such as reducing visibility and thus risk, but still resonate with unsavory efforts to control men's expression.

There was ultimately some resistance against these efforts to suppress participants' presentations of self. JD, who regularly dressed in women's clothing, found that acting masculine and straight around his mother was counterproductive: "I try to act a certain way, and then when I act a certain way to appease her, to please her, then it's like, 'Whatever, you're still the same,' well, yeah, of course you still gonna see the same lyin' ass JD, because I'm actin' a certain way to please you!" And beyond that, in the case of several participants including JD and Dollars, they resented their stepfathers' negative attitudes toward their gayness and gender presentation, which they presumed affected their mothers' acceptance of their lives. Furthermore, a strained or absent relationship with family members made participants indignant about their ill treatment. Rashad's dad wasn't around, but that side of the family doesn't accept his sexuality; Oz's dad called his sexuality a "phase" despite not raising him or knowing him well; ATL's brother insults him for being gay, but calls him any time he needs something; and so on. This tension is perhaps especially striking in Derrick's case, where his father calls him a fag, "gets irritated" when Derrick "does gay stuff," and told him that he "ain't raise no faggot"; indeed, he was incarcerated for eight of Derrick's first 18 years, which Derrick and Derrick's mother reminded him about when he tried to pick a fight.

"We Ain't Got No Faggot Brother"

Several of the above examples include the homophobic slur *fag/faggot* used by participants' family members to describe them or other gay men. Although not all men called fags are gay—indeed, the slur is directed at heterosexual young men often[12]—it nonetheless exists as a way to insult gender non-conformity and/or gayness. When heterosexual males said *fag/faggot*, participants did not always interpret it as inherently derogatory.[13] While it could be used dismissively to address a person who is ridiculous in some way ("Quit bein' a fag"), participants still had to process how they felt about these uses since they do identify as gay. In the case of family members, they may have experienced the word in hurtful ways, but most saw its use differently over time. Silas explained, "Whenever my dad used to call me a faggot, or queer, it used to bother me, but now I know, my dad's a hillbilly, it's just the way he talks, he doesn't mean anything by it, it's just him, so I just laugh it off." Derrick also said he was able to laugh it off or respond by cussing his dad out.

One of the times that participants disapproved of friends and family using "fag" was when it was done in anger. Of his brothers, Reese reported, "I don't know how to understand them, because when I first came out, they was like, 'You ain't no little faggot, we ain't got no faggot brother,' but now like, I don't know if it's just a straight thing where when they get mad at you, [they say] 'you fuckin' faggot,' I don't know if they're really understanding." Brandon experienced a similar scenario: "All my sisters used to call me a faggot growin' up. They still do call me faggots every time we get into an argument. But, it don't bother me no more."

Johnny also noted that "a lot of straight friends, if you get mad at them, that's the first thing they want to say to you: 'Oh, you're gay' and all that, that's the first thing everybody wanna bring up." Their gayness became the go-to insult that was always true, and usually could be construed negatively. Derrick also experienced this with his father calling him a fag: "When he get pissed at me, he likes to call me out my name. And I laugh at him, and he gets so irritated about me bein' [gay], and I don't know why."

King isn't out to most of his dad's side of the family, because he said they were from "down South" and "really homophobic." His father knew, however, and used "fag" as an insult. King explained, "Boys that show more feminine [mannerisms], [like] if they show that (snapping fingers, wobbling head) 'Yes baby girl, oh girl,' that stuff, and dress like girls, he'll say 'fag,' or 'that little gay boy,' most of the time it's 'that little fag,' [especially] if they're really flamboyant about themselves." King would give a shocked look to his father when he used the word, and his dad would reply with, "You're not a fag, I'm just saying, *that* fag," to which King replied he was "over" (not interested in hearing). That is, although his father tried to mark his use of *fag/faggot* as reserved for certain types of gay men, King believed that his father harbors at least some of that negativity about him. King would rather ignore these incidents than get into it.

This discussion is not meant to make light of such instances, as being called *fag/faggot* resulted in many negative familial interactions. JD reported that his relationship with his mother went "down the drain" as a result of his stepfather calling him a faggot, which he experienced as abuse. Such interactions extend into homophobic comments that do not contain the word "fag," but still target gay identity. For example, Joe clarified that although his dad doesn't call him a faggot anymore, he always changes the subject to focus on Joe's sexuality and teases him for it, which Joe said he "hates" because it is so "nerve-wracking." Kevin said he has no respect for his stepfather because he will crack gay jokes at his expense, while Derrick's father will insult him by comparing him to a flamboyant person with the comment, "They gayer than you!" Although these are serious occurrences, they typically did not result in physical altercations with family members. In a telling comment, Dollars said flatly, "I don't respond off people's verbal abuse, because I've heard it from my family." In instances that included extensive verbal or physical altercations, participants more often focused on discussing their negative reactions to "fag" as an epithet that marks and aggressively insults atypical gender presentation, same-sex affection, or gay symbolism ("Shut the fuck up, you little faggot") by strangers or acquaintances. The familial uses described here were irritating, but the latter, more antagonistic use by non-family persons could (and often did) spark an altercation.

Making Sense of Negative Reactions

Participants readily attributed negative reactions to religiosity. Tony stated definitively, "most Christians don't like homosexuality." Derrick said his grandma was upset with him for coming out because "she was always into God," while Bird's family told him that his sexuality was not right and that he will go to hell. Ali attributed his mom's and grandmother's hesitation to accept him to their Christianity. He explained, "They all let me know that they don't support it, or they don't agree with it, but they my family, they love me, so they ain't gon' change how they act or how they feel about me. It's been the same, they just don't like the fact that I'm gay." Greg also believed this was what underscored his mother's dislike of his sexuality: "She just don't accept the fact that I'm gay, [because of] her religion and what our family say." Josh and his family actually had to switch churches due to him bringing a gay friend with him. D.C. was even subjected to a public demonstration of his "sin": "My dad took me to church and embarrassed me by havin' me go up, and having the priest place his hand on my head, like it was an exorcism or somethin.'"

The religious men in my sample wanted to discuss "homosexuality" and religion from a philosophical and moral perspective. Both Brian and Tony discussed the Bible (and its different versions) and how it affected people's viewpoints, including their own. Jeremiah, Boog, and Oz viewed their same-sex attractions and sexual behaviors as a sin, but did not think it would send them to hell. Max and Casper also spoke about how churchgoers or clergy may want to pass judgment on them, but everyone sins and they did not want to be singled out for being gay. And Dollars and Joe had actually been dissuaded from attending church because they felt uncomfortable knowing that churchgoers might bash their sexuality. Greg even had trouble coming to terms with his sexuality because of his religion: "I always had an attraction to boys, but I never knew what it was, and I never went with it, cuz, you know, the Bible says a man's supposed to be with a woman, so I tried to portray as that."

Religion also intersected with other cultural factors to frame reactions to participants' coming out. Most participants were hesitant to make any racialized comments about how different racial/ethnic groups treat gay people, but religiosity may provide both its own explanation and a conceptual bridge to race. That is, certain interpretations of Biblical scripture can fuel anti-gay sentiment; additionally, the influence of the church within Black communities is undeniable and enduring, and has been criticized for being a driving force of homophobia within Black communities.[14] It is also understandable for participants to favor religion over race as an explanation of homophobia: if they feel that the racial or ethnic communities they were born into largely disapprove of their identity, they have a low sense of belonging. However, if they can attribute homophobic sentiments to a particular belief system (religion), these can be separated from the people expressing those beliefs, and perhaps allows participants to feel less deterministic about encountering homophobia in their communities of origin.

As stated above, it was less common for participants to think that anti-gay attitudes hinged on race. Derrick said he had "never known no difference" between Black families and white families. In terms of homophobia, Greg denied that it was heightened in any group, and instead suggested it was a problem across society at large. Though, he noted, "some Black families can be hard, I will say that." Although Adidas reasoned that the treatment of gay people ultimately depended on the family's history of dealing with groups of people unlike themselves, he did have a theory about Black families' reactions: "In the Black community, when you're gay, they think that you're gonna start wearin' girl clothes, and like, you're just gonna become automatically flamboyant, and I think that's a lotta guys' predicament, when they think their son's gay. Like, 'Oh, my son's gay, he about to start wearing skirts, he's about to start wearin' pink,' and stuff like that. That doesn't happen. I feel like that's one of the main reasons why guys think, 'I don't want my son to be gay,' and stuff like that." In this case, the issue may instead be related to misogyny, and heteronormative expectations for males. Negative, misogynistic interactions between participants and their male family members[15] were not at all uncommon, as these examples suggest. Ali commented, "My brothers, they're just boys, regular boys, they're not gay, so of course they're not gon' agree with it if they're not gay." He went on to clarify that not all straight boys have a problem with gay boys, though some do because "they're not gay," implying they disagree *because* they are straight. One academic explanation of these phenomena ties Black masculinity and homophobia to Black nationalism, which then renders effeminacy as closely connected with both weakness and whiteness, constructing Black gay men (especially those who are effeminate) as race traitors.[16]

Other Black participants were also willing to discuss how their racial or ethnic identities factored into negative responses to their gayness, but were more explicit in asserting their beliefs in racial differences. Max boldly stated, "Not to be racist, but white people seem to accept more who you are before you know who you are, versus Black people tryna push who you are on you before you know who you are." Rashad said, "It's nervous at times, just bein' Black and gay, cuz you don't never know what you can get into." When I asked him for detail about being Black and gay, he suggested that Black gay men "get bashed," particularly if gay people dress in drag or are animated. Darius was particularly willing to indict the Black community:

See, in the Black community, bein' gay is not the best option. It is not, that's the last option you wanna tell somebody. Cuz, they're very violent with gay people, so it's like, okay, don't tell them, that be the last group of people you tell. That's why it be so hard for Black gays to tell they parents and stuff like that, because 9 times out of 10, your parent will put chu out there, too. They will go tell they friends, their kids will overhear it, and it's out there. Cuz that's how my mother is, like, once I told her, the whole neighborhood knew, and I was like, I can't tell you nothin'! So, that's why we kinda never really clicked, I never really clicked with nobody, cuz you can't tell people nothin' nowadays, unless you want them to hear it. And then, the stuff you want them to hear, they don't listen to you. So, it's like, a meaningless way to say anything.

Darius's narrative reveals not only his general apprehension regarding attitudes toward gay people within society and the Black community, but also his deep-seated mistrust of his mother, who was incarcerated for six years during his childhood. For young men like Darius who fear losing ties to their families of origin and the respect of peers in their ethnic or racial communities, the decision to come out and befriend other gay youth is wrought with uncertainty: they may gain support from one community, but lose acceptance in another. This is consistent with prior research that suggests queer youth of color may feel the need to "choose" between their sexual identity and their racial identity.[17] Additionally, some heterosexual Black people see LGBTQ Black people as denying their blackness because they associate homosexuality with white culture; this leads many queer people of color to feel conflict because they perceive (or actually experience) racism in queer communities and heterosexism in Black communities.[18] Commenting on such tensions, Bird said, "Sometimes I find it very hard for me in this society because I'm young, I'm gay, and I'm Black. And sometimes that's still not a good thing, and . . . it's really really really hard to not think like that."

The nexus between race, culture, religion, and gay identity is best illustrated in Jordan's narrative. Jordan emigrated from East Africa to the U.S. at the age of 13 when his parents "won" the green card lottery. He mentioned that his family was religious, "family oriented," "conservative about family issues," and intimately connected to the African immigrant community in Columbus. I asked how they reacted when he came out. He replied:

> JORDAN: They were pretty (pause) not-so-into-it. (chuckles) . . . At least the way they said it, they were like, "We don't really support it, but you're still family, so we can't really turn our back on you."
>
> VP: Did they think that it was going to reflect on them at all?
>
> JORDAN: Mmm-hmm [yes]. Cuz people are pretty ignorant, and they think that you can raise your child to be gay, or it's like, a sickness or something you now have.
>
> VP: Do you think it has more to do with something culturally, like, because of where they're from, or because of their religion?
>
> JORDAN: I think both, cuz the Catholic Church condemns homosexuality, and then you have [my home country] that has sodomy laws in place, and so they both work together into it.

He later added that when he saw members of the African community, they treated him as if he were sick or mentally ill, and although it was upsetting, he would brush it off and doesn't "read too much into it." Interestingly, he noted that the African community did not want to associate with African American communities in Columbus, because they viewed them as immoral, "ghetto," and believed that they were as depicted in "rap videos." When I asked if he could be out in his home country, he hedged: "I probably could get away with it in certain circles, but I couldn't just do that and just be out, and go hold hands with a guy and make out in the middle of the street." So, although his identity wasn't seen as culturally acceptable, moving to the U.S. has allowed him freedom that could not have been realized in his birthplace. Although American queer persons may face misogyny and homophobia, they cannot be legally prosecuted for their gay identity or same-sex sexual behavior; the same cannot be said for queer people globally.[19]

How to Create a Respectable Gay Identity

Identity formation, disclosure, and performance are all interactional processes; this chapter focused primarily on how my research participants balanced cultural expectations and their own values as they learned how to create a respectable gay identity. Participants described their experiences as children—many were accused of being effeminate or gay at young ages, primarily if they had any interests in gender-atypical activities and behavior. In order to counteract such assumptions, they engaged in strategies such as outright denial and having girlfriends as "cover-ups." However, once they began to make sense of their same-sex attractions and identities, they came out to at least some people in their lives. Despite their apprehensions and the messages they had heard (some directly from the individuals they came out to), reactions to these disclosures were not uniformly negative, though many from family members were tainted with less than full acceptance. Participants attributed negative reactions primarily to religiosity, but also to cultural factors such as race and ethnicity, as well as expectations of heteronormative masculinity espoused by fathers and brothers. Such meanings and interactions illustrate forces of misogyny and heterosexism—endemic in our society, they permeate identity formation processes and inter-personal exchanges. It is with these meanings and reactions in mind that participants' interactions with others, including their peers, their romantic interests, and their fellow gang members, are appropriately framed for subsequent chapters.

Participants' experiences with gay identity formation are similar to those found in the literature, even among older queer people. I was struck by sociologist Dana Rosenfeld's findings with gay and lesbian elders, some of whom formed their gay identities as early as the 1920s. Those who formed these identities before the late 1960s had vastly different experiences than those who did so in the late 1960s or after, due to events like the Stonewall Riots and the gay liberation movement. She identifies them as having discreditable and accredited identities, respectively. The pre-liberation cohort developed their identities under a "stigmatizing discourse," whereas the latter did so in a milieu where gay folks rejected being oppressed for their desires and encouraged other gays and lesbians to stop "colluding in their own destruction due to cowardice, ignorance, or self-hatred."[20] For example, the "discreditable" cohort did not appreciate gay people who "flaunted" their sexuality, came out publicly, and participated in gay pride events, primarily because they saw too many possibilities for marginalization to arise from such actions. Many years later, the men in my study seem to have come out in a similar milieu, where they felt the need to hide their sexuality to avoid stigma. They were told not to flaunt, not to be gay in public, not to let out that big secret. And yet, in the vein of the accredited identity, participants wanted not to hide it, not to drag others into the deception, not to be disrespected by their families of origin. They wanted to make it right.

2

Who's the Fag?

Negotiating Gayness and Visibility

I had been in the field and conducting interviews for this study for over two years, and had heard the words "fag" and "faggot" a dizzying number of times. In interviews alone, these words appeared well over 400 times. I used a Microsoft Word function to count them and, as if it actually had a brain, the program flashed these words on the screen: "That shows up a lot!"

On numerous occasions, the first time a participant used it to refer to another gay man with me and wasn't quoting what someone else said, he would call attention to his usage. After using the word, it was common for a participant to stop talking and laugh, or apologize, or try to explain it away. Jeremy called it "a habit," while M6 said, "I use that word but I don't mean it offensively . . . that's just how we refer to each other out here. I saw you roll your eyes, but no offense." I don't think I rolled my eyes, but I'll bet I visibly reacted early on in my data collection by widening them.

Because of its frequency I must have become totally desensitized, because I started using it occasionally in the field with participants, both in making jokes and talking matter-of-factly about others. There was also no shortage of other misogynistic things I encountered, no doubt influenced by my fairly masculine gender presentation and the fact that I dated women, but also the reality that many participants spent most of their time with other males.

Some time after my study concluded, I was talking with a queer female friend about someone we both knew. I didn't know he was gay, but she mentioned that he was. He was somewhat feminine and well-dressed and I did suspect his gayness, but didn't know for sure. As soon as the words came out of my mouth, I realized I had made a mistake.

"Oh, is he a big ol' faggot?"

Stunned silence from my friend.

I myself went through the same pause, nervous laugh, excuse, and apology. I attempted a feeble justification: I have dealt with the word so much lately that it sort of lost its forbidden flair, and I'm part of the queer community who has had the word lodged at it. So was she, though, and she didn't dig it. Ultimately I apologized, but the conversation was soured.

I still think of that moment a long time later and the questions I asked myself. Am I allowed to use that word? Was I using it in a misogynistic or homophobic way? Should it be taboo among the communities that are arguably entitled to use it? Maybe, it occurred to me, since I am not male, I shouldn't be using it. Should anyone?

* * *

Calling forth the "fag"—and calling out those who are alleged to be one—is a way that people informally police men, with the hope of shaming them into sexual and gender conformity. This epithet is not only used to shame them for feminine behaviors or for being open about their gay sexual identities, but to punish them as well. It is meant to mark them as different and inferior. The cultural construction of "the fag" existed alongside participants' journeys to self-identification and disclosures. During my data collection, it quickly became apparent that *fag/faggot* referenced a series of context-specific meanings, each with different intentions and consequences. Although I had suspected that these words would arise in a project focusing on constructions and negotiations of masculine and gay identities, I could not have predicted their importance in how participants made sense of social interactions with various others: family members, friends, and even strangers. In interviews and fieldwork, participants both referenced and actively used these words, and I became attuned to how they made sense of the exact same word under very different contexts.

"Faggot," though it also can refer to a cigarette or a bundle of sticks or metal rods, has existed as an insult for gay men for about 100 years in the United States. In its original usage, dating back hundreds of years, it referred to heretics and burning them, and it was even used as a disparaging term for women.[1] It is little wonder that its more recent life is as an insult for gay or effeminate men. Despite its existence as a hurtful pejorative, some gay individuals and liberation groups have used *fag/faggot* to refer to themselves or other gay men for several decades, suggesting an in-group/out-group dynamic to the word as well. Fag is arguably the least reclaimed of the well-known gay slurs, as there are a number of "queer studies" departments across the country, and some cities feature a "Dyke March" and also a contingent of "Dykes on Bikes" during Pride festivals. I explicitly explore the salient image of "the fag" and its implications for identity negotiation, which also contributes insights about the meanings that urban gay men of color ascribe to this word.

Because gender patrolling can involve not just verbal epithets but also physical violence against the transgressor, gay men's motivations for avoiding effeminacy are grounded both in concerns about social status and in practical concerns such as visibility and thus physical safety. Constructing a gay identity separate from being "the fag," then, is not only a matter of one's own personal desires or sensibilities, but a consideration for the interactional aspects of social life: for which gender transgressions will they be held accountable, and to whom? Whether a man has successfully presented a conventionally masculine persona is partly determined by his success in distancing himself from mannerisms or attitudes considered feminine or gay, which are devalued. A guiding concern of what to avoid is what sociologist C. J. Pascoe might deem "the threatening specter of the fag"[2]—a failure to achieve a gender presentation that inspires confidence in one's masculinity and heterosexuality. The previous chapter suggested that such considerations factor not only into identity formation, but into identity disclosures and presentation. Furthermore, factors such as race, culture, and gang membership can structure individuals' presentations of self but also their self-perceptions, as they view themselves partially through the lens of how others view them or could view them. Thus, all of these considerations can have significant effects on their senses of self, their opinions of other queer people, and their opinions of what a respectable gay identity entails.

This chapter builds on the previous one by moving beyond a discussion of cultural messages participants had heard regarding how a "fag" looks and acts, to the values they have internalized about acceptable and unacceptable masculine and gay identities. Participants were well-versed in who "the fag" was and, as a result, they constructed extensive boundaries between appropriate and inappropriate behavior for gay men. However, these boundaries often proved to be general guide-lines, which could be transgressed under particular circumstances. As I discuss throughout, there exists a palpable tension between idealized masculine behavior, which allows a man to gain masculine status with others and general society, and accepting the full range of how gender is enacted. The tension exists precisely because acceptance of gender fluid-ity has been so stifled in many participants' lives. I conclude the chapter by discussing an evening spent at a vogue ball, where these boundaries became even more fluid and where femininity could be celebrated.

"What's Up, Fag?"

The men in my study used the words *fag/faggot* in many varied ways, some of which were reminiscent of the ways heterosexual males used them. Similar, though not completely analogous gradations were evident in the use of *fag/faggot* among gay and bisexual men. Most importantly, although historically an extremely loaded term, *fag/faggot* had little connotation on its own, and instead had shifting meanings that were context-dependent, even among other gay men.

Johnny insulted a rival gay gang by calling them "a bunch of fags" and agreed that he would fight over being called a fag, but also relayed this when I asked if "fag" was only used negatively:

> Uhh-uhh [no]. Like, you could be like, "Whatchu doin', fag?" And I'll be like, "Aww, nuttin', chillin'," you know. I don't always take it offensive. . . . Like, if somebody walk up to me and they don't know me, say for instance I'm at a gay club and somebody be like, "What's up, fag?" I'ma look like, "I don't know you like that to be callin' me no fag," you know what I'm sayin', even if he is gay too. It's disrespectful for you to just walk up to me and call me a fag and you don't know me. . . . So, it just depends on the circumstances, like, in the situation and all of that.

Thus, "fag" could be used as a social greeting for a fellow gay or bisexual man, though some participants like Johnny specified that this use was more likely to occur without incident among gay men who knew each other. As mentioned, participants frequently used the term themselves, usually being reflexive about saying it only because they were saying it to me. This illustrates complicated in-group/out-group dynamics in using this typically pejorative term.

A reclaimed or reappropriated word is a term that was formerly used as a slur, but has been semantically transformed by members of the maligned group, who may instead utilize it in an oppositional or positive manner.[3] Linguist Robin Brontsema suggests that the use of epithets by the "targets" of those insults can be a "self-emancipation that defies hegemonic linguistic ownership and the (ab)use of power."[4] Reclaimed words are usually offensive to the in-group when used by outsiders, especially in light of historically grounded power relations (such as the controversy over the use of "nigga"). When in-groups are very diverse, this can present challenges to the uniform acceptance of the reclaimed word. In this case, the men in my study may have felt somewhat uncomfortable with their use of *fag/faggot* because I am female. While I am part of the queer community more broadly and they recognized me as such, when it comes to the use of this particular word, they may have essentially placed me in an out-group. In this case, I may very well be there.

There is no indication that *fag/faggot* has been reclaimed on any large scale, and although my findings do suggest some level of reclamation among friends, they also support a continued negative association between these gay epithets and poorly regarded social behavior. On this note, *fag/faggot* was also used to other[5] and shame flamboyant gay men who were acting loud, dramatic, feminine, or generally "too gay." In a related way, *fag/faggot* was used to describe stereotypically effeminate activities or grooming habits. These included vogue dancing or wearing skinny jeans, regarding which some participants declared, "I don't do that faggot shit." However, some of these declarations are context-dependent. Not two hours after Baby told me that he didn't do "faggot shit" like voguing, I saw him pull a few vogue moves on a makeshift dance floor in Aga's bedroom after he and his friends pushed a mattress up against the wall to make space. Baby laughed as he saw me watching from the doorway, caught his stocking cap as it fell off of his head during a move, and added that he didn't perform at competitive vogue balls; rather, he "just needed the exercise."

Finally, gay men used the term in other forms to describe reactive behavior, such as acting in aggressive and flamboyant ways simultaneously to deal with conflict ("fagging out"). Thus, as a signal of its dynamic uses, *fag/faggot* was employed as a noun, an adjective, and even a verb. I detail all of these uses more in the next section.

Criminological literature on bias crime victimization would suggest that at least one of these uses of *fag/faggot* is familiar to criminologists: that of an anti-gay slur that is associated with heterosexist violence and marginalization. Other linguistic attributes, such as contradictions between in-group and out-group usages, are likely recognizable to many social scientists. However, an in-depth analysis of *fag/faggot* reveals insights far beyond its status as an epithet that has been occasionally and situationally reclaimed; it also indicates pervasive societal expectations that demand normative masculinity and discourage femininity among men, regardless of sexual orientation. That is, even among a group whose members have been called fags in an attempt to mandate their behavior, homophobic and misogynistic uses of *fag/faggot* persist. Set largely against a backdrop of negative perceptions of gay men, calling another gay man a fag was one way to create and enforce boundaries between appropriate and inappropriate behavior, and thus construct a respectable gay identity. Participants' negative uses of the term did not always map onto their heterosexual family/friends' usages of it, suggesting that at least some of the standards for respectable gay identity and gender presentation arose in queer circles, though they were likely influenced by outsiders' expectations of them.

"The Fag"

Participants simultaneously condemned the use of "fag" not just as a form of disrespect to themselves and the gay community, but as an insult that connected them to a portion of the gay community to which they did *not* want to belong. Their descriptions of who was "the fag" or who was "too gay" help illustrate the value they placed on traditional masculine behavior. To be accepted and respected as gay was seen as challenge enough; were participants to be associated with the folk devil of "the fag," it would endanger their claim to masculine respectability.

Virtually no one had anything positive to say about "the faggot." Spiderman stated, "A fag would be somebody that acts gay, dress gay. You wear tights, you 'Girl this, girl that,' just actin' gay." When I asked Darius to expand on how someone "acts gay," he replied: "Oh my God, they switch! They wear colorful clothes, they get all these type of piercins, their haircuts. Their voice is like a lil girl, and you be lookin' like, 'You grown! Act like you got some balls between your legs.' And then they wear the gayest shoes! Half the time, they wear girls' shoes! And I be lookin' like, 'What?' And they loud, some of 'em be loud for no reason." Regarding other negative "gay" behaviors, Johnny explained that "fags" could be "messy" and "gossip so much"; Jeremiah believed that feminine gay guys who "are out on the scene, stay in a lot of drama." He also suggested that because they date within the same circles of people, diseases are more prevalent. ATL added, "Faggots are nasty, them nasty punks. . . . Basically, in our dictionary from down south, a faggot is nasty people that goes up, lay [have sex], and give people diseases and all this and that." It is unsurprising that negative cultural stereotypes of gay men, such as alleged promiscuity and disease spreading,[6] have made their way into some participants' meaning system as associated with feminine gay men.

Stereotypically feminine grooming behavior was frequently mentioned for how a "gay boy" "acts gay." Brad stated that flamboyant gay men were "not my type of people." He explained that his friends work on cars and hang out in garages or the woods—bastions of "country" masculinity, with which he as a white male from a rural area identified—while flamboyant gay guys talk about getting their hair, nails, or eyebrows done, and are loud. What follows are two examples of men who might engage in these grooming behaviors semi-regularly; Elijah in his daily life, and Jeremy when he is in women's clothing (perhaps for drag performances, but sometimes off the stage, as well). However, they take issue with other "faggots" who engage in these behaviors either too often or in unacceptable ways. Elijah said, "I don't want chu to be switchin' your hips, paintin' your nails, straightenin' your hair, dyein' your hair, you know? Leave that to me! And I don't even do most of that. I mean, I dye my hair, but I dye my hair and it still look masculine. Or, I paint my nails, but I paint it a clear coat. You know? Like, it's gay people out there who get acrylic on they nails, and get extensions, that is disgusting to me! Don't come around me like that." Jeremy's comments also suggest themes of being loud, stereotypical, and sexually aggressive:

Gay boys can be too much! Like, if you around straight boys, gay boys tend to act more gay-er, and that's prolly why that's a turn-off to them. It's just the way the fag-, I mean, the gay boys—it's a habit! (laughs) It's a habit to call 'em that. . . . It's the way they carry theirselves. Like, if I was to bring a straight boy in my lil clique around, not all of 'em, but a few, will queen out. And then start tryna make passes, which make him uncomfortable. Which piss me off, which get them upset! (laughs) . . . If I'm around a straight boy, 9 outta 10 times, I have on hair, I have my nails done, I do. And I know how to talk, you feel me? If I'm gonna dress a female, I'm going to act like a female. I'm not going to still say all the gay slangs, and [my friends] be in here, like, "What's the T [what's up], bitch?" and "That's a gag," and "Gurl, that is the—" I don't have time for that. And so now the straight boy lookin' at them, like, "Okay, umm, I gotta go," and I be like, "Are you sure?" and they be like, "Yeah, I'ma call you later," and then they'll text me, "Man, I don't wanna be around all them fags," and this and that. I'm like, "Y'all don't know how to act when boys is around! Y'all wanna queen out. Fuckin' faggots!" When I do say it like that, they don't do nothin' but laugh and stuff. They'll be like, "Who you talkin' to?" They think I be playin', but I be dead serious!

Jeremy notes several things that he claims irritate straight men: gay men acting flamboyant, hitting on them, and presenting as male but acting in feminine ways. Being flamboyant was seen as something unnecessary and aggravating. In nearly an exhausted way, Rocc asserted, "You can be gay, but you don't have to be flamboyant." Bird stated, "I always carried myself as a man, because we *are* men, ya know. I am a man so I have to have that backbone as a man instead of a flaming gay guy, cuz most of them don't have backbones." But interestingly, Bird enjoys wearing makeup because it heightens his feminine facial features and thus his attractiveness, while Jeremy regularly explores a fluid gender presentation: "I have my days when I feel real boy-ish, then I don't know, sometimes my voice just get like, hella deep, and I can't control it. So, I just goes wit it. But then sometimes, my voice can get real high-pitched, and I just put the hair in, and let's go! You never know who I'ma be." Rigid standards against acting gay or feminine thus are not as clear-cut as they may seem. As an expression of identity, artistry, or beauty, femininity could be acceptable, but when it crossed a line into increased visibility and thus could garner *unwanted* attention, it became problematic.

"Fags Is Not My Type": Visibility and Safety

Being flamboyant or being a "faggot" was associated with increased visibility. Although sexual orientation is not inherently visible, participants were well aware that non-normative cues would cause others to make the conceptual leap that they were gay, and then might attempt to patrol their identities. One strategy to avoid anti-gay harassment was to not call too much attention to oneself by not being feminine, and to modify one's behavior so as not to be read as gay. Eric stated, "I have my [flamboyant] moments, but it's not like an all-day every day thing." Bird said, "When I meet people, I might come off gay, but I try to not come off what they expect me to be. Like, 'Oh, you look gay, but do you act gay?' No, I don't." Boog suggested that the necessity of a uniformly masculine presentation has decreased over the years, but still influences his behavior: "I wouldn't necessarily try to be tough now, back then I probably would have, but I still have this image, so yeah, I'd probably act tough, act a different way, talk about girls, do the things they [other men/gang members] do, just to fit in." While many situations encouraged participants to tone down their effeminacy or gayness, such as hanging out with other masculine men, certain situations presented themselves as chances to "act gay." Batman explained, "With my gay friends, a lot of them are more feminine. I might pick up that trait when I'm around them, and we just might talk about guys, or whatever, and with my straight friends the whole persona is different. I don't know, it's like having two personalities. I act more straight with straight friends and act more gay with gay friends, pretty much. [My gay friends] bring it out. Their fabulousness and rainbowness just makes me happy, so I'm just like, (singing) 'Ohhhhhh.'" Logically, Batman's gay friends allowed him a safe space to express his same-sex attractions and to explore his gender presentation. However, the vast majority of spaces, especially public ones, were not seen to be the time or place for freedom in presentation.

Whether men were mostly out or not, hanging with flamboyant gay guys could bring their own sexuality into the spotlight within the larger society. Masculine-acting friends or boyfriends assisted in the goal of staying hidden, as they were often mistaken for straight. Several men spoke exactly to the issue of safety in public. Elijah said, "I don't want nobody that's more feminine than me. I would like for them not to even look gay, at all, you know? So, if I wanted to just walk around with the dude, we both wouldn't be called fags." Others agreed, and specifically made the distinction between friends and love interests. Javier explained, "[I like] basically masculine guys that's not—you know, if I was walking down the street with 'em, somebody could say that's my friend, not my boyfriend, you know what I'm saying? I don't want nobody who's twistin' [dancing/"switching"] walkin' down the street with me. . . . I have all kinds of friends that's like that. I love 'em, but I don't wanna date nobody that's like that." Oz shared a similar sentiment:

> I don't like flamboyant guys. I like guys who know that they're guys. If they're dressed like girls, really girly, that's not my type. We can be friends, [but] can't be nothin' else. If I wanna be with a girl, I could be with a girl. If I wanna be with a guy, he could be gay, as long as he still knows he's a male, we're good. That's what really turns me on, cuz he still knows he's a guy, and he dresses like a guy, and acts like a guy, and it's like, when we go out, won't people know that we're gay unless we're hugged-up.

Presumably, anyone can be friends with anyone else, but if a man is in public with another man who is flamboyant, participants knew that their own sexual orientation would become visible, or at least may be subject to inspection and questioning.

Concerns about interpersonal interactions also extended from the public sphere to private settings, such as with friends and in the home. That is, concerns about visibility, status, and safety were present in interactions with strangers *and* with valued others, especially for members of straight gangs. Spiderman explained that his type of guy was someone who he could take around his friends and they wouldn't know they were dating. He said, "I feel like, if I take you around my friends, and you actin' all gay, then [they'll say], 'Why you hangin' out wit this fag?'" The same goes for Adidas with his family. He thought his low-key personality "wouldn't fit someone else's personality that's really flamboyant," and he didn't want to date someone who was "super flamboyant" or "super gay." He wants someone who "I can bring them around the parents, and they won't be like, 'Oh, that's too much,' or 'That's too gay,' or someone will be like, 'Are they friends, or is that boy gay or not?' I kind of want it to be in between." King said he'd rather date a man who is "solid about his stuff, and don't do the marching in the parade, but he knows that he gay." There are few actions more visible than marching in the gay pride parade—a literal celebration of the ability to be out and express being gay in public.

Not only would hanging out with straight-acting guys help conceal participants' own sexual orientations, it would shield them from other negative perceptions. Raphael stated that although he was not trying to be judgmental, he "just can't be seen with a feminine person" because he thought "all attention" was going to be on him, and he wondered what people were going to say. He followed that up quickly by saying that he didn't care what people said, thereby trying to establish some independence from salient cultural messages, but clearly he does care on some level. Silas's comments illustrated these tensions between having one's own opinion but not wanting to be affected by others' opinions of them:

> I just don't like being around a lot of gay people, like a crowd of gay people, it makes me feel very self-conscious and uncomfortable. . . . Because of the way they're acting, and people will be looking at me, and I wonder what they're thinking about me. I'm pretty self-conscious when it comes to that stuff, because I know what I think about other people, when I look at them, and I'm sure I'm not the only person who thinks like that. . . . And they judge you. . . . [Gay people are] superficial, and I'm not superficial. . . . I care what I look like, but I'm not like, a princess about it, I don't go tanning every day at the tanning bed, I don't get my eyebrows done, I don't get my nails done, and I'm not trying to look sexy for the next person. I'm just me, and if you hang around with a lot of gay people, that is how they are. They just want to be "it." I'm just me, I'm not "it."

Especially in light of participants' concerns regarding their masculine gender presentation and involvement in traditionally masculine behavior and criminality (such as gang membership), becoming visibly "gay" and thus a target for close scrutiny were sources of anxiety. This anxiety is partly what drives situational identity negotiation, pulling participants back to a neutral or masculine presentation. The ways participants make sense of such tensions provides insight into how and why they arrived at their own sensibilities about how a gay man should act.

Perhaps unsurprisingly, the majority of participants preferred traditionally masculine guys, sometimes "straight-acting" (or even heretofore straight) guys. This was true regardless of where the participant was on the spectrum of gender presentation. For example, Kevin reported, "I'm a feminine boy by myself, I don't need another princess walkin' around." A few very traditionally masculine participants did like feminine guys, and others reported no physical preference, but the preference against femininity was overwhelming and often very strongly worded. Reese prefaced his comment of "You're not a girl, don't try to be one" with "I do not like flamboyant gay men." Spiderman stated definitively, "I don't mess with [have sex with/date] fags. Fags is not my type." Even Boss, who reported no preference, explained, "I do like a boy cuz he's a boy, you know? Not a boy that wants to be a girl. I might as well just be wit a girl." Boss's sentiments echoed common refrains regarding gay orientation. I heard several comments that were nearly identical. Marcus said: "I'm a boy, and I like boys, so I wanna be wit a boy, not somebody that acts like a girl." Rocc rationalized, "If I wanted somebody to act like a female, I'd just date a female." Of feminine guys, Toby claimed, "I feel like they remind me of a girl, so I don't wanna really be with that." And Nate playfully noted, "I want a dude that look like a dude, act like a dude. Cuz, if I want a girl, I can get a girl. I was bisexual once."

Participants also specified signals of gay culture to be associated with visibility and with what they considered to be less-than-desirable behavior. Nate explained, "I really don't judge or discriminate, but I don't go for the girly-girl dudes, like, just too much loud, and stuff like that. That's femme, wearin' the skinny jeans, and just, vogue. (pause) Well, I'm not gonna say that, cuz I have been wit a couple that vogue, but the girly-girl type just turn me off. It's nothin' there." Nate essentially sums up other men's concerns with a three-item list: femme, skinny jeans, and vogue. Although Nate clarified what he meant, "vogue" was a regular code term for femininity and flamboyance; indeed, even Javier's comment above about not wanting someone to walk down the street "twistin'" can reference vogue moves and performativity. Baby called vogue balls "faggot shit"; Jeremiah didn't like the "drama" of the "gay scene"; Javier and Juan felt that feminine men were a "turn-off" to them; and Max claimed that in light of his large, muscular stature and mannerisms, the only way someone could tell he was gay was if they saw him wearing skinny jeans, which he did on occasion.

Aga even went so far as to connect masculine behavior with hetero-sexual behavior: "I like to date boys that are masculine, that act like boys. Those that don't portray themselves to be gay, that act straight." Perhaps in light of negative perceptions about effeminacy in general and effemi-nate behavior enacted by men in particular, various (and diverse) gay male communities do seem to voice an overall preference for norma-tively masculine men as romantic and sexual partners.[7] These interview excerpts are at the nexus of comments that are inherently dismissive of effeminacy and gay culture, but also likely reflect practical consider-ations regarding visibility, safety, and status.

Flexible Preferences

Despite such strong declarations, participants wanted to allow for some flexibility regarding the gender presentation of their friends or intimate partners. While Toby did say, "I like guys who act like guys, and guys that are not feminine," he also clarified, "I don't mind a little bit of feminine." Greg noted that while a romantic partner can do a little bit of "gay stuff" here and there, he shouldn't be "gay" all the time. Sometimes, the feminin-ity of the man was not so much the issue as whether or not he was involved in gay drama. Nate and Darius both said they didn't want to date feminine guys, but clarified some of their hesitation. Nate explained, "I like in-between, I guess, like myself, that's discreet, that's not known out through Columbus, and stuff like that. I just don't mess wit them. . . . But I wouldn't say masculine, I'd prolly say in-between guys." Darius similarly specified:

> The [type of] dude I like, he gotta be laid-back, ain't all in that drama, and into all the gay stuff. Like, I don't really like the lil gay scene or whatever, I mean, I appreciate it, and I accept it, but I live a regular life, like a straight dude, like any heterosexual. It's just, I talk to a male. . . . And I don't really like feminine boys. Like, you can have a lil feminine, but chu cain't be too feminine, like, all this and all of that (making sweeping hand gestures), no, that's gay! That's gay! I don't like gay boys. (laughs) Well, you see what I'm sayin', like, flamboyant.

Darius soon reiterated, "I just don't wanna be around a lotta drama. I just wanna live a regular life." Even the use of Nate's phrases such as "not known" and "discreet" evoke a sense of anonymity and being hidden, the opposite of queer visibility.[8] It should be clear that these concerns are related to those expressed by others, capturing various considerations regarding their preferences for blending in, and are not unique to Nate's or Darius's narratives.

Of course, some participants with preferences wanted to rise above restrictive rules for other people, especially because of societal judgments on gay identity. Boss explained,

> I think in the beginning, I was more attracted to guys that looked straight that are really gay . . . because I didn't want anybody to know, I didn't wanna be wit somebody that looked gay, or was just out there, or anything like that, but now, I can be wit a feminine guy too, and be wit a masculine guy. I don't really have a preference if they're feminine or if they're masculine, it's more of who they are, and how well we get along, and that type of thing, versus, I think I'm past the stage of judgin' people. I wanna judge somebody for who they are, not for the way that . . . they act . . . or they look.

And Dollars went beyond this to say that his own mannerisms could determine whom he wanted to be with: "If I'm feelin' feminine, and I have my skinny jeans, (laughs) I don't want to date another feminine guy. I would want somebody who's masculine, and if I'm masculine, I wanna date somebody who's feminine." Ultimately, such statements are an acknowledgement of maturation processes, changing preferences, and moves toward accepting differences. Identity formation occurs over time and is affected by interactional processes, such as the homophobic and misogynistic reactions experienced by participants, after which they are able to critically reflect on how restrictive gender patrolling can be.

Even Darius, who had much to say regarding feminine men and flamboyant behavior, realized why they might be so loud, colorful, and flamboyant: "I understand some of the reasons why some of 'em like that, cuz gay people go through a lot. Cuz, I went through a lot, so, if I went through a lot, it ain't no tellin' what the next person went through." Darius's willingness to detail stigmatized "gay behavior" perhaps belies his subsequent vacillation regarding the importance of these behaviors to gay resistance. Such measures even include "fagging out," a method of acting in aggressive and flamboyant ways simultaneously. Although Darius can appreciate the use of defense mechanisms to deal with gender harassment and anti-gay sentiment, he is conflicted about it. Because he desires to assimilate into "regular life," flamboyant gay behavior by his friends or romantic partners would mark him as gay and therefore render him visible to the larger society. Darius's hoodie, backwards hat, tattoos, and loose fitting, low-worn dark blue jeans aid in his masculine gender presentation and invisibility as a gay man. Despite (or perhaps *because of*) his history of rejection by his friends, family, and gang due to his sexuality, he suggests he is like "any heterosexual."

Despite the preference for masculine partners, I was surprised when participants were critical of their sexual or romantic partners who did not want to come out. The group they were specifically referring to was men who they called "the trade": masculine and straight-acting guys who are either gay or bisexual, or who at least have sex with men, but will not claim any identity other than heterosexual. A mantra I frequently heard was, "You cannot date the trade." One day, when hanging out with Aga, Imani, and Ali, the subject of the trade came up:

VP: Would you ever date the trade?

IMANI: The trade is good for one thing, and that's dick.

AGA: O-kay [agreed].

IMANI: I can't ever see myself in a relationship with the trade.

AGA: The trade is too stressful.

IMANI: I had to get this tranny together [give her a reality check], she said, "I'm in a relationship with the trade." I said, "Does your trade take you out in public, Miss Thang? No, I don't think so."

VP: Why are these trades not out?

AGA: They're scared.

ALI: Because of they rep! Some of them are hood niggas.

The reason the trade was considered stressful was because of the scenarios that sometimes arose precisely because they were not out or not open about relationships, including interference from jealous girlfriends, amorous ex-girlfriends, demanding "baby mamas," "homeboys" who encouraged them to get with girls, family and friends who they would never introduce, and so on. Trades were simultaneously eroticized by most participants for their rugged masculinity and their "hoodness"; my guys sometimes even slipped into fantasies during our conversations. What continued after the conversation above was Imani imagining a "hood nigga" who sold drugs, and he started drifting off into daydreamland, saying, "Yes, just come in wit'cho baggy outfit." Aga contributed to the vision (or maybe he was telling Imani to calm down?), "Keep yo' boots on." Imani quickly added that he would prefer jocks, though.

It is paradoxical that participants could want partners who were not visibly gay so that the two of them could blend in, but would be dissatisfied with the trade who blended in almost completely to the point that it caused strain. It seems, however, that the issue is about intent and identity: straight-acting guys are just *pretending* to be straight, whereas the trade seem to be *convinced* that they are straight, or are fundamentally unwilling to proclaim their sexuality because of their peers' expectations. They want to maintain their masculine and straight "rep" (reputation). Men may well identify as straight and engage in sexual acts with other men,[9] but my participants didn't see that as a viable state of being. Ali even suggested that I should ask future participants if they would date the trade (and I did start doing so), ostensibly because of the disagreements among gay male communities and what men's answers could signal about their preferences.

"That's So Gay": Internalization of Cultural Messages

In sum, fags are "too gay" in that they are unnecessarily loud, dramatic, femininely groomed, or otherwise inappropriately behaved for a man. Boog even went so far as to suggest that feminine gay guys are not real men. As discussed, heterosexual men may try to police and control the behavior of non-heterosexual men, and my findings suggest that gay men also try to construct boundaries around ideal gay male behavior. Although some men deemed feminine behavior a "turn-off," often their concerns were external in nature. That is, participants were fine with flamboyant gay men at least some of the time, especially in private, but did not like being in public with them because of the "attention" and negative reactions they elicited. Flamboyant gay men presented an obstacle to their strategic or sustained public identification as masculine (and even straight); this identity work continued during the interview when they expressed their displeasure with the actions of "fags."

What beliefs contribute to this dislike and disapproval of men who are "too gay"? It could be argued that participants' internalized homophobia is behind these sentiments. Internalized homophobia describes an individual's acceptance of and agreement with their own sexual stigma, which refers broadly to the "negative regard, inferior status, and relative powerlessness that society collectively accords anyone associated with nonheterosexual behaviors, identity, relationships, or communities."[10] It can include an unwillingness to publicly identify as gay, the perception that there is a stigma associated with being gay, a lack of social comfort with gay men, and the belief that being gay is morally and religiously unacceptable.[11]

Internalized homophobia has been linked with health-related risk behaviors such as alcohol use, illicit drug use, smoking, and high-risk sexual behaviors,[12] and is compounded with racial stigma for Latino and Black men.[13] The formation of gay identity may even be impeded by internalized homophobia,[14] as the stigma against homosexuality discourages LGB individuals from discussing their sexual desires or activities with their peer groups or families. This creates identity confusion when a young person avoids her/his sexual feelings because s/he has internalized society's views on these feelings, specifically, that they are unacceptable.[15]

Internalized homophobia is also associated with adverse psychological symptoms, such as shame, guilt, and low self-esteem,[16] as well as lower relationship satisfaction, shorter relationships, a lower proportion of social time spent with gay people, low membership in gay/bisexual groups, and low disclosure of sexual orientation.[17] Although some participants report not having a lot of gay friends or hanging out with a lot of gay people, every participant but one was recruited through another gay or transgender person, whether it was their boyfriend, a friend, or myself. Finally, for those who are less "out" than others, this is likely a result of foreseeable violence or rejection by fellow gang members, friends, and biological family members, instead of (or at least in addition to) internalized homophobia.

Although homophobia may be internalized as shame, gay individuals can also engage in "enacted sexual stigma" by shunning other gay individuals or by using anti-gay epithets.[18] Clearly, participants used anti-gay epithets to refer to other gay men who they perceived to be inappropriately gendered, but they also used these terms to refer to their friends, which suggests some level of word reclamation. This may also be reflective of a cultural milieu where phrases and terms such as "that's so gay" and *fag/faggot* have entered the lexicon and are routinely used to refer to other non-normative or devalued behaviors.[19]

Depending on their life stage, participants engaged in both passing, which is hiding one's sexuality, and covering, which is downplaying but not hiding one's sexual identity. Both are assimilationist strategies—for example, Darius's claim of being like "any heterosexual" is similar to one many other queer people speak: "we're just like you [straight people]." Though, if Darius and others have to say it, it casts some doubt. In his legal analysis of covering, Kenji Yoshino suggests that "assimilation can be an *effect* of discrimination as well as an *evasion* of it."[20] That is, sexual identity covering and marginalization work in mutually reinforcing ways, where the desire to be treated equally manifests in downplaying differences, and may very well help one avoid being treated inequitably.

"Faggot Shit" for Queer Consumption: My First Vogue Ball

Although there were misgivings about feminine, flamboyant, and/or obviously "gay" behavior in public, many of my study participants competed in or at least attended vogue balls, where the other attendees and audience were made up overwhelmingly of LGBTQ people and the events were held in semi-private settings. After spending much time watching participants practice their dance moves, I was anxious to finally be able to attend a ball to see several of them compete. Not to be confused with ballroom dancing, these balls included several competitive performance categories for voguing, modeling, emceeing, and "realness." Vogue is a stylized type of dance that juxtaposes exaggerated, fluid gestures with angular posing. My participants typically competed in the vogue performance and "realness" categories, though some also competed in the modeling ("runway") categories. They belonged to various vogue houses, and not all members of the same gang were members of the same house. Vogue "houses" are essentially teams of competitors who are united under a house mother or father (of any sex or gender), and although members of vogue houses do not necessarily live together under one roof, some do. They are comprised primarily of gay or transgender members who support each other socially, and perhaps even financially.

A few minutes before midnight in early January 2012, after about an hour and a half of driving, talking, and listening to music, we (me, Imani, Ricky, ATL, and another friend of theirs) get to the location of the Magic Masquerade, a vogue ball. We followed a crowd of 5–10 people filing in to the building, because there were no signs outside showing us where to go. We walked up a flight of stairs to the second floor of what appears to be a small office building. It is clearly vacant, with a tattered "For rent" sign in one of the windows. We run into a tall, striking woman in the stairwell, who greets me quietly. I don't recognize her, until I realize it's Aga, another participant in my study. Her eyes give her away. I tell her how great she looks, and she thanks me.

A table is positioned near the entry of the room where we each pay the $10 door charge. Inside, the linoleum floor tiles are stained and cracked, the blinds are yellowed, and there is a cloud of cigarette and marijuana smoke lingering just above our heads that dissipates near the panels of the vaulted ceiling. The ball was supposed to start at midnight but didn't start until 1:30 a.m. It ended at about 3:30 a.m.

Among the categories of this evening's ball was "Thug Realness," which is the "Banjee Realness" of today's vogue balls. In *Paris Is Burning*, the acclaimed documentary from 1990 about vogue balls, "Banjee" was described by the host of an event as "Lookin' like a boy that probly robbed you before you came to Paris's ball!" Another competitor commented, "It's really a case of going back into the closet." And still others suggested that banjee realness was a way to go through life more comfortably without being negatively affected by the prejudices of society.[21] Although it was not specified that the competitors in tonight's category must appear to be straight, just thuggish, it is undeniable that straightness is implied to some extent. The category featured guys with "grills" (removable inlays of metal jewelry worn over their teeth), sagging pants, big "bling" in the form of chains around their necks; some smoked blunts of marijuana and/or tobacco on the "runway." If a contestant was convincing as a thug, he was allowed to compete; otherwise, he was "chopped" and eliminated from that round of competition, as with all other categories.

I knew about 12 people there and in one night, I got to see 3 of my participants in drag. One was Aga; another one was Jeremy during the time he performed in one of the categories. The third had to skip going to the ball with us because his "date" (client for sex) for the evening fell through and he therefore had no money to pay the door charge, but when I got to his house, he was still wearing a form-fitting tank top and tights, makeup, and a black wig for the intended date. He was very convincing in his presentation, and I didn't realize he "dressed up for money," which was a coded phrase that participants used to mean selling sex while wearing women's clothes. Oddly enough, the theme of the ball was magic, and I know that some of my other guys did turn a "trick" to be able to pay to get there. I was also surprised to see some of them in attendance, including Darius, who was particularly critical of flamboyant gay men, especially as sex partners. Interestingly, he was there to see his boyfriend Johnny compete in the vogue performance category, which features exaggerated movements/dancing, colorful costumes, and feminine gestures such as hair flipping, even among men who had short hair; they would flick their wrists back just above their shoulder to communicate the gesture.

Vogue performance was actually the most anticipated and largest category of the night, where lots of attendees battled it out dressed in "Jack in the box" effects. An "effect" is a vogue term for a costume, makeup, and/or accessories, meant to suggest that a good one will cause the judges and audience to register some desired reaction. Effects ranged from lycra or even velvet body suits of varying colors and styles, jester outfits, clownlike facepaint, boas, neon pink or green wigs, and other very ostentatious get-ups. A fabulous effect was referred to as "sickening."

There were probably 150 people there total, and I was the only white person and one of an estimated three women who were assigned female at birth (which my participants called "real girls" or "the fish"), but there may have been more. Accordingly, I suppose, the women's bathroom had no towels or toilet paper (though I managed to get some napkins from the "bar"), the toilet barely flushed, and there was no running water or soap to wash my hands. The sink was fully crusted with rust and lime; I was told that no one ever washes their hands in the bathroom at a ball. They piss, gossip, fix their effect, and maybe do a little coke, so they're not complaining about the conditions.

The ball organizers were not checking any IDs, but were selling $3 cocktails and $5 chicken and fries that they cooked from bags of frozen food in a backroom kitchen area. I did have a cocktail before the ball started and ended up holding the empty plastic cup almost the whole night because I didn't see a trash can and didn't want to throw it on the floor. My guys waited until we left to roundly make fun of me for not tossing it just anywhere, like everyone else did. I didn't realize it was that noticeable until Imani got a big laugh from everyone when he teased, "Gurl, she just stood there with her lil cup in her hand!"

Over the course of the whole night, the only people who talked to me were people I knew, the doorperson, the bartender, and only one other person. He was African American, early 40s, mostly staying on the wall as I was. This was the entire conversation:

MAN: This yo first time comin' to somethin' like this?
VP: Yeah, it is.
MAN: You enjoyin' yoself? Do you like it?
VP: Oh yeah, I'm having a great time.
MAN: Do you like, own this place and rent it out or somethin'?
VP: Oh, no. No.
MAN: (nodding, smiling)

Later in the car, when I told my companions this, they thought it was hilarious that this dude figured the only white woman in the room was there because she was checking up on what "those homos" were doing with her property.

I recount this evening for several reasons, the first and most obvious of which is clear: that through vogue balls and the camaraderie participants received from their "houses" (teams), they were provided with a space to explore the fluid continuum of gender presentation and performance. They could do so in an environment where judges, organizers, mentors, and audiences would externally validate their performance, and they even had a chance at winning some cash if they won the category. Historically, vogue houses have been a way for young queer people to belong to a supportive group, express themselves creatively, and earn cash prizes, all of which are particularly important considering pervasive social and economic marginalization, especially for young gay and transgender youth of color. In this way, gender patrolling in the ballroom scene operates as a test of the "realness" of whatever you are presenting as; not what you were assigned at birth or what society expects you to be, but the dramatized portrayal[22] of a gender or personality type. Tellingly, were I as a butchy woman to enter one of the feminine realness categories, I probably would be "chopped" from the competition immediately. That night I was wearing gray slacks, a plaid button up with the sleeves rolled up to my elbows, and Adidas shoes; my hair short but shaggy. Certainly not the portrait of idealized feminine beauty.

This account also illustrates just how inauthentic I appeared in this event marked as "faggot shit," a male space where feminine "realness" was a performance or a state of mind, in a setting historically valued and occupied by queer communities of color. Although my companions for the evening laughed long and hard about my encounter with the patron, it stands out for me as a defining moment of fieldwork. It made me wonder, "Is that what everyone else here is thinking? Do they feel nervous or on display? How will my presence affect my participants' reputations within the ball scene, if at all?" I felt a twinge of guilt that my presence (driven by a desire to see my participants in a setting they enjoyed) was interpreted as an act of control by at least some attendees. More generally, I questioned how participants themselves interacted with me, and if they felt like they needed to be guarded, or if they felt uncomfortable having such involved contact with a white person. My study's participants of color tended to have friendship networks that were largely racially homogeneous, and I was typically the only white person *and* person assigned as female at birth ("real girl") in the crew.[23]

For all of the narrative effort spent on demarcating when it was inappropriate to be flamboyant, colorful, loud, or a faggot, vogue balls are moments for such displays to be celebrated and competed over. And we the audience were there to be entertained and to appreciate it. Hell, we *paid* to get in, and as for "owning" the place, the performers certainly did that.

Maintaining Order

Tellingly, the use of anti-gay epithets such as *fag/faggot*, which are imbued with harmful social meanings for queer people, were used by participants in diverse ways. These included affectionately referring to other members of their community, but also insulting feminine gay men. Participants discussed the characteristics of a "fag," including how he dresses, acts, grooms himself, interacts with straight men, and so on. They were seen as objects of scorn and embarrassment, and were devalued as friends and as romantic partners. Generally, a "fag" had crossed an invisible boundary into territory that was too feminine, too flamboyant, too loud/dramatic, and, essentially, too gay. However, such boundaries could be transgressed regularly, depending on where the man was, who was around, and whether participants were sympathetic to encouraging other gay men to be themselves. It was well understood that shaming flamboyant gay men was perhaps inappropriate in light of lifelong efforts by others to control them. The same social pressures are likely what caused participants to adhere to strict guidelines in the first place. At the vogue ball, a place where "faggot shit" was celebrated even among some of the most traditionally masculine participants, such happenings represent only brief respites from everyday expectations.

This meaning system represents what John Kitsuse, former president of the Society for the Study of Social Problems, calls "tertiary deviance": how people who are considered deviant assess, confront, and reject negative identity labels, ultimately turning their identity into a positive one. This is similar to the process of reclaimed words discussed earlier: using "fag" in a friendly way, despite its history as a word of scorn. Kitsuse adds that the concept of tertiary deviance lets us explore "how it is possible for the stigmatized, ridiculed and despised to confront their own complicity in the maintenance of their degraded status, to recover and accept the suppressed anger and rage as their own, to transform shame into guilt, guilt into moral indignation, and victim into activist."[24] Indeed, the analyses in this chapter and the previous one suggest that my participants were resistant to negative cultural messages about gay men in general and about themselves in particular. However, they simultaneously upheld at least some of those values when they too patrolled and denigrated flamboyant or feminine men. Some made clear that they were very aware of their "complicity" in perpetuating the lower status of the "fag," and although they might have disliked doing so, sometimes concerns such as safety overrode concerns about community. Regardless, their misgivings did not stop them from spending time with their gay friends, celebrating gay culture, fighting back against anti-gay harassment, and even forming gay gangs as projects of resistance. The analyses in the next two parts of this book speak better to the latter elements of the tertiary deviance process—moral indignation and moving beyond victimhood—but still explore complicity.

PART II

Gay Gangsters and Their Gangs

3

Gay Gangs Becoming "Known"

Respect, Violence, and Chosen Family

About a year into my study, I was still trying to access the current gay gangs in Columbus. I knew they had to exist, as I had interviewed former or inactive members of gay gangs, but I just wasn't having any luck making contact with someone who was active in one currently. I basically needed someone who was willing to let me into their world. One of my participants who had been a member of two straight gangs had informed me that he not only knew "a whole lotta Bloods that are gay," but also of an entire gang in Columbus that was gay. However, he doubted that other (non-gay) members of the Bloods would take them seriously. He stated definitively, "I wouldn't think they would be recognized by a real Blood gang," mostly because he thought their group would be small and therefore relatively powerless in the masculine games that control the streets. He also clearly doubted that gay gangs were similar to the Blood set he belonged to and sets like them, with a telling use of the modifier "real."

I spoke to another member of a straight gang that was not modeled after any of the nationally recognized gangs, such as the Crips, Bloods, or Gangster Disciples. He suggested that gay gang members' acceptance in gangs could very well differ by which gangs their sets were affiliated with: "Like, it depends. The GDs, never happening, never happening, if they find out you're gay, that's it. The Bloods, they don't really care." Of course, he had told me that he was not a member of either group, but had known different sets while on the streets and in prison. I happened to mention that I had heard about an all-gay gang, but was not able to interview them yet. He suggested, "The 55s and X2 both has fags in them, but somebody is kinda yanking your chain, making you go on a goose chase hunt, like, 'Oh, vampires are sucking blood in the basements of clubs.'" Although I'm sure that some people find a vampire underworld to be more believable than all-gay gangs, I was not one of them. I remained undeterred.

* * *

By October 2011—another year later—my wild goose chase was finally over. This was primarily due to interviewing Imani and his many referrals, starting with members of his gang, the Royal Family. Although I knew Imani from years prior and we first reconnected in June 2010, I had trouble getting ahold of him since then, and as it turned out, he wasn't officially a member of a gay gang until shortly before I finally interviewed him. One referral from his gang was Johnny. As Johnny and I neared the end of his interview, he told me more about the gay scene in Columbus, particularly its all-gay gangs. We talked about the Royal Family, but he also wanted to tell me all about the Boys of Bang, a rival gay gang also known as the "B.o.B." He wrapped up recounting their sordid history of fighting, drug use, and escorting with this advice: "You would want to interview them, you would. They would be nice to you and stuff like that, they not mean like that, but chu would want ta get ahold of them, I would want chu to interview them. Cuz you would be interested in that. You really would, and I would be interested too, I wanna know like, what makes them do the things that they do? I really do." I too wondered what made them do the things they do. Members of the B.o.B. were "known," or established in the gay community, and were arguably the most notorious, feared, and loathed gay clique in Columbus. The B.o.B.'s reputation around town was that they were fierce fighters who would do major damage (to people and property) over minor slights. They had 10 to 12 core members, with another 20 or so who were loosely affiliated or had been affiliated in the past. I was able to interview five current or former members of the B.o.B. At the time, their gang had lost members and was in a period of transition as a result of their past conflicts.

Although I eventually spoke to men in a number of gay cliques, the majority of my study's participants in gay gangs belonged to the Boys of Bang (B.o.B.), the Royal Family, or the Firing Squad. The Royal Family, to whom Johnny belonged, had 15 to 20 members, about 10 of whom were regularly involved in the group's activities. I was able to interview nine of these men. The group also had another 10 or 15 friends who lived out of state, but whom they claimed as members of the family. While they did fight around town, this was not a major part of their reputation. Instead, the Royal Family was well-known in the ballroom scene, a semi-underground competitive dance scene that connected several urban areas' gay populations. Although members of the gang belonged to different "houses" (teams) in the dance scene, this did not at all interfere with their group membership.

The Firing Squad was a bit smaller, with 10 to 15 members (three of whom I interviewed, and I met a fourth). They had a reputation for skilled fighting, but not necessarily frequent fighting anymore. In fact, of the three groups, they seemed to be the least entrenched in the "drama" of Columbus's so-called "ghetto gay scene." Interestingly, this group comprised totally of gay males also had an auxiliary straight female group who hung out with them and brawled with them when needed. Despite past problems with the B.o.B., the Firing Squad's loyalties were more closely aligned with the B.o.B. than the Royal Family.

All members of these three gay gangs were adults, spanning from those in their late teens to a few in their early 30s, though as each gang had been in existence for several years, some had joined in adolescence. They all had a public presence in the Columbus gay scene, and none was affiliated with a particular part of town. Although these three gangs had participated in intergroup conflicts and were willing to cast aspersions on each other, some had members who were also friends, family members, and romantic interests of men in opposing gay cliques. There were also many friend, familial, and dating relationships between gay cliques and straight cliques that existed without formal rivalries. The gay gangs had, for lack of a better phrase, a love/hate relationship with each other. I couldn't wait to learn more, and would soon enough. Later that evening after Johnny's interview, I interviewed a former core member of the B.o.B., and in the weeks that followed, conducted a number of interviews that shed additional light not only on the social world of these three gay gangs, but on the experiences and identities of young men in gay gangs more generally.

In this chapter, I specifically discuss the gay gangs, their members, and the social world of these groups in Columbus. Twenty-six participants were or had been members of one or more gangs with a majority of gay, lesbian, or bisexual members.[1] Typically, the majority-gay gangs were 100 percent or nearly 100 percent GLB members; I refer to them simply as "gay gangs." At the time of the interview, participants were or had been members of 13 unique gay gangs; several had belonged to two or more cliques, with one reporting current or former membership in three different gay cliques. It was common for me to interview or spend time in the field with multiple members of the same gay gang, which was not the case with the straight gangs. Many of our outings included members of different gay gangs, and we were sometimes accompanied by men in straight gangs. That is, the gay networks of the gay gangs' members were much more extensive than those of the straight gangs' gay members.

Some of the themes I explore include how members of gay gangs joined these groups, the activities they engaged in with their gangs, and the importance of the group to their lives. Regarding gay identity, one overarching theme was clear: participants were able to be relatively unconcerned about impression management related to their sexual identities, and thus more likely to articulate the camaraderie they felt with fellow gang members.

Getting into Gay Gangs

The gay gangs represented in my sample were characterized by one major and obvious difference from the straight gangs: while straight gangs were often organized by space (such as neighborhoods or drug-selling turf), gay gangs were organized around a shared sexual identity. In fact, some members of the same gay gang lived more than 10 miles from each other. For the most part, the gay gangs originated from gay friendship groups who then grew and took on a life of their own. In fact, many research participants who belonged to gay gangs played a role in the formation of the gang itself. These groups and the gangs they became developed organically, often from a combination of school friends, cousins, love interests, and/or peers met at programs providing outreach to and services intended for gay youth. Aga of the Royal Family remembered, "I've known them for like, a long time. Some years! Hurricane's my cousin, and Johnny, I've known him since sixth grade. Baby, I met him and we been cool since I first met him, and he introduced me to Javier, and then after Javier, we just, me, and Johnny and Baby and

Javier, we just all got together, and been together since." Ricky of the Heavyweights recalled:

> It all got put together between [20]07 and '08. . . . I moved here in '05, I started goin' out in '06, and that's when me and my best friend started kickin' it, like all the time. . . . We started putting people together. And we would all go out on Sundays, and we'd meet up at a bar, downtown off of High Street, and it'd be 10 of us, 11 of us, sitting in a bar, with a group of, you know, other people, the gay people that are there, and we're just causin' a big scene. And then that's how we all banded together, we were all just loud, ghetto. . . . Like, one person knew another person, and another person knew another person, and then once we see you, once one person sees one person, they got introduced to another person. That's how everybody got together.

After some time together, they decided to make their groups "legit" with symbols of cohesion, such as a name. Casper told me this about the B.o.B.'s history:

> Well, we was kids, so we was all like, 14 and 15 and 16, and we all was like, "We should make up a name for our lil [group]." Because it was two groups, okay, it was me, and two other people, and we were our lonesome, and it was one person, he was by hisself, and it was like, five or six other people, and they were in their little clan that they grew up, when they was [much] younger, and we all met up at [an HIV prevention program], and we all clicked, so we all was like, "We need a name for ourselves."

Regarding his joining of the B.o.B., Tony said, "I was messin' wit [hanging out with] them for a long time, it just like, it naturally happened, I guess. I just fell right in." Josh echoed this, saying he joined by "Just hangin' out, just like, one family, big family, a gay family!" In these ways, many of the men in gay gangs reported being a part of the gang from the beginning; they were involved before and during the transition from "just friends" to an official clique.

Because participants had a hand in forming the gang, their reasons to "join" per se were often not articulated. However, their reasons for becoming involved with a gang encompassed a number of the motivations that are evident in the gang literature and are shared by gay members of straight gangs. These include respect, reputation (what they called being "known"), belonging, or because friends or family were in the gang. Take, for example, Derrick's reasons for joining the B.o.B., and how he joined: "I wanted to be in a big crowd, I wanted to be known, well, actually, I am known now, now that I'm older, I was known when I was younger, too, I don't know how, but my name had just got out there like that, people just started to like me and stuff like that, get to know me, pretty much. . . . I just started hangin' out with them, like with my cousins and them, my cousin is from the B.o.B., you probly heard about him. . . . Yeah, then I got to know everybody." Although several men in straight gangs talked about being "known," it was much more likely for members of gay gangs to use this language. Prior research on becoming "known" in the context of gang members largely relies on their willingness to use violence to build a reputation as a "real" gang member and to avoid future conflicts and status challenges.[2] Members of gay gangs also suggested that being "known" provided status and insulation from challenges, but someone could be "known" for any number of skills or attributes. These included fighting, dancing, looking good, and making money. But it also referred to them being known as openly gay and thus as a player in the gay scene. A gay gang allowed for the visibility and structure to get a man's name and characteristics into the world to become "known."

Before I began this study, I surmised that gay young people might join gangs to protect themselves against homophobic bullying or harassment, especially since that was a key insight the limited literature on all-gay or all-lesbian gangs could offer. Specifically, scholar-activist Dominique Johnson found that the young women who formed Dykes Taking Over, an all-lesbian gang in Philadelphia, did so in response to anti-lesbian harassment in school.[3] My experience with LGBTQ advocacy and my knowledge of queer young people's school experiences also led me to suspect that this might be the case. To my surprise, no participant explicitly mentioned joining a gang specifically to protect himself against anti-gay harassment. However, participants' experiences with school-based homophobic bullying and harassment combined with their other life experiences to produce an environment favorable to gang joining.[4] Interestingly, in contrast to a common depiction from the gang literature and a number of the men in straight gangs, physical protection (in general) did not seem to be articulated as a reason for joining, but relational factors such wanting a place to belong, reputation, and social support were often provided. The gang literature demonstrates that young people join gangs for reasons such as seeking a sense of belonging, because friends or family are involved, to have fun, to gain protection, to get respect, and to resist repression and exclusion.[5] In light of negative peer, familial, and societal reactions to their sexual identities, combined with instances of physical unsafety, motivations such as "a sense of belonging" and "to get respect" likely hold special significance for gay youth.

Men joined gay gangs at about age 18, which was almost four years older than the average age at joining for straight gangs. The average length of time men had been or were presently in the gang was three and a half years, and the vast majority of the members of gay gangs were still involved with their gangs. The fact that gay identity is the organizing characteristic of gay gangs likely explains why their members joined later than men in straight gangs. Despite the fact that many of the men in my study knew they were attracted to other males from a young age and identified as gay by or during their early teens, many did not start to come out to peers or family members until high school or later. They did not necessarily hang out with a group of other gay youth before coming out, unless they had fortuitously become friends with those individuals, perhaps without being aware of each other's sexuality. Upon coming out, their peer groups changed in ways that reflected an increased interest in friendships and romantic relationships with other gay males. For example, Max started hanging out with his crew because it included a boy he liked, and because he "started to get uncomfortable with the straight people."

The older ages at gang joining may also be because the gangs themselves shifted to "official" groups after existing for some time as non-gang peer networks.[6] Just as Casper's clique—the B.o.B.—decided they needed a name for themselves to be a fully formed group, Jeremiah's crew—the Firing Squad—went through a similar transformation: "It's not a group that you just joined, it was like, we all grew up together, and as life went on, we all kinda just—I met a friend, he met a friend, add 'em to the group, and we just grew as [we] grew up. We all been knowin' each other since like, middle school, elementary school. . . . [Just two years ago], we actually came up with a name, and decided to make it a legit group." Boss, another member of the Firing Squad, echoed this: "I think as we began to hang around, we all became more of like, a gang, versus, it wasn't just originally like that." He said that he and his friends created their crew "out of nowhere" after repeatedly getting drunk and/or high, going out to the club, and "after the club, we'd fight somebody. There was always drama with somebody." Thus, their crew also was born, at least partially, of intergroup conflict.[7] Perhaps unsurprisingly, Boss noted that the "originals" did not have to prove themselves in an initiation ritual, but that newcomers did have to prove themselves by fighting. Similarly, several members of straight gangs who joined by being a long-term neighborhood resident or family member also said that non-resident or non-familial hopefuls had to endure jumping-in rituals. That does not mean that certain requirements for gay gangs weren't still in place; for example, Boss also stated that to be accepted as a member of the Firing Squad, "Everybody in the group had to be some type of cute." As such, the requirements of this gay gang were also consistent with ways to become "known" in the Columbus gay scene—an understandable mandate considering they were jockeying for position within that scene.

Also important to note is that only two men described scenarios involving violence that seemed to function as initiation rituals. Imani detailed an encounter between his posse and a group of college males who were calling them fags, following them, and throwing things at them. Although he was not an official member at the time, because he participated in this chance conflict and held his own in fighting, the group wanted him to join. Imani was initially introduced to the clique (which he called a "family-type thing") by his "gay mother." He had started to hang out with this group prior to the encounter, and they began to refer to him in familial terms. However, it was his willingness to fight (thus solidifying his rapport with the group) and his skill that essentially fast-tracked his membership in the Royal Family. It reduced the time he would have spent getting closer to the clique in order for his membership to develop organically. Another man in a gay gang, ATL, had not even spent time with his crew before joining the group. After saying, "We weren't friends at all before I joined. I had to fight them," he recounted:

I was at a club, and I was dancin', and one of them boys, I guess I bumped one of 'em, and he didn't like it at all, so he brung someone else over there. And I told him I was sorry or whatever, and I apologized, but it seem like shade[8] kept throwin', like, they'll throw somethin', or walk by and bump me, and I was like, fuck it. At the end of the club, it is what it is when we step out the door.

After they left the club, he fought four members of the group, and said that he was "gettin' the best [of them]," which alerted the leader to his potential. What started as a fight over an unintentional bump ended with the leader of the clique taking an interest in helping ATL navigate the gay scene by making him "her gay child," or protégé.[9] He became the leader's gay child after two months. Although this also was not meant as an initiation, ATL has now framed it as one, beginning his narrative of gang joining as if it were explicitly an initiation ritual.

Imani's and ATL's respective paths to gang joining are especially useful theoretically. Although they are technically deviant cases with respect to the rest of the participants, these examples help to clarify and substantiate the patterns illustrated in the rest of the narratives from men in gay gangs. In both cases, Imani and ATL still had to spend a couple of months with their crews so that the groups' members could get a feel for and develop trust in them. Their fights with gang members present, which ultimately represented an initiation ritual, did not fully replace the time normally spent building rapport. However, it seems that something of use can be substituted for part of that time. Other accounts of gang members joining or "falling in" typically described the friendship that existed between the new member and existing members. The gangs wanted him for his personality traits, not necessarily something tangible that he could contribute to the gang (like being good at fighting or making money). However, both Imani's and ATL's fighting prowess marked them as being of immediate usefulness to cliques who obviously fought with other crews or individuals with some frequency.

It is perhaps all of the shared history and experiences among members of gay crews that caused them to eschew initiation rituals; they had grown up together and come out together. If members of these tight-knit groups deemed a new person to be worthy of their time, this constituted sufficient acceptance. Although they acknowledged that their groups were gangs, they were much more likely to use other terms that communicated the social aspects of these groups, such as "cliques" or "families."[10] While several members of straight gangs also described their crews as "families," about two-thirds of the members of gay gangs described their groups as such. They repeatedly used language to reinforce this idea, such as utilizing familial relational terms ("uncle") or even the word "family" in their gang's name. And, as with other gang members, gay and straight, fellow gang members were sometimes actual blood relatives.

I return later to this theme of gay gangs as chosen families, but should emphasize that these individuals were drawn from neighborhoods and familial backgrounds similar to those of the men who joined straight gangs, and yet they still joined gay gangs. They presumably had opportunities to join straight cliques, but did not. For example, Derrick's father had been gang involved for Derrick's entire life, while a number of Imani's cousins and extended family members were gang members. However, instead of joining a neighborhood gang or following in the footsteps of their heterosexual family members, Derrick and Imani joined gangs comprised exclusively of other gay people. Also, the homes where Casper and Derrick lived were nearly right around the corner from the homes where Raphael and Jayden lived. Although all four identified as gay or bisexual, two chose to join a gay gang while the other two joined (separate) straight gangs. The key difference was access: at the time that they joined their gangs, Raphael and Jayden did not have extensive friendship networks of other gay people but had opportunities in their neighborhoods, while Casper and Derrick were involved with a close-knit group of gay people whose group morphed into a gang over time. Being out, at least to some extent, and knowing a critical mass of gay people were necessary conditions to joining (or forming) gay gangs.

What Do Gay Gangs Do?

Men in gay gangs engaged in a variety of legal and illegal behaviors, often first stressing the legal behaviors. With their gangs, members liked to go to the movies, nightclubs, parties, each other's houses, vogue balls, out to eat, and out of town. Of the Royal Family's activities, Baby summed it up well: "Basically what you do when you're young: Everything!" Enjoying being young and having fun with friends was a recurrent theme. Of his gang, the Firing Squad, Jeremiah suggested, "Really we are a fun group. We dance, we drink, we smoke, we cook, and go out to the club, shop, fight. We do everything together, like, we're together 24/7! If we're not all together in one spot, we're together in little groups. We're never just by ourselves." Jeremiah mentions fighting, which also emerged as a frequent activity, but not initially in most participants' descriptions.

Not only were the members of gay gangs engaged in typical young adult activities, but they also articulated what would be regarded as pro-social behaviors: they helped each other study, look for and obtain legitimate employment, and gave each other advice on important matters. Several even mentioned attending "family reunions," or large gatherings of their clique's members, some of whom had moved out of state. Take, for example, JD's description of his crew (the Royal Family) and their activities:

> I actually kinda feel like we're all supportive as a family, like one of us done had the other [one's back], . . . It's actually very supportive, we try to keep each other out of trouble, and for the most part, encourage each other to do better. Like, if somebody's not workin', then hey, get your ass up and get a job! For real! Like, just sittin' around, layin' around every day ain't gon' get you nothin'! If you ain't got yo education, go to school and get it now. Now, the question is, if they wanna be helped or not. If they don't, then oh well! I mean, I can't force nobody that don't wanna do nothin' theyself. . . . [We] go out to eat, to the movies, out of town, things like that. Travel, kind of. Things families should do. You know, be supportive of each other, and also have fun, and live life! We go to the bars, stuff like that! Parks, cookouts, . . . Even family reunions and stuff like that.

JD's depiction of his gang as his family is especially salient: they are engaged in productive activities and in helping each other succeed in work, school, and life—*things families should do*. Jeremy described the ways his clique worked together as a team by cleaning the house, cooking breakfast, and helping each other stay out of major trouble. However, as I will soon detail, these families were also involved in illicit activities such as interpersonal violence, theft, and sex work.

As a reflection of these varied activities, the time I spent with gay gangs included our watching television or YouTube videos, dancing and listening to music, eating dinner, playing pool or video games, going to clubs, gossiping, shopping, drinking and/or smoking, and traveling out of town for dance competitions. These were basically the same things they did with other gay friends or romantic interests who were not gang involved. I also engaged in many activities with participants individually (that is, outside of their gangs), which included those listed above and other outings such as barhopping, house parties, and attending the Columbus Pride Parade. On occasion, I even kept them company while they babysat relatives, did housework, or, in one case, recovered from surgery. I was also privy to seeing them sell drugs and arrange "dates" during which they would sell sex,[11] but these activities comprised a substantially smaller share of their time than legal activities.[12] This is especially true in light of the fact that many were busy attending school, working, or both, at least several days per week.

A few of the illegal behaviors they described were much more likely to occur within the gay gangs than the straight or hybrid gangs. Specifically, many of the instances of crafting and escorting occurred within gay gangs, though not exclusively. "Crafting" encompassed a series of financial crimes of varying degrees of skill. The lower-skill activities included lying to businesses to obtain free goods and services, returning stolen merchandise to retail establishments for cash or store credit, and intentionally overdrawing bank accounts. Some activities required a bit more specialization and risk, such as purchasing stolen credit card numbers for personal use, while the most sophisticated acts included building and cashing fraudulent checks or creating false paystubs so they could file bogus tax returns. In fact, several men had been involved with gay cliques whose illicit profits were generated almost exclusively from crafting; Johnny and Josh had each been a member of such groups, while Hurricane had been a member of *two* such groups. "Escorting" (also known as "turning dates") involved selling sex or erotic services to others, usually older men.

The extent of selling sex acts (whether one's own or pimping someone else) among the members of gay gangs was substantial: 18 of the 26 men had been involved in these activities. Thus, it was an integral part of my conversations with the members of the gay gangs. Important to note here is that some men learned how to escort from other members of their gangs, such as Casper of the B.o.B.:

Some of us were escorts, way back when we first learned about it, and the abilities of it, and stuff. . . . My first time was when I had just turned 18, didn't have no job, and it was quick money. It was people out there that wanted to pay for it [sex], so. . . . Well, they [the ones who taught me] learned from someone older that taught them, so they was just teachin' me how to be safe, what are the pros and the cons of it, how to make sure they're not . . . the police or anything, and junk like that.

Both crafting and escorting typically entailed learning the "tricks of the trade" from fellow crew members who were seasoned. When using the Internet to sell sex, participants learned how to not get flagged for removal or caught in a sting, by skillfully using a heavily coded lexicon and posting pictures from a cache of false ones, as well as learning to read cues that would help them select innocuous clients who would pay the agreed-upon price. When selling sex on public streets, they learned where to go, how to dress (sometimes dressing in women's clothing, makeup, and wigs to work the "tranny stroll"), and how to comport themselves to be seen as a desirable "date." All of these strategies were communicated and utilized not only to maximize potential earning, but to minimize ever-present risks to health and safety, as well as the threat of detection by authorities. Participants preferred to sell sex via the Internet, because arranging dates on the street carried lower status, lower pay, and higher risk.

The men who crafted and escorted reported that they were involved in these crimes for instrumental reasons. In recounting all of the money that could be made through crafting, participants noted that the activities included in the term entailed a substantial risk of being caught, especially with new fraud-detection technologies. For example, Hurricane had been incarcerated in an adult institution for fraud, theft, and possession of criminal tools; Johnny spent time in a juvenile facility for similar charges he incurred as part of the same gay gang Hurricane belonged to prior (they both would later join the Royal Family). And of course, the aforementioned risks of escorting were also perceived to be serious.

Although there *were* men in straight gangs who escorted, this was typically done at night, outside of the view and judgment of their fellow gang members, and perhaps aided by technology. On his ability to hide his sex work and sexual identity from his straight gang, Darius exclaimed, "That's why I'm glad cell phones was invented!" He and other closeted gang members acted in stereotypically masculine and heterosexual ways in front of their fellow gang members, so their escorting remained largely hidden. In this way, selling sex was a gang member activity, but not a gang activity. That is, individual men in straight gangs escorted, but not with or for the benefit of their gang.

Although men in gay gangs escorted with the aid of or with their gangs, they too did not directly share the profits with their gangs (as with the participants who were members of straight gangs and sold drugs), but sometimes shared them with other members. For example, if a fellow gang member had actually set up the date for them, referred a client to them when he was sick or unavailable to make the "date," helped with their advertising materials, or co-participated in the sex acts, some portion of the profits might be passed on to him. However, these deals were pre-negotiated between gang members in particular instances and were usually not part of a regular pattern of practice. And, in contrast to the escorts in straight gangs, escorts in gay gangs did not have to hide their involvement, as it was likely that fellow gang members had taught them or were also involved. Interestingly, although studies on males who buy and sell sex have existed since the mid-20th century, such as criminologist Albert Reiss's well-known "queers and peers" study on gang members who sold sex to older men,[13] these studies often did not focus on gay-identified male sex workers, but instead on how those young men retained their heterosexual social identities.[14] The men in gay gangs make no such attempts to hide their gayness when selling sex to older men; the gay world seemed to provide them with opportunities to make money in these ways. Thus, these activities were not as heavily stigmatized.

Another observable difference between the activities of the straight gangs and the gay gangs is the presence of drug sales. Some men in gay gangs did sell drugs, but for those who did, their drug selling took place primarily outside of the context of their gang. Several members of gay gangs clarified that neither they nor their fellow gang members sold drugs, but they all did "smoke them" (mostly marijuana). These differences are likely the result of a combination of factors. Specifically, because their groups were not organized around space, it may have been more difficult to have any sort of centralized territory where they sold drugs and controlled the drug transactions in that area. It may also be due in part to stereotypes of the gay community that they perceived to exist relating to drug use, and thus they did not want to perpetuate drug abuse within their community.

Handling Conflicts

Despite stereotypes of gay men that might exist, men in gay gangs were involved in serious (and often public) violent behavior. They fought with individual or groups of men who had harassed them for being gay, and with other cliques, gay and straight. Gay gangs were essentially equal opportunity fighters and were quick to defend each other against any aggressive party. Putting it succinctly about his close friends and fellow clique members, Aga said, "We don't be playin' about our brothers and sisters and my [gay] kids."

Regarding heterosexual community members, anti-gay harassment was often a clear motivation for fighting, but any rudeness from straight men could spark a fight. I asked participants what they and their gay crews would fight straight people over. Casper's response was illustrative of the general consensus, besides anti-gay harassment: "Respect too, because a lot of 'em would try to disrespect. Like I said, we would be on the bus or somewhere, anywhere, and someone would disrespect us, and all it take is for one (snaps fingers), and then we're all up, stuff like that." Casper clearly communicated the group dynamic here: when one member of the gang was affronted, the others were too, and were willing to respond. Jeremy added that his group was "real close" and they "take up for each other," especially "if somebody was to disrespect one of [us] in public." Josh was willing to take this one step further to articulate what could constitute disrespect and cause a conflict: "If they say somethin', or anything! Anything that pisses us off." Occasionally, these conflicts were directly related to gay identity and same-sex sexual behavior, but not necessarily because of offensive language. When I asked Derrick what might cause his clique to fight with straight people, he replied, "Prolly sometimes bringin' them out the closet, or sayin' you did somethin' wit 'em [sexually], or they just call you faggots, call you out your name, or somethin', that's stuff to fight about." That is, a person with a heterosexual public persona who is engaged in clandestine same-sex sexual activity (or accused of doing so) might initiate a conflict when his private behavior has been revealed.

These data are inconsistent with early research on gay gang members, which suggested that gay men could not be "out" to their gangs without facing serious consequences, and gay gang members felt the need to engage in gay-bashing scenarios to maintain their masculine (and heterosexual) status within their gangs.[15] Of course, this disconnect is related in part to the fact that these are all-gay gangs. When it comes to anti-gay harassment, my participants not only did not victimize other members of the gay community, they defended them. These discrepancies between my sample and prior research are likely attributable to the fact that all of the members of gay gangs were out and proud of their gay identities, partially evidenced precisely by the type of gangs they joined. Indeed, not even the participants in straight gangs violently gay bashed. The only people discussed in this study who bashed on gay folks were the members of straight gangs who were presumed to be gay and closeted.

Interestingly, men in gay gangs *do* commit violence against other gay men, but it is typically as a result of gang rivalry, retaliation, and power struggles. While gay cliques did have violent conflicts with straight cliques, it was much more likely for their *rivals* to be other gay cliques. Unlike in straight gangs, conflicts were not organized around geography; rather, they originated from threats to identity or reputation in ways that were not as direct as those experienced by men in territorial or neighborhood-based (straight) gangs. That is, the gay gangs did not claim ownership of any given neighborhood and had less obvious symbology: an insult to a color, number, street name, or housing project rarely got anyone in gay gangs worked up. But a rumor, a sideways glance, a dismissive hand gesture, a shoulder bump, or a suggestive text sent to an already-partnered man was taken seriously and could involve the whole clique in a retaliatory conflict.

Fights took place in metropolitan parks and nightclub parking lots, but also in front of and even inside gang members' homes. I heard about several intergroup fights from multiple participants in each clique that was involved. For at least a short time, there was ongoing "beef" (conflict) between the Royal Family and the B.o.B., as well as between the B.o.B. and the Firing Squad. One storied confrontation resulted in the convictions and incarcerations of some members of the B.o.B.—who were also required to make restitution payments—because they not only "tore up" Johnny and Javier's apartment and garage, but also seriously injured Javier by punching him, stabbing him, and beating him with blunt objects. For his injuries, Javier required stitches, surgery, and hospitalization. I was given detailed information on this incident from several parties who were there (as well as several who were not), as context to explain the intergroup tension. The fact that the narrative was readily available and consistent across accounts communicates both the seriousness of the real outcomes of the conflict for all parties, as well as its prominence in the gay gangs' social histories.

Despite this, members of the Royal Family, including Johnny, remained friends with certain members of the B.o.B., even referring them to my study. These lasting relationships were due to life experiences they had shared before this conflict, fictive kin relationships (such as being the "gay child" of a member of the B.o.B.), or due to the fact that they were extended family members, especially cousins.

As mentioned earlier, members of the B.o.B. were "known" in the gay community, as individuals and as a gang, and typically for reasons related to their extreme behavior. As such, the B.o.B. was a hot topic of discussion, as they were simultaneously despised and almost revered for their fierceness. Early in his interview, Ricky mentioned the B.o.B.; when I asked if he was a member, he replied flatly, "No. I don't go around beating up women just because I'm bored." Johnny also thought they had hair-trigger tempers:

Everybody, like, every person, every gay boy that's in the B.o.B. gang has an actual brother, like a real brother or a real family member that's in a real gang. So it's like, they used to all of that ghetto stuff, so they combined it in a lil ghetto form, a ghetto gay form, so that's why they always fightin' at the club, even if you look at them wrong, they will walk up to you on the dance floor and be dancin', and like, bump you real hard, or they'll start pointin' in yo face, and shit like that, that's what they do. And want you, like, they'll try to force you to swing on them first. . . . Like they'll throw you off, you'll think they dancin', gettin' it, and they just walk up on you and just hit chu! You'll be like, "Wow."

He also recounted a story where someone in the B.o.B. threw a bottle at a driver's head because they thought he had looked at them wrong—the driver needed stitches around his eye as a result. After Johnny's comment about the B.o.B.'s family members in "real gangs," I asked if he thought the B.o.B. was a "real gang." He replied that yes, "B.o.B. is a real gang. . . . The court system know about B.o.B., and the police and all of that know about it. They off the chain!" He said he used to be closer with them, but they were too "banjee" (which he explained as meaning "ghetto") and he wanted to stay away from that. Max, the on/off boyfriend of a former member of the B.o.B. agreed: "Rashad's group of friends were, that's a gang, I'm not gon' lie, it is, like, the way their things happen, it's a gang." He went on to explain that people might not see them as a gang because they're gay, but that being gay shouldn't have a "stereotype" because there are all "different types" of gay people. Despite being made up of gay[16] members, the B.o.B. was seen as a "real gang" because of their ongoing involvement in violence, which was seen by members and non-members alike as senseless and extreme. Because this classification of "real gang" rests partially on their inappropriate use of violence, participants have necessarily judged larger patterns of gang violence to be similarly gratuitous. These comments also represent attempts to "other" the B.o.B. crew, by depicting them as irrational, ghetto, and wild ("off the chain").

Members of the B.o.B. freely spoke about the extensiveness of their group's violent activities, especially in gay clubs; the group's members would even focus on fighting at the club in their descriptions of their group activities. Take this exchange with Josh, for example, after he had earlier mentioned the violence of his crew:

VP: What kinds of things you guys do together? Like, what would you do as a group?

JOSH: I mean, we go to the mall, the movies, hang out, chill at one another's house, sleepovers,[17] there's different stuff that we do.

VP: Do you guys ever get in fights?

JOSH: (laughs) Yeah, at the club. It be a lot of fightin'! (laughs)

. . .

VP: So, you would fight with other groups, other gay groups, what would you guys fight over?

JOSH: It be over dumb stuff, like, in the club, [if we] don't like that person, or just. (pause) Just a fight. I don't know, it just be crazy stuff! Like, it'll just happen, and you'll just be like—"Oh my gosh, did that just happen?" Well I mean, things have changed a lot, errybody calmed down, a lot, just cuz errybody gettin' older.

Or consider this statement from Derrick regarding when the B.o.B. would fight with other cliques: "When somebody in the club will say somethin' stupid, or people that we just didn't like, we'd fight 'em. Stuff like that. Most of the time, [they'd get] jumped too. . . . Like, [they would] get all up in your face, and all this and that, talkin' shit, and then that's when we just round everybody up, and it be on, and . . . it probably be other people in there that have groups too, so we just all fightin'." Although I did not specifically ask Derrick about gay clubs, this was his go-to example: his gay clique fighting other gay cliques at a gay night-club. It also came up in his original description of the B.o.B.'s activities: "We used to go to the club, drink, chill, they had parties, kicked it. Like, we used to fight at the clubs and stuff like that too, and just have fun." The B.o.B. was thus engaged in violent behavior in public, semi-public, and private spaces as a facet of their gang activities.

However, these same members of the B.o.B. gang now expressed harsh appraisals of the group's previous behavior. Josh called the violence "dumb" and "crazy," but stated that the B.o.B.'s members had "calmed down," not only because they had gotten older, but because "there's no need to just fight people, go around beatin' people up." However, Derrick pointed out that they would still fight other people as a group if necessary; Rashad offered that the B.o.B. had just recently posted a fight of theirs to Facebook. Rashad noted that his decision to lessen his involvement with the crew was because he did not "wanna be known as somebody who is known for fighting." Although being "known" in the gay community was a desired status among participants, Rashad and others would prefer to be known for their achievements, attractiveness, or other personal qualities; violence was not necessarily their *preferred* way of becoming "known." Furthermore, it could carry harsh penalties and, in some ways, did not even support the B.o.B.'s claims that they were tough and thick-skinned, insofar as they were easily offended and would bully others by picking fights for no reason. Of the B.o.B.'s inter-gang violence, Rashad explained:

> [W]hen I got 18, I stopped, because you can go to jail, and some stuff they were doin', like bustin' out people's windows and stuff, like, I would hear it, cuz I stopped goin' out, and it was too much at the club. Every weekend they're fighting, every gay event they're fighting. It'd be too much, and it became them pickin' fights with people, and it was just like. (pause) People are entitled to say what they want. If you can say what you want to people, you can't expect somebody for you to say somethin', and they cain't say nothin' back to you. So, that's how I look at it, cuz that's how they are. They expect to say stuff, and if you say somethin' back, we're gonna jump you, or we're gonna do this, like, you can't do that! If you dish it out, you should be able to get it back. That's how I feel about it. So, don't dish it out, if you cain't get it back.

That is, the B.o.B.'s irrational violence not only put them at risk of arrest and disturbed the peace among members of the gay community and within gay venues that they previously enjoyed attending, but, according to Rashad, it perhaps even suggested an underlying fragility of the B.o.B.'s members. Derrick described their intragang environment as "a bunch of drama." He said that the B.o.B. "used to fight each other and then get back cool, and I didn't understand that either."[18]

Although the B.o.B. was especially "known" for fighting, other gay cliques fought, with both the B.o.B. and additional cliques. For example, Boss chose to hang out with members of the Firing Squad instead of the Royal Family or the B.o.B., suggesting that the Firing Squad was "a gangster-gangster type of atmosphere." The challenge the B.o.B. represented to other crews was thrilling to him and his crew:

> A member in their group had just died because of some stuff that had just happened with them, and they had just done a lot of crazy stuff, and I heard stories about them, like, everybody said they don't fight fair, they use crowbars, . . . Everybody knew who they were, and they already had

this rep. And everybody was scared of them. Everybody was scared of them! Like, I don't care who you're talkin' 'bout, everybody was scared of B.o.B. because of the shit that they had done in the past, surroundin' people's cars, and tippin' their cars and stuff over, bustin' they windows out, and goin' up to their house and runnin' up in they house draggin' 'em out, then fightin' them and stuff like that, and goin' outta town and fightin', and then they had repped, you know, they had lost somebody in they group, and that supposedly made them stronger, and made them even more threatful, and showed that they were even more daring, and stuff like that.

He added that their daring excited him and he "wanted to see who these tough bitches are!" The serious violence of the B.o.B., as evidenced by their willingness to use weapons, destroy property, outnumber opponents, and even enter someone's home to assault them, became part of their reputation that other gangs, like the Firing Squad, sought to challenge. Repping (representing or displaying their gang membership), in this context, clearly encompassed the same sorts of public declarations of gang identity evident in the straight gangs' behaviors, but was even more salient as it related to Columbus's urban gay scenes. Reputation, such as being "known," was important to the men in my study and was difficult to achieve.[19] The gay cliques provided an avenue through which to become visible within the urban gay scene, whose dynamics were certainly affected by intergroup competition and conflict. Of the Royal Family, Imani noted: "Our posse is known, cuz like, a lot of people know us, and I wouldn't wanna be in no lame posse. Cuz I don't, mmm-mmm [no], I don't wanna go nowhere and [them] be like, 'Who is that?' (laughs) But it's like, if you say my name to people, they'll know who I am. And it's not just because of the lil posse thing, it's like, especially in the Ohio gay scene, you gotta really work to get a name for yoself out here." Relatedly, Casper shed some light on why the B.o.B. may have begun to fight so much in gay clubs. He remembered, "When we first came out, a lot of people were testy, like they would test us, just because we were new to the crowd, so it was more of respect fighting." He said these groups were "older," "already there" (more established), and "jealous," and tested the B.o.B.'s mettle "like a new student comin' to the school," in Casper's words. Rashad added, "It was fun at first, [because] you fought for your respect." Evidently, fighting over reputation or unfettered access to gay clubs was one way to become "known." In fact, the closest entities to "turf" that the gay gangs fought over were those gay nightclubs. Even this example of territory represents a proxy for gay identity. They weren't defending their right to move freely in their block or neighborhood, or protecting the place where they grew up; they were fighting to be able to drink, dance, and pick up romantic partners without competition and to be left alone in the places where they could be themselves.

Conflicts were partly attributed to the perceived "competition" that existed in Columbus's gay scene, though not all of it was exclusively gang-related. Johnny explained what he saw as being wrong with the scene that he and the gay gangs inhabited:

> Don't nobody really get along, it really can't be no parties and stuff down here [in Columbus] because there's a fight at the club every weekend. It's like, everybody really don't get along with each other, and that's the problem with this scene. I wouldn't necessarily say that it's ghetto. It's one group of gay people that do like to fight, and they is ghetto, but . . . the main problem with the gay scene up here is that it's segregated. Everybody wanna be catty, talk behind everybody's back, diss this person so this person won't talk to them, and it's all about competition up here.

As described above, the "ghetto" group he is referring to is the B.o.B., but the "cattiness" and "dissing" permeate throughout the scene. Furthermore, if participants wanted to be involved in the scene and the gay clubs, they also had to accept some level of "trashy" or dramatic behavior. King explained this about members of the scene: "Sometimes they do clock you [call you out], now that I'm on the right path, and I keep my nose clean, don't get me wrong, I like some drama, but I don't like a lot of it, because I obsess too much. Sometimes I'd say, 'Let me see the drama, I want to see this,' but now that I'm 21, I feel like I done got old, old-young, so I can't have a lot of trashy, but I do want it just a little bit." That is, the competition and "drama" were entertaining to young people, but could also be consuming and exhausting. Even Bird, who did not belong to a gay gang, had experienced the players in the "ghetto gay scene" to be "jealous" of people who are attractive, and to have "a lot of hate and a lot of drama and just a lot of negative."

But what else were the gay gangs fighting over in these spaces? When I asked Bob about the origin of the many conflicts at a popular gay club, he explained that it was about "boys" and "he said, she said" gossip and "drama." He added: "Just about really their boyfriends talkin' to somebody else, and it was a lot of unfaithfulness that was in the gay relationships. And they wanted to fight that person or this person said somethin' about me, or lied on me, or, uhh, what else? Really like, petty stuff, where . . . they be talkin' about each other, and they'll then get mad of course, and argue, you know, start fightin' or something." As additional evidence that many of these conflicts involved jealousy, infidelity, or gossip, the phrases "his/my/somebody's boyfriend" and "drama" regularly appeared near to each other in participants' narratives about these fights. Jeremiah offered this when asked what his clique (the Firing Squad) fought with other crews about: "Honestly, stupid stuff. Like, somebody thought somebody said somethin' about somebody in the club, somebody pointed at the wrong person. We fought over, like, little stupid stuff, but it wasn't little stupid stuff, but it was. You have to hear about the fight to actually know how it comes out. But, it was stupid stuff. But for me it was more pride, but on their end, it was more stupid." Jealousy, gossip, and immaturity even caused members of some gangs to fight with each other, but they usually "got over it" because it was, as Jeremiah suggested, "little stupid stuff." Tony said members of his clique would fight with each other or with rival cliques over "lil stuff that get us aggravated and annoyed." Jeremy said that within his group, "We probably do blow up at each other every once in awhile," including over his pet peeve, which was people pointing their fingers in his face while arguing with him. To a friend who had this bad habit, he warned, "Boo, you my sista, and I love you, but that finger's gonna getchu hurt!" While in the moment, participants felt that these encounters required action, but they also acknowledged afterwards that such fights were unimportant by using terms like "petty" or "little stuff."

As further illustration of the way that "beef" manifested within a troubled intergroup dynamic, Boss denied that he was a direct player in his many gang fights:

I don't never feel like I personally had beef with anybody, I was just sorta, like, a part of it, I was sorta one of the fighters, so I was sorta like, there. But I still to this day, never truly had an individual or a one-on-one beef, where someone was mad at me. I feel like, when they were mad at me, they were mad cuz I kicked they ass, but they was never mad at me over somethin' that I done to them, or betrayal, or anything like that, and they was just mad, like, "What does he have to do wit it, why did I fight him?" Or, you know, somethin' like that. It was never like, "Oh, I don't like him cuz he did [something]," or anything like that, because at one point, I was cool with them B.o.B., but I knew I was never gonna be able to be a part of Firing Squad and be cool wit B.o.B. at the same time. So, at the same time, I never really wanted to be cool with them, I just never really had a reason to beef with them until Firing Squad were beefin' wit them.

Gang rivalry structured part of Boss's social life and affected his ability to avoid conflict when he could have otherwise. Boss's role in the gang is akin to the "foot soldier" role some men in straight, hierarchical gangs described, at least in the sense that he did "dirty work" for the gang, even if he did not personally dislike the people he fought. When one member of the group was affronted, even when the circumstances were unclear, action was necessary.

Participants described disrespect as the core of the problem in many fights, some of which started with fairly innocuous events, such as one person accidentally bumping into another or being asked about a prior romantic partner. Nightclub scenes are likely to produce masculinity challenges, perhaps due to the presence of alcohol and bystanders, so minor occurrences such as inadvertent bumps can escalate into serious violence.[20]

A description of a violent encounter I witnessed exemplifies these contextual themes. Although I saw much play-fighting and even an-noyed roughhousing among friends, family members, and boyfriends, I was present for only one clear-cut assault during all of my time in the field. It took place at a gay club in Columbus, one with a reputation for such fights on a certain themed night of the week. A participant in my study (who I will refer to as Participant X) confronted another member of the gay scene over allegedly spreading a "rumor" that Participant X had tested positive for HIV. I have chosen to obscure the participant's name not only because he committed an assault in my presence, but also because, based on some of his statements during his interview, it is very likely that this "rumor" regarding his HIV-positive serostatus was indeed true, despite his assertion to me that he was HIV-negative. For example, when asked about safer sex practices, he said, "I keep condoms in my coat, in my bag, I stay protected. I have to have condoms, cuz I don't have time to be tryin' ta kill somebody." That is, his concern seemed less about maintaining his own health and (professed) negative serostatus and more about maintaining his sexual partners' health, and is perhaps a direct reference to statutes that criminalize the transmission of HIV. Although he made these comments in front of his fellow crew members, I did not ask any of them about his remarks due to concerns about his privacy and group norms that prohibit such questions. Regardless, Participant X confronted the community member about his claims as X's torso and right hand were held back by friends. Seemingly before the community member could fully respond to the allegations, Participant X slapped him across the head and face with his left hand, which remained free. Bystanders put their bodies between the two and Participant X stormed off. They did not fight again later that night, and no one was forcibly removed from the club, presumably due to the fast escalation and subsequent quick dispersion of the crowd.

This encounter was the topic of conversation that night for two reasons: first, the community member's comments were deemed to be unacceptable, even if he had reason to believe they were true. Asking someone outright for his serostatus, speculating publicly on his serostatus, and/or "outing" another person's positive serostatus were all taboo and socially unacceptable in Columbus's gay scene. The community member's activities would certainly qualify not only as gossip, but disrespect as well. Second, everyone was surprised that Participant X actually swung on the community member, and thought it was comical that the slap caused this person's hat to go from an angled yet forward-facing position to a near backward-facing position. The consensus seemed to be that he got exactly what he deserved at the hands of Participant X (a literal smackdown), and should think twice in the future before engaging in such conduct.

That conflict was without a doubt particularly salient to participants because it was related to HIV, the deadly virus that has had a pervasive influence on gay communities for over 30 years and infection with which is still stigmatized. That is, even in an age of education and harm reduction, being HIV-positive is already regarded negatively. Furthermore, obscuring the truth about one's status when one is sexually active was deemed irresponsible (though, was still engaged in by some of the HIV-positive participants in my study). However, accusing someone of this egregious behavior was taken very seriously due to the negative consequences it could have on an HIV-negative person's reputation, as the aspersions it casts on one's serostatus are not shaken off easily.

Gay Gangs: A Family Affair

Although inter- and intragang conflicts often occurred among gay cliques, their members also reported near-familial relationships with fellow gang members. From the familial terms that they used to the ways the group was important to their lives, gay gangs were also fictive kinship networks or, as they are more fittingly called in this case, chosen families.

Gang Structures and Roles

Earlier, I discussed how gaining a sense of belonging by joining a gang likely holds unique significance for queer people. Regarding their sense of belongingness within their gay gangs, when I asked participants to mark on a bull's-eye their status (how "core" they were) within their gangs,[21] most reported being in the innermost rings, some at the center-most point of the target. As illustration of the gay gangs' generally diffuse leadership, Imani noted before he marked his spot in the innermost ring that his chosen placement depended on "how many people can fit in the center." That is, he thought I might place a restriction on how many could be considered core, but in his group, many were core members. Although he was not one of the "shot callers," he said he could call the shots if he wanted to. Illustrating a similar understanding of the group's organizational structure and ability of the members to have a say in the group's activities, Baby also put himself in the innermost ring, "Cuz I'm mostly the influence of who's the center. . . . I influence the mind of the center most, more than anybody that's out this way [in the core of the clique]." Still additional members of the clique also marked themselves in the innermost ring, but everyone acknowledged that Javier was at the centermost point and the head of the crew, along with another member who had a hand in forming and growing the crew, but who was not necessarily involved in the group's day-to-day happenings anymore.

This diffuse leadership was evident in my field experiences and especially in my recruitment processes. There were no particular gatekeepers to other gang members, meaning that referrals came from multiple members of each group. Most of the members of gay gangs were referred to my study by members of their own or other gay gangs. I often conducted interviews when other members of their gangs were present, where they were free to fill in forgotten details and challenge their friends' statements.[22] In interviews with the Royal Family, nearly every other member who was present interrupted at least once (and often multiple times). No one perceived that they were relegated to a lower status, as evidenced by their willingness to interject, sometimes with pointed appraisals of their friends' comments or behaviors. This contrasted sharply with the straight gangs, where I very rarely interviewed multiple members of the same gang, either because participants did not think there were any other gay members, or because they did not spend time with gay friends and straight fellow gang members at the same time.

Although their proximity to the core fluctuated over time, members of the gay gangs largely portrayed themselves as integral and necessary members of their crews. They saw themselves as meaningful members of their street families, who had a say in what happened. The words they used to describe their roles communicated this. For example, Silas described himself as the "ringleader"; Jeremiah called himself the "heart." Ricky exclaimed, "Of course I'm in the core! Of course! I wouldn't be anywhere else," while Oz suggested, "Shoot, they can't do nothin' without me, they love me!" Javier, Jeremiah, and Rashad (current or former leaders of the Royal Family, the Firing Squad, and the B.o.B., respectively) all acknowledged that their status in their crews was directly related to their age and/or to how long they had been involved in the gay scene. In this way, although the gay gangs' leadership was age-graded, young and new members were still integrally involved in these groups and were appreciated. But beyond this, the leaders also had formed identities as problem solvers. This was evidenced by their willingness to give of their time and resources to help others; all three also did so through prosocial channels such as their chosen professions or their volunteer work.

These roles in the gang as problem solvers and providers of resources were evident in certain gang members' daily lives. For example, King, the leader of Hot Cent (another gay gang), maintained how needed and vital he was to members of his community. Just during the time of our interview, someone returned a shop vacuum they had borrowed from him; another person picked up King's old cell phone so he could borrow it for the weekend; while another person called him to ask when their sports team's practice was that afternoon (and called again to clarify when the next competition was). With specific reference to these men's gangs, they would loan fellow members money, let them borrow their cars or cell phones, help them get jobs where they worked, or assist them in filling out paperwork for school or financial aid.

They also would lend their problem-solving skills to interpersonal interactions that needed outside assistance. Utilizing fictive kinship structures that are common both in queer communities and in communities of color,[23] gang members would refer to themselves or fellow gang members as "uncles," "brothers," or even "moms," highlighting the relationships among their chosen families. Taking great pride in his adoption of his "gay daughter" (a male in his clique), Jeremy said, "She's a work in progress, but as a mutha, a gay mutha, I will shape her up, and she will be the gay I know she was destined to be!" Some even saw it as their duty to keep the family together and sane. Javier described how he tries to lead the Royal Family: "[They] ask me for advice, all of that, so I try to keep everybody together you know? We always havin' fights. Somebody always have it out with each other. But I try to bring them back together and all that." With his gay gang Unstoppables, ATL felt a responsibility: "I have to get errybody, like say if the family, if we gettin' involved to it, tryna battle each other, I have to be the one that's like, 'No, we out here for errybody, for the other ones, we can't fight each other, we like family!' So, I have to keep that role goin', family-wise, but otherwise, in the streets there ain't nobody else, you know? It is what it is." Ricky put his helping role explicitly in familial terms: "I'm like that mom. . . . I wouldn't say mom, but in the gay community, even though I'm a male, I would be considered a mom because I'm a little more femi-nine. But, I'm like that mom that they would come to, and they would talk to, and they'd be like, 'Well, I feel this kinda way about this kind of situation,' and I'd just sit there and listen and give them my opinion. And it's like, 'I feel better now.' So, I'm like their counselor, I'll put it like that. But I can kick it with them (laughs)." Just as siblings have rivalries and family members have falling-outs, it was expected that some level of turmoil would exist in the gang, and it fell to the more mature or insightful members to mediate conflicts and to look out for the emotional well-being of the group's members.

Tellingly, only one member of a straight gang (Brad) suggested that part of his gang role was to "pacify" fellow gang members and "make sure no one was fightin' over no bullshit." In this case, it was a prison gang whose unified front was directly related to their ability to prevent injury of their members and to secure their economic assets within inmate subcultures. Interestingly, the group often used the term "brother" to refer to fellow members, but this term was not used in the near-familial way the gay gangs meant it when they referred to their members.

There was considerable variation among the members of straight gangs' descriptions of how integral they were to their gangs, but importantly, some of them suggested they were on the very outskirts of the gang. In contrast, no member of a gay gang placed himself that far from the center. In fact, the only times members of gay gangs placed themselves outside of the two innermost rings of the bull's-eye were when they had just joined or had experienced serious conflict with fellow members in the recent past. At the time of my data collection, it is likely that the Firing Squad and the Royal Family enjoyed more group cohesion than the B.o.B. precisely because of the B.o.B.'s overwhelming reputation for chaos, but the B.o.B. still spent time together and had each other's backs, with Derrick stating, "we all still like family."

Identity Negotiation within Chosen Families

Beyond the increased cohesiveness of their gangs, clearly, gay men in gay gangs did not face the same issues with coming out or impression management that the gay men in straight gangs did. Not only did they feel comfortable with other gang members, they actually reported feeling more comfortable with their gangs than with any other group. For many, these gangs comprised their primary friendship networks.

Beyond that, the fact that everyone else in the group was gay meant that a man did not have to put forth effort to hide his sexual orientation, and did not have to modify his gender presentation substantially. As will soon be discussed, in straight gangs, gay identity was considered to be the antithesis of masculinity and therefore was unacceptable behavior. For example, Elijah felt pressure to stay closeted in a straight gang so as not to negatively impact his own group's reputation and dynamics. Elijah's later experience with the Firing Squad, an all-gay gang, stood in stark contrast: They brought him into the group and appreciated him for who he was. In fact, he hoped to eventually open a small business with several other members of his clique.

Not only were rules of traditional masculinity relaxed for men in gay gangs as compared to straight gangs, I often heard that, when they were with their cliques, members of gay gangs could act "more gay" and "less masculine" than they could with their biological family members. As described in earlier chapters, "more gay" was inextricably linked with a loosening of masculine gender norms; being "more gay" meant that they could engage in a variety of activities that were taboo within their families and within the larger society. These included wearing tight-fitting or revealing clothes, enacting exaggerated mannerisms, modifying the tenor of their voice to a different pitch, using (gay) slang terminology with impunity, engaging in public displays of affection with their romantic partners, and more. Nonetheless, although participants felt free to act "more gay," they likely were careful not to act "too gay" for fear of being ostracized for being "the fag." Recall that two of the attributes related to internalized homophobia were spending a low proportion of social time with gay people and having low membership in gay/bisexual groups. The men in gay gangs overwhelmingly spent their social time with other gay people and necessarily spent much of their time in GLB groups, which were their gangs and primary friendship networks. So, while they may still hold some heterosexist ideas about their gender and sexual identity presentation, the members of gay gangs do not enact sexual stigma by avoiding spending time with other gay people.

I mentioned earlier that, without prompting, about two-thirds of the members of gay gangs volunteered that their gangs were more like families, even choosing the word "family" to appear in their name in the case of the Royal Family. This boundary construction started early in the interview. One of my screening questions was whether the participant was in a gang, clique, crew, set, posse, or organization. The list became so long because participants had used all of those words to describe their groups, which has been well-documented elsewhere.[24] Most of the participants in gay gangs settled on "clique," but wanted to clarify. For example, of the B.o.B., Casper remarked, "We were more or less of a clique, more of a group, I mean, more of a family, cuz we all was real tight, and we all knew each other's families, and we all came out together, for real." That comment was made in the context of how important the B.o.B. was to his identity and his daily life during the time that he was a member. Of the Firing Squad, Jeremiah stated, "It would be more like a clique, or a family." Later, when I asked him to elaborate on why he wouldn't use the word "gang," he clarified:

> We're not out here standin' on corners, we're not out here shootin' people for no reason, we're not out here battlin' people over turf, or anything like that, and we don't have anything to claim. Like, we're not out here tryna prove somethin', umm, we call ourselves a clique because we're around each other 24/7 and we always have each other's back, but at the same time, I feel like gangs are territorial, so they feel like they have to get somethin', or they're out there for somethin'. We're not out here to prove anything, or anything like that, we don't have anything to prove, we're just out here livin', and helpin', supportin' each other.

Indeed, while they were battling over "territory" in the form of gay venues and did seek to "prove" their tenacity and group loyalty, Jeremiah tried to convey that this should not be conceptualized in the same way as the turf wars of urban street gangs. Based on other narratives, gay gang members did want to "prove" something in the club with minor interpersonal violence, but as Jeremiah noted, it wasn't life-threatening violence *for no reason*. That is, he wanted to mark his group's behavior as justifiable and not excessive. Perhaps one of the reasons members of gay gangs did not join neighborhood-based straight gangs is because of this particularly negative opinion of youth street gangs as unnecessarily violent and risky. It is likely much easier to rationalize the violence of a close friendship group when the group began engaging in those sorts of behaviors out of perceived necessity, as a result of intergroup competition instead of an economic or symbolic motive.

Jeremiah was not the only one who wanted to avoid the word "gang," but participants acknowledged that the distinction was perhaps nonexistent to outsiders. Take this exchange with Ricky:

> VP: And are you currently a member of a gang, or a clique?
> RICKY: I wouldn't call it a gang, most people would, but I would really call it like a family affiliation. But we'll put it that way.
> VP: Okay. But you think most people would call it a gang, why?
> RICKY: Yeah, just cuz we hang out so often, and we cause a lot of trouble. (laughs)

The "trouble" he mentioned was escorting, crafting, and fighting, activities the members of his gang often engaged in, both with and without fellow members. King's gang even had a conversation about how to define their group; in his recounting of the conversation, he vacillates between terms:

> If we gotta do what we gotta do, we gon' ride as a group, so yeah I'm a gang member, but we say organization. We said, "Why should we call ourselves a gang?" And one dude said, "We should pull [challenge] the stereotype about being gay and being gangster." I said, "Anybody can be a gangster, even a gay boy can be a gangster, even if he really feminine," so I said that we shouldn't call ourselves a gang. We did at one point in the game, until I stepped over and said no, and took that position and being the head of the operations, I said "No, we gonna be called an organization, how 'bout that? It would be better." I guess you could say we're a gang.

"Organization" sounded more serious, businesslike, and less likely to arouse suspicions of formal authorities. And indeed, King's group's escorting was much more organized than that of the other gay gangs, with many of the group's members working out of the same home. But of course, King made a claim to equality by emphasizing that a feminine gay male could be a gangster *if he wants to be*, even if this is shocking to some.

While the members of gay gangs did acknowledge that they belonged to a gang (regardless of the words its members called it), connections to other members were often deeply felt and genuine. Speaking of the Royal Family, Bob said that the group was important to him, as they had taught him a lot. JD told me: "I click wit everybody, but I just don't click wit people like that, you know what I mean? I feel like, I would never find a group of friends like this, ever again. . . . I feel like it's somethin' spiritual, too. I don't know. Like, we're meant to be together." Regarding his own feelings about the Royal Family, Javier stated it was "very important" for him to be a member of this group: "Cuz I love 'em all. I've known most of 'em for years, since I been living here. . . . And they're very close to me, and they was there when my mom passed. All them came to my mom's funeral and stuff. . . . They really was there, and I really appreciate them, and I love 'em for it." Aga directly compared the Royal Family to his family of origin: "As far as my real family, I love my real family, and stuff like that, although they get on my nerves, my gay family understands me more than my regular family does, because I be around my gay family a lot, and I don't like my real family, they just too much." For its members, the Royal Family represented either a close approximation of or even a preferable alternative to their biological families. Due to shared experiences, especially their histories of same-sex sexual attraction and coming out, gay gangs were safe spaces for sexual identity disclosure and coping with gay-related stress. Anthropologist Kath Weston notes that the support networks gays and lesbians form may be as strong as or stronger than any biological family because they are *chosen* families; this is especially true in light of the societal and familial rejection LGBTQ people sometimes face.[25] Although some members of gay gangs suggested that one of the activities they engaged in was fighting with each other over "drama" (thus the necessity for the peacemakers mentioned earlier), overall, they had generally positive perceptions about the affective quality of these relationships. This is summed up well by Hurricane: "These is my babies. I love 'em dearly. They be actin' funny as hell sometimes, but I love 'em."

Paradoxically, gay gangs were "safe spaces" for these young men, but urban street gangs are fairly *unsafe* spaces, including these same gay gangs. They were places where members could truly be themselves, and express more than just their sexual identities. They received camaraderie and caring from fellow gay people when they didn't receive it from their biological families. However, they simultaneously were involved in illegal activities such as fighting, sex work, and theft, often with their gangs. These activities opened them up to health and safety risks, as well as the risk of arrest and incarceration, but allowed them to make money and support themselves. Gang membership also helped them to carve out a niche in the Columbus gay scene where they sought status and respect, which was particularly salient in light of the pervasive disrespect they faced as gay males.

Are Gay Gangs All That Queer?

The social worlds of gay gangs like the B.o.B., the Royal Family, and the Firing Squad illustrate a complex picture of gang membership and gang members' identities. All-gay gangs present a strong challenge to the stereotypically heterosexual depiction of street gangs, for instance in their members' abilities to be out and accepted by fellow gang members. For men in gay gangs, negotiation of their gay identities focused on becoming "known" within the gay community and creating a public gay persona—quite the opposite of what might be expected when discussing straight gangs. Gay gangs were typically friendship groups that evolved into gangs over time, and were organized around a shared sexual identity. Initiation rituals were almost nonexistent, since participants were with their gangs from their inception, and most reported being core members of groups that had diffuse leadership. Most also preferred to call their gangs "families" or "cliques," in an effort to communicate the social, supportive, and positive aspects of these groups.

While they did engage in a number of prosocial activities, members of gay gangs also crafted and escorted, as they perceived these opportunities to be available to them as gay men. In addition, they fought to defend each other, whether it was from anti-gay harassment enacted by straight men, or from threats made by rival gay crews. Conflicts between gay cliques originated from issues such as disrespect, gossip, and access to gay clubs (the closest entity to "territory" in the world of the gay gangs). But even these fierce rivalries were flexible; some members of gay gangs were the friends, family members, and romantic interests of men in opposing gay cliques. And, just as all families fight, they even fought among themselves, though they were typically able to move beyond these conflicts. After all, their gangs allowed them a space to really be themselves and to develop their gay identities, without the fear of heterosexual rejection. They had no reason to remain closeted and were free to be out and proud; the same cannot be said for men in gangs with an overwhelming majority of heterosexual members.

Gay gangs seem quite queer, or different from straight gangs and those described in previous gang scholarship, but they aren't completely dissimilar. Members of gay gangs may explore gender fluidity and express genuine affection for their fellow gang members, but they still engaged in various illegal activities, refused to be disrespected, and fought with their enemies, many of whom were in rival gay gangs. They resisted economic marginalization by engaging in illicit money-making activities with their gangs, and resisted social marginalization by forming community from which they could draw status. Being a member of a gay gang was one of the ways they attempted to construct identities as gay men who were to be taken seriously. The queerness of gay gangs arguably lies in the ways they proudly proclaim gay identity partially *through the activities their gangs are involved in*; they fight over it and form tight-knit cliques to bolster each other's identity as gay men worthy of belonging.

Thinking of the gay gangs and how they become known, I am reminded of the many ways resistance and subversion can occur, all within the context of gang membership and identity. For example, Norma Mendoza-Denton's study of gang-involved young women described how they used a system of makeup, hairstyling, and fashion to signify their gang membership, portray a tough persona, and highlight their refusal to adhere to either Latina or Euro-American gender roles. Speaking about the strength in being noticed for her beauty while simultaneously appearing tough and unapproachable, one participant stated, "People look at you, but nobody fucks with you."[26] Men in gay gangs similarly draw on masculine tropes of fighting and gang membership to structure the ways they gain reputation and status, but ultimately subvert expectations since their public identities are based on their sexual identity. They strive to be noticed and known for being gay, but not fucked with.

4

"In the Game"

The Experiences of Gay Men in Straight Gangs

Forgoing the use of my GPS and deferring to Spiderman's claims that he'll get us to the club the fastest way possible, we drive through his neighborhood until we reach the highway. Windows up as the on-ramp ends, I yell at another driver who doesn't want to let me over before finally merging into the middle lane. Knowing that we'll be on this road for a few miles and he has me all to himself, Spiderman asks me excitedly, "So what did you think of him? Did he tell you somethin' good?"

I hesitate for one second because I'm initially unclear of who he means. During the course of the day, I conducted three interviews, hung out with whichever neighborhood friends dropped by, and had dinner with about eight other people. In total, they represented no less than six gangs. It then becomes clear to me: He's talking about his boyfriend, James. I have come to learn the significance of the car as confessional in fieldwork, so I know that he doesn't necessarily want my opinion about James; he just wants to be able to tell me his.

"Definitely," I say, and pause again, this time intentionally.

"I knew he would! He was kinda like, iffy about the whole thing when I first told him. But, I'm glad he did! I been knowin' him for a long time, and I've known a lotta niggas, and he's really *that nigga*.[1] You know? That nigga that showed me the love that nobody else ever showed me."

"Mmm," I mumble. Again I pause, in a way that I think communicates I know what he means. In Spiderman's interview, he was very clear about his feelings for his boyfriend: although off-and-on (especially in light of James's other relationship with a woman), he said they had contemplated exchanging rings with each other in their own private ceremony, and James is the only man he trusts enough to have unprotected sex with. But in many ways, I don't know what he means, from a personal perspective. Both James and Spiderman spent 10 or more years with their straight gangs, with James still reporting active membership and Spider-man saying he was still "kind of" involved. These two men are engaged in a five-year intimate relationship that very few people in their neighborhoods or families know about, and which their gangs certainly are not aware of. During his interview, Spiderman told me this about James:

> I'm his only guy, and I'm his first guy. He said I exposed him to it. (laughs) And, he loves me a lot, and he was kinda pourin' out his feelins, but he don't know how to tell his friends either, cuz he don't know what their reaction will be, cuz he hardcore, he a nigga! When he over here with me, and my friends here, he feel open, but he don't know how to do it on the outside wit other people. Like, "Naw, I can't do it. They prolly feel different about me, then." But he said he considers himself bisexual, but he just cain't let nobody know, cuz he don't know how they would feel, or react. Or, he'd lose love from people, and stuff like that.

The way Spiderman represented James's story was quite accurate to James's own narrative, but I don't offer up that information. Spiderman knows I won't, even if I'd like to.

Still thinking of the complexities of their relationship, I remained silent. As if he read my mind, he continues: "And like, I know stuff is hard for him. I know he got a kid, and a girl[friend], and he in the game, and all that. But I know he loves me. And I love him too."

* * *

Despite their commitment to each other, it is not surprising that neither Spiderman nor James were out to their gangs. Although considerable progress has been made toward LGBTQ equality in the Western world, same-sex sexual behavior is still stigmatized in their communities, as discussed, and perhaps especially so in gangs. Due to their involvement in violent and other masculine status-conferring activities, gangs are typically regarded as hypermasculine groups. A hypermasculine environment is not particularly forgiving of unconventional masculinity or same-sex sexual activity. Furthermore, existing research and recent events would suggest that perhaps these misgivings about coming out to the gang are justified. Gay men have been tortured by gang members;[2] some gangs have formal rules against same-sex sexual activity;[3] over 50 years of gang research has chronicled anti-gay attitudes;[4] and the limited research on a handful of male gang members who were gay, bisexual, or questioning their sexual identity suggests that they gay bashed with their gangs to gain masculine status and conceal their sexual identities from fellow gang members, from whom they feared violence.[5]

However, it would be reductive to depend on this limited literature to ascertain the experiences of gay-identified male gang members. In fact, what we think we know about them raises far more questions than answers about their activities and interactions with fellow gang members. Whether gay gang members have experiences similar to presumably heterosexual gang members, as described in the gang literature, is also unclear.[6]

Certain characteristics of a gang's structure impact members' experiences. Specifically, just as a gang's sex composition influences gender dynamics and behavior, the sexual orientations of the gang's members do, as well. Scholars who study gangs and gender suggest that the ratio of male to female gang members affects both males' and females' relative involvement in delinquency/violence, efforts to control female gang members' behavior, females' motivations to attain similar achievements within the gang as males, and how females behave toward each other, sometimes in marginalizing ways.[7] Likewise, the gang's proportion of gay, lesbian, or bisexual people holds consequential implications for gang experience.

Nineteen participants were or had been members of gangs comprised of more than three-quarters straight members. They represented 20 different straight gangs; two men had been members of more than one straight gang, and two had belonged to the same straight gang. This chapter attempts to fill gaps in knowledge by exploring important issues for men like James and Spiderman, who are members of straight (primarily heterosexual) and thus largely heteronormative gangs. I will evaluate their reasons for and processes involved in joining a gang; the activities they engaged in with their gangs; and how the decision to disclose (or conceal) their sexual orientation to the gang has shaped their experience. After having discussed the gay gangs in the previous chapter, focusing now on straight gangs allows me to illustrate how gangs with many versus few gay members are alike and different, especially for gay members, whether they are out or closeted.

Gang Joining

Many forces shape young people's entry into gangs. The decision to join a gang is typically regarded as the result of "pushes," such as risk factors for gang membership, and "pulls," such as the perceived benefits that the gang can provide to members. Risk factors for gang joining that have received consistent support in the literature include negative life events, a lack of parental supervision, and having delinquent friends.[8] Reasons youth give for joining gangs include wanting fun, protection, respect, money, a sense of belonging, and because family members or friends are involved.[9] For young people in urban areas, this often occurs within the context of their facing multiple marginality, such as racism, repression, and economic exclusion,[10] and thus their gang membership can be conceptualized as an act of resistance.[11] As was seen in the previous chapter, gang members sometimes refer to their groups as "families," not only because of the perceived benefits gangs can provide that their families of origin could not, but also because fellow gang members may be actual biological relatives.[12] As I detail below, the young men in straight gangs told gang joining stories that were quite similar to those found in the broader gang literature.

The straight gangs in my study were organized largely around geography, be it the neighborhood in general, or a certain area where members sold drugs, tagged (sprayed graffiti), or otherwise controlled the space. As illustration of this point, when asked generally about the neighborhood he grew up in, Spiderman first mentioned that it was "a Blood neighborhood"; Brandon said that his neighborhood was "mostly gangsters and hoodrats." Fellow gang members were often family members. Rocc, whose brother introduced him to drug selling and gang life, described the connection between neighborhood, family, and social structure when he discussed who joined his gang:

> Anybody from [that area] that's claimin' Crip or whatever, and grew up in that culture kinda, and if you was gon' do somethin' and you was connected [then you joined]. And it's kinda, like, generational, you know? Like, if your uncle did it, your brother prolly did it, you do it, you know? And that's how people knew each other. It's kinda like, a family. Like, people grew up in the same struggle, and wanted a way out, and if I knew

you, and we were cool, and I knew your family, and we were cool, and you wanted a way out, come fuck [hang out] wit me, I gotchu.

Rocc's quote alludes to some of the familial and neighborhood reasons why young people, including these young men, join gangs. For example, Boog, Darius, Toby, and James all joined because they thought gangs could offer protection, support, and resources their biological families had not and never could provide for them while in dangerous neighborhoods. Darius suggested that because his family "wasn't there" for him, he had to join a gang to preserve his safety because he "needed some protection" from fights and other people: "I didn't have nobody, so it was like, if I did get into it wit somebody, I was gettin' jumped on." Of this group, he noted, "It was an actual gang gang, like, the shoot, kill, fight, all that typa gang." Toby also joined a gang to prevent trials by neighborhood peers, explaining it was "because we was new to the neighborhood, and basically, that's the only way they was gonna accept us livin' there. I didn't wanna have to every day get up and fight everybody in the neighborhood. I just decided to join."

James went so far as to classify experiences with parental neglect, abuse, lack of a father figure, and neighborhood violence as a part of certain young men's experience that helps propel them into gangs. When I asked him to tell me a little bit about his family and then his neighborhood growing up, he replied:

Uhh, family, fuck that. (laughs) Uhh. (pause) Wow. Grew up, I had to be like, the head honcho, you know? Be the one that's holdin' down the household, dad wadn't there, left, asshole, oh well. Don't care to meet him, don't wanna meet him. Better off without him. Uhh, I don't know. Shit's just average, well, not average shit, but typical Black male shit. No father figure, joinin' a gang, abused when I was young, raped, fucked up my head. Made me paranoid, made me seek mental help, you know, fuck that, man, just fuck that. That's why I smoke so much weed, just to calm me down. (laughs) . . . [I grew up in] a pretty rough neighborhood. Them people were dyin', like, in front of you, yeah. (scoffs) Like, somebody can die right in front of you, and it's just another day, like, "Man, yep, you know, so-and-so died."

James also detailed the serious drug activity in his neighborhood that produced "zombies" who looked "crazy in the face." When I asked if he had been involved with drug sales prior to joining the gang, he again attributed his delinquency and gang involvement to traumatic experiences in his life and how they affected his thinking: "It just happened when I got raped. After that, I said fuck life, fuck everything. If I'ma die, I'ma die for somethin' serious, gettin' paid, to give to my kid. That's all that matters to me, for real." James said he had been physically abused by his mother to the point that he had "permanent marks" on him, and had been sexually abused by his mother's then-boyfriend. Experiencing trauma in families of origin can contribute to young people seeking alternate support structures in the form of gangs. Neighborhood context is also important to frame young people's involvement in gangs and crime; in James's case, the neighborhood is a site of violence already, evidently desensitizing him ("somebody can die right in front of you, and it's just another day"), and driving his willingness to engage in illegal activities that could help him provide for his young son. James fatalistically describes this cycle of poverty, familial discord, and crime/violence as "typical Black male shit."

Boog also reported seeing gangs and violence in the neighborhood as a child, and even being attracted to that aspect of gang life as an adolescent in light of familial neglect: "I was excited with the more violence, the more people, the better off, I just wanted to make trouble. I feel like I wasn't getting love [from my family], so I didn't want nobody to be happy in my life, nobody. . . . I mean, my friends, my brothers, the gangs, they showed love. Whether it's the wrong kind of love, it's the love you need at that time." Boog had an idea of what awaited him in the gang: his gang-involved older brother "didn't live to see 18" because he had been murdered, shot twice in the head. Regarding gang violence, he suggested, "If you gon' live by it, you gon' die by it, that's the rule." In this way, Boog saw gang and criminal involvement in his neighborhood as a culture, as Rocc suggested. And, as further illustration of the generational features of some participants' gangs, Rocc, Raphael, Adidas, and Elijah joined so they could spend additional time with some of their family members, who were gang involved.

I asked each participant how old he was when he either joined a straight gang or helped form one; on average, they joined at about 14. This is consistent with many self-report studies of gang members, which suggest the peak age of gang involvement to be 14 or 15.[13] Almost all of the young men in straight gangs joined existing groups. They did so in both ritualistic and relational ways. Nearly half of the men in straight gangs reported an initiation ritual for at least one of their crews, all of which included violence. For example, hopefuls may have to commit a crime, such as robbery or an act of violence against a rival gang member,[14] or be "jumped in." Elijah had to "put in work" by doing both: getting beaten up and then committing a robbery with his brother. Toby's "jumping in" ritual consisted of being "beat up" by his gang's members for about 10 minutes, during which he was able to fight back. Spiderman said that getting jumped in by a gang means that "you gotta let 'em beat chu up!" He added, "You not supposed to [fight back], but some of 'em let chu, just to see where your skills is, to see if you're really down for the clique." The jumping-in process can also be linked to the gang's mythology, as James's account of joining his gang illustrates:

> I had to get my ass whooped. . . . In the Bloods, we go under the five-point star, everything is five, everything to the right, everything is red, red and brown, when blood dries, it's brown, and that's one of our colors. . . . But, I took five steps, and got jumped. Even before gettin' jumped, they lined up in a row, it's like two rows, five right here, five right here, as soon as you walk in, they swinging on you, you take five steps and you gotta stop, and then that's when the old heads is at the end, like, the people that's in control of it, take five more steps, and that's when you can swing back, and then after that, you in.

Although many of the straight groups did adopt the symbology, colors, and names of nationally recognized gangs such as the Bloods, most were "homegrown" without formal attachments to other sets of the larger gang. This homegrown quality has been seen in other gang research in Columbus and elsewhere.[15]

Another violent initiation ritual involved assaulting and/or robbing someone, especially someone who the OGs (original gangsters, or important/longstanding members) or other higher-ups wanted to retaliate against. Boog explained: "My initiation was to rob somebody that one of the members was having a problem with. . . . It's always gonna be the other adversary, the gang you got a problem with, or somebody that the OG have a problem with, because you always gonna have a OG, it's just like military rank. [W]hen you come in, you just a foot soldier, you do what you told to do." Similarly, Brad said he joined by "just bein' a soldier. Uhh, crashin' out on people. They'd be like, 'Hey, dude owes money and he ain't paid, go get 'em,' so I'd go beat 'em up, or fight 'em.'" As suggested by participants and gang research, these rituals served several functions. First, they demonstrated whether the new recruit was tough, and perhaps had useful fighting skills. Spiderman's fellow gang members wanted to see if his skills showed he could be "down" (ready to fight) for the clique, while Jayden "earned his stripes" by fighting members of other crews. Second, the ritual provided an introduction to the structure of the gang and, in some cases, its associated mythology and symbology. Note, for example, the reliance on stars, the number five, and red/brown for James's gang initiation ritual, or the hierarchical and military references in Boog's, Brad's, and Jayden's talk. (Brad also said it took years of being a soldier to get to his "spot" as "captain" of his set.) Third, initiation was useful for the OGs, who sought retaliation against those who had wronged them. And finally, the group endeavor served to reinforce the solidarity of all involved, and prove the recruit will be loyal to the gang.[16]

Regarding men who joined their gangs in non-ritualistic ways, sometimes they had to do almost nothing in order to join. It was not uncommon for there to be little-to-no formal transition from being a neighborhood resident or member of a peer network to being a gang member. Regarding his gang, DJ said, "I didn't really join, I was already in it, because that's where I stayed." Echoing this, Dollars noted that he and his cousin were gang involved, stating, "It was just automatically joined if you grew up out there." And finally, familial or romantic relationships could allow for smooth entry into the gang, such as D.C.'s sexual relationship with an existing gang member.

Gang Activities

As these gangs were comprised of friends and family members, it is not surprising that much of the time spent with fellow gang members did not include harmful illegal activity. Indeed, research shows that gang members talk about violence and crime much more frequently than they engage in it.[17] When asked what sorts of things they did together, a common refrain was "Smoke, chill," followed by descriptions of several other activities, both legal and illegal. In addition to typical adolescent pursuits such as sports and "hanging out," which is the most commonly reported activity of gang members,[18] participants engaged in a large variety of criminal acts with their gangs, which encompassed violent, property, and drug offenses. Although comparatively little of all gang members' time is spent engaging in illegal activity,[19] gang members are far more likely to engage in delinquency and violence than non-gang youths.[20]

Gay men in straight gangs provided narratives of gang life very similar to those reflected in the extant literature. Time within the gang was spent participating in recreational activities or otherwise "chilling" with each other, selling drugs, and fighting other crews. Several men's accounts of their gangs' activities are illustrative:

> JAYDEN: Smoked, chill, and just—I wouldn't say too much like, umm, play ball and shit, and just chill out. Now, like, might shoot off a gun every now and then. Might fight with other gangs, there is another gang out there that they fight with. . . . I guess just bein' in the same neighborhood and claimin' this, and they claimin' that, and they just be fightin', like, they'll throw up [claim] they hood, and then somebody else throw up [a gang sign], and then they just wanna fight, yeah. It be like that. . . . Like, hoods, cuz that's what it's by now, ain't nobody like, "Oh, Bloods, Crips," no, it goes by hoods, you feel what I'm sayin'?

> SPIDERMAN: Steal cars, break into houses. If we see somebody that wasn't from the hood, we'd talk shit to 'em, or we might go fight 'em, or somethin' like that. We set a couple of fires. Skipped school together, or when we did go to school, we'd act a fool. (laughs) That's basically it, same thing over and over. . . . We were sellin' weed, and then we caught ourself tryna sell powder, and that's the stuff you sniff up your nose. . . . We might go out, kick it at the club or somethin', play some game of pools, or dice. . . . I [tagged] probably like twice.

DJ: Umm, just chill. Sometimes maybe fight, but mostly chill, go to the pool when it's summer time. . . . Play basketball. Play football. . . . I would look out [while they sold drugs] a couple times. . . . The little kids, well, us, we would just steal. We'd go to the store and steal. We might steal a car, maybe, if we knew the keys was in there, and it was runnin'. . . . We broke into a house a couple times, didn't get caught, so we wanted to stop it while we was ahead. (laughs) . . . [We would fight with] other neighborhoods, if we didn't like how you was co-min' at us. Or, if we ain't like you period, we would fight you.

As is suggested by these examples, when conflicts with other crews were described, they were discussed in such a way that communicated the territorial nature of these groups. That is, much of the violence they described arose from what amounted to "turf battles" between different crews, such as multiple crews staking a claim to the same neighborhood, someone being in the "wrong" neighborhood, or a rival group generally threatening their gang's reputation.[21] Spiderman explained how fights would start between his and other crews:

Basically they was talkin' shit. They might say our group is, we punks, or we whack, we cain't do this, we cain't do that. Or they can beat our ass, and stuff like that. It's just basically how we got into fights, too. Or like, say, okay, where I'm at, that's the Blood neighborhood, and we might have a cousin or somebody that live out there, and you comin' into the Blood neighborhood to visit them, but chu got all blue on, and that's who we'd talk shit to, like, "Aww, you in our hood now, we beat cho ass, . . . you need to get up outta here," stuff like that, and we end up fightin' like that, too.

Thus, the gangs sought to address challenges to their group's reputation or their group's territory by besting their opponents in physical fights. This also points to the frequently retaliatory nature of territorial gang violence. Boog suggested, "If you do something to me, it gonna always be a response, if you did something to my brother, there gonna be a response, tit for tat."

On this point, in Boog's case, his move from his home state to Ohio meant that he did not have to deal with retaliatory gang violence, since his main rivals were out of state: "I ain't gotta look over my back, when

I go in the store, I ain't gotta worry about who might be sittin outside." He reported actually being shot at within the first week of a recent visit to his hometown. But Boog still wavered on whether or not he felt safe in his Columbus East Side neighborhood due to a sense of fatalism and perceived risk: "I feel safe, very safe. Well, I ain't gonna say very safe, because a stray bullet can kill you!" Regarding this uneasiness and potential for the unknown that has been shaped by neighborhood and gang violence, Jayden said that he felt safe because he grew up in his neighborhood. He also cautioned, "You still have to watch your back, because you never know what could happen." In fact, he was in a conflict with someone who was threatening to kill him over some "dumb stuff."

Fights also occurred when the gangs encountered someone from a different neighborhood while in public places, which were considered neutral (or, possibly, up-for-grabs) territory. Public places that were the sites of intergang conflict, which gang scholar Scott Decker refers to as "staging grounds for violence,"[22] included clubs or community celebrations, such as the downtown Fourth of July fireworks display ("The Boom"). Toby suggested, "We'll go to the Fair, or the Boom, Ribfest, just be out there just startin' stuff. They'll be like, 'Oh, go over there and hit him.' I'd go over there, punch him, and then his people run up, and we all be out there fightin'." Thus, this defense of the neighborhood group extended even beyond the boundaries of the neighborhood. Rocc expounded on this: "It's called reppin'. Like, if we were out at the Ribfest, or whatever, everybody was together, everybody wore they color, and we were goin' out lookin' for fights, brawls. Hit somebody in red, dodge out [leave], like, everything before the police came. It was kinda like a game, you know?" Violence also transcended beyond rival crews; non-gang-affiliated ("random") people were sometimes targets. Elijah suggested that he and his brother "had to do the dirty work" of his gang and said this involved "beatin' somebody up if they know they don't belong in the [neighborhood], or just beatin' a random person up as they walkin' down the street." When Greg told me about his gang's involvement in what he deemed "fighting people for no reason," he began by asking me, "Have you ever heard of the game Knockout?" Toby also described it: "[We'd] play Knockout. . . . Knockout, basically, is like goin' to another neighborhood, and randomly walkin' around the neighborhood, whoever you see, just punch 'em. And then run, and just keep doin' it. Over and over and over again, no matter who it is." Perhaps especially telling regarding violence existing alongside gang members' other youthful activities is their transformations of it into a source of entertainment, as "play" or a "game."

Over half of the men in straight gangs had sold drugs, most with their crews, which suggests another reason for these gangs to protect their territory. Beyond representing the neighborhood they felt ownership over, the neighborhood doubled as drug-dealing turf and therefore was an economic asset to be protected. Boog noted, "It's always about money, and more power." Individuals who are gang involved have also been shown to sell drugs at higher rates than those who are not gang involved.[23] The drug economy provides many gang members with a primary source of money, but also an enterprise from which they can derive status.[24] Sociologist Martín Sánchez-Jankowski suggests gang members' motivation to engage in lucrative pursuits such as vehicle theft and drug sales is a result of their "entrepreneurial spirit"; attributes of this spirit include competitiveness, being able to plan and to take risks, and finally, a drive to accumulate money, material possessions, and status.[25]

On this note of risk, involvement in these various illicit pursuits also increases gang members' susceptibility to violent victimization.[26] This could be from their clients or other drug sellers. For men involved in the underground economy, there are limited legal avenues for recourse. This produces additional motivation for them to respond violently to customers and competitors to collect debts, exact revenge, or give themselves an advantage.[27] Some men, like Boog, made efforts to convey that the victims of his violence were "particular" individuals who were acceptable targets because they were also "in the game," meaning gang or drug involved. Beyond that, the risk of being formally punished was low because they had little legal recourse, and the potential payoffs were considerable: "You knew they had money, you knew they had dope, and all the other stuff was bonus. So they always gonna give you something. My thing in robbing, why rob somebody that's only gonna have $100 or $200, and they too many consequences after the fact if you get caught. . . . Yeah, go for drug dealers, who they gonna call? The police and tell them? 'Oh, I just got robbed for my drugs and—' Okay." However, others suggested their fellow gang members might victimize them if they made mistakes while selling. Brandon, a reluctant drug seller, discussed serious consequences:

> I just wasn't comfortable wit it, because first, I was scared of jail. I was forced to sell drugs, because they was like, "If you don't sell this—" and I saw people who was out there that lost their drugs on accident, but the person that had them sellin' did not know that they lost it, so they would end up gettin' hurt, they would end up gettin' shot, end up [with their] house gettin' shot up, or somethin' like that, and I always thought like, maybe if I lost somebody's drugs, then the same thing would happen to me.

Brandon's apprehension was not so much rooted in moral concerns about drug selling (though many drug sellers did discuss ethical considerations in selling), but in his value to the gang being based on his ability to deftly sell drugs.

Roles in drug selling did not always entail violence—several participants, for instance, had been involved as a lookout, a holder, or a courier (someone who transported the drugs). Lookouts could also be utilized for robberies, whether or not they were drug related. Lesser roles in drug selling were often age-based or strategic. For example, Dollars's gang counted on the fact that he did not look like the typical drug seller. They knew he was gay, which was atypical for men in straight gangs, and "with me being who I was, and how I dress, the police never thought I sold, so they never stopped me." Thus, the gang would call on him when they were short: "If they didn't have it, I would have it, and then they would call me, and I'd be like, 'Well, here.' But I didn't know how to do the scaling and stuff, until later on." Similarly, Joe's age made him the most logical choice for holding his group's drugs: "Seein' how I was so young, they was like, 'Okay, we gon' have to hide this stuff.' And it was like, 'Oh, use Joe.' And I'm like, 'Oh? Why me? They might check me too?' They was like, 'Aw, naw, naw, you young!' Me being stupid, I hid it. And I hid it on myself. And thank God the cops didn't come and search us (laughs)." Participants who were involved in hand-to-hand drug transactions reported a variety of economic structures: some were able to keep all of their profit from selling, some returned a percentage to the gang, and others reported returning all of the money to the gang, but would then benefit from what the gang bought with the money.

It should be clear that, although these gang members engaged in many age-appropriate recreational activities, violence was a regular part of gang life, as has been shown in the literature. In the gang context, violence can be used to respond to threats, either to the safety of members or to turf and economic interests; as a vehicle to join or leave the gang; as a way to gain status; and in retaliation for violence committed against group members by rival gangs. Given these varied uses, my participants and other gang members describe violence as a central feature of their gang experience.[28]

Violence not only became a fairly routine part of participants' gang lives, it left lasting impacts that they felt and could be seen even by outsiders. As described above, Boog said that he still could not visit his home state and old neighborhood without fearing for his safety or actually being victimized. Although he was still peripherally involved with a Blood set in Columbus at the time we spoke, he reported not only that he did not engage in violence anymore, but that he viewed himself as more guarded and less social as a result of his continued viewing of and engagement in violence over his lifetime. Beyond mental scars, several men made a point to tell me about broken bones or show me physical scars from injuries sustained during gang activity. These included Raphael's scar from his gang initiation, Darius's scar from getting pistol whipped by a rival gang member, and Toby's "marks everywhere" and James's "couple a little scars" from stabbing injuries sustained during intergang fights. Also relevant to note is that eight of the 12 men who had carried a gun or used one to commit a crime were in straight gangs.

Paradoxically, although some participants joined gangs to gain protection, joining also increased their chances of victimization.[29] For example, Boog explained that the gang afforded him some level of protection on the street, in reform school, and prison, but in order to maintain the protection that the gang offered him, he had to engage in violence. Interestingly, he joined his first gang in reform school for protection before ever being victimized, but became a victim of violence as a result of his involvement. The same goes for Darius and Toby, who joined because they wanted protection, but were then initiated into serious violence after joining. Sociologist Victor Rios refers to this as the "gang double bind": inner-city boys of color fight to prevent their future victimization, but their involvement in violence only leads to more potential for victimization.[30] However, this was not the only "double bind" facing gay members of straight gangs.

"I Really Don't Get to Be Myself": Identity Negotiation in Straight Gangs

A recurrent theme in participants' narratives was the need to negotiate their sexual identities in ways that did not conflict with the masculine status they had built up during their gang involvement and were trying to maintain. The extent to which members of straight gangs had to conceal their involvement with the gay community (in the form of friends, boyfriends, or clients) depended primarily on whether or not they were "out" to their gangs, and also on the proportion of members of their gangs who were gay, lesbian, or bisexual. Men in gangs made up almost exclusively of heterosexual members often had to hide their sexuality. This was achieved by presenting a normatively masculine persona to the gang, becoming romantically involved with females, and also by controlling information regarding their sexual identity. Several came out, sometimes with violent consequences.

"I Didn't Wanna Be the Fag"

Of the 19 men who were or had been members of straight gangs, 15 chose not to come out (disclose their sexual identities) to those gangs. The decision to not come out was based primarily on these men's concerns that they would face negative repercussions in the forms of damage to their reputation or threats to their physical safety. They suggested they were living separate lives, which could not intersect. James said, "Me around my peoples, my gang, and then me around my man, you know what I'm sayin', two different things, basically." When I asked if there were times when he could really be himself, not putting anything on, just being him, he replied, "When I'm by myself." No energy spent on impression management is needed when a man is alone.

Although not officially out to his former crew, Elijah had a feeling that his family members (also fellow gang members) knew he was gay, but did not want him to mention it while with the gang. Not only would it invite challenges to him, but it would cast aspersions on his family members and the gang. That is, misogynistic and homophobic cultural messages devalue anything other than conventional heterosexual masculinity, and being openly gay in this context would be very likely to attract gender patrolling. Regarding this straight gang and gangs like it, Elijah painted the following portrait: "I don't think they accept gay people now. (laughs) . . . I don't think any group would, though! Why would you want a gay dude sittin' on the block witchu? (laughing) Y'all all wear baggy pants, and he got on skinny jeans. Like, what that look like? That's embarrassing (laughs)." Elijah's use of *accept* likely means *allow to join*, but it also undeniably refers to the gang's intolerance of gay men. And of course, he assumed a gay man would not share the masculine and urban style of his fellow (heterosexual) gang members. This is perhaps because Elijah himself engaged in stereotypically feminine grooming behaviors by dyeing his hair and using clear coat on his nails, but clarified that this can be done in ways that "still look masculine" in comparison to other forms of grooming that he considered to be extreme among gay males. Toby had a similar feeling. He quipped, "Who wants to have a gay guy in their gang? Nobody gonna take 'em serious. Like, 'Y'all got a gay dude in y'all's group, y'all not hard.' And I just didn't wanna put 'em through that." Interestingly, the perception that gay gang members are not as "hard" as straight ones and thus are unsuitable for membership mirrors the views of some gang members (of both sexes) that gang males are "harder" than gang females, and gangs *without* females are "harder" than gangs *with* females.[31]

Of course, image and reputation were important components of respectable masculinity and gang membership. This was also evident in Part I of this book regarding the cultural messages pertaining to gay men, gay men of color, and men deemed to be "the fag," a denigrated public identity. Thus, there was pressure, especially within the gang context, to enact a masculine and non-gay public persona. Rocc elaborated:

> In the hood, we was never really exposed to it, because it was a taboo. So if they were gay, you didn't know it, and if they were, they was the fag. Everybody knew the fag! And I didn't wanna be the fag. (laughs) . . . [T]hey don't really get to see me, they see this persona of Rocc, this always fight, always ready, they see that side. And I really don't get to be myself around these people, simply because their expectations of who I'm supposed to be, or what they've seen previously, to give them an idea of who I am.

Because of the pressure to not be "the fag" (openly gay or feminine) and instead to be ready for violence, Rocc identified how gang life was inconsistent with his and other young gay men's abilities to be themselves. Rocc's sexuality is indeed part of who he is, but it is a part he felt he could not reveal. Toby had similar concerns regarding his safety and status:

> [After my first same-sex sexual experience,] I continued to stay in the closet, though. Just because I had a reputation, like, a part of a. (pause) You could call it a gang. In [my old neighborhood], so I woulda had to maintain myself as a boy. . . . Cuz I feel like, if I was openly gay, they woulda kicked me out the gang, or not let me be in a gang, and I woulda got picked on. So, I just didn't wanna go through that. And, I didn't wanna come out the closet, cuz my family, I was scared of what they was gonna say. . . . [The gang would] treat me different, yeah. They wouldn't have been openly acceptin', they probably think I'd try to mess with [have sex with] one of them. I mean, I probably would've, but they didn't know that. (laughs)

Tellingly, Toby implied that being openly gay is inconsistent with "maintain[ing] myself *as a boy*"; that is, straight gangs are heteronormative environments that presume gay men do not possess the requisite attributes to be regarded as men, let alone possess the toughness needed for gang membership. He did not want to put his source of protection at risk, nor his reputation, and certainly didn't want to be suspected of sexual impropriety. Toby also made a point to state that although he suspected some of the higher-ups in his gang were also gay but not out, "they never will be [out]." When I asked why he thought that was, he replied, "They're just scared of what errybody's gonna say. They don't wanna be judged." Boog went so far as to claim that gay gang members *must* stay closeted in order to maintain their relationships with fellow gang members:

> They had to be [closeted]. It's just how you got to be! Because you'd rather not, people realize it with us being male and bisexual, and say you come out to somebody, everybody gonna have they opinion, you gon' lose some friends, and you gon' keep some friends. That's how you gon' figure out who the real friends are. So that's what you majority worried about. I got

this far, I got all these niggas with me, and now I got to tell them, and they find out I'm bisexual, who gon' mess with me? There's a lot of things.

Toby and Boog's comments on the nexus of image and outcome are related primarily to perception and ambiguous changes in others' opinions of them. However, the potential outcomes could be even more direct and serious than threats to reputation, and instead threaten their actual physical safety. When asked if he personally would come out to his gang, Boog replied:

> I can't open that to certain people, because it's just like, being disrespectful to what you live by, and that's definitely a no-no in the gang, in the Blood gang. . . . It was more like a pride thing, and because I respect the code. More or less my pride. I felt like people was just gonna make an opinion about me. At that time, a lil bit, I cared about how certain family members would feel about me, even though I had this kinda hatred toward them, because I felt like I was neglected, you know? I really cared, so it was more or less the pride and then the code. [In the code, being gay is] not tolerated. That would be automatic action. So, they would try to hurt me, maybe kill me, you never know. . . . It's safer to not [come out]. Never!

Still on the subject of why he wouldn't come out, Boog then expanded on these comments by considering the ways new gang members jockey for position within the group: "Somebody can always take your place, somebody always want what you have in the gang. You controlling people, you up there, of course somebody gon' want to sit in your seat, be acknowledged, yeah, so you can't trust anybody. You have some that will bounce for you, that's the majority of the soldiers and the young boys that's trying to get into the game, them the most volatile of the gang, is the younger." The ratio of dependable older friends to volatile younger members also spelled potential disaster for his coming out, due to his perception that the younger ones were more willing to engage in violence, especially to take the status he had worked so long to achieve. Jayden suggested that in the past, many of his fellow gang members were volatile. He was not sure of his sexual identity during the height of his gang involvement and still had not told his gang about his sexuality: "To be real, more back in the day, they was more hectic, like, if you say somethin' to 'em, they'll just hit you for no apparent reason. Yeah, and it can be a whole bunch of 'em just come at you at once, just start wailin' on you, I done see that, so, I mean, that's why I really didn't come out [to them], but now they don't say nuttin' cuz I'm grown, and I'll tell them straight out, and I do keep a pistol in my thang, so I mean, that's why." In Jayden's case, although his gang's members seemed to have become less volatile over time, he feared violence from them primarily because he had experienced violence without knowing the reason; coming out would ostensibly give them a reason to want to harm him and might incite their violence. Jayden had to match their perceived volatility by carrying a gun with him everywhere so he would not be the target of their unprovoked attacks.

Furthermore, because gay identity is perceived to be linked to behavior regarded as less than masculine, gay men could be targeted for gender- and sexuality-based violence. Although only one man explicitly mentioned rape as punishment for gay identity, D.C.'s story is illustrative of the varied fears associated with coming out:

> D.C.: I heard from one of my friends that were in the same gang, or claimed, that one of the older people did [rape someone]. So it's just like, oh, okay. That was weird. So, I stopped talkin' to that person who I heard it about. I didn't talk to that person at all, cuz I ain't look at him the same. It was actually like, a gay-bash type rape. So, they beat the gay boy up, and then they raped him. It's like, okay, so, what if that was me, if I wasn't as cool with them? So, I stopped talking to a lot of them. And I just slowly started moving on with my own life. It took a minute, cuz they kept comin' around, (laughs) some of them. Once I got into high school, like, the middle of my freshman year, it slowed down.
> VP: Were you concerned that you were gonna be the victim of an assault like that if they found out you were gay?
> D.C.: Yeah. Umm (pause) I was concerned, but then I wasn't because of the person I was havin' sex with. And he told me I didn't have nothin' to worry about, so. (pause) But, I felt like I did, so that's why I ain't come out the closet until later on, in my freshman year.

Perhaps the most telling part of D.C.'s comments is his reference to his inner monologue: "What if that was me?" He was musing of his similarity to the rape victim, or at least that he possesses the qualities that are hated and punished, and thus doubted whether he could actually be protected from violence, especially by his same-sex partner.

Fears of violent retaliation are not wholly unreasonable; Brad had to literally fight his way out of his gang when his own gay relationship with Reese was discovered. Brad's gang was unique in two ways. One was its form: a prison gang that was also a neo-Nazi hate group, which followed the tenets of the Aryan Brotherhood.[32] The second was that they spent time "bashing" on gay inmates by staying away from them, not offering them any protection or a spot in the gang, and "talking shit" about them. Two members of the gang physically attacked one man who "went gay" after he tattooed "VOID" over the large swastika tattoo on his own chest. Of course, the affront was not only to the gang's symbology (though he was not a member) but also to their neo-Nazi ideals, as well as their beliefs that being gay is inappropriate. A very heteronormative group, they spent most of their time "talking about girls, getting high, and working out," according to Brad. These warnings were not enough to deter Brad from carrying on a romantic relationship while incarcerated, but he eventually had to answer for it.

Brad fought twice as a result of the attention he drew spending time with Reese, another study participant who was his boyfriend while incarcerated and still at the time of the interview. The first fight occurred because a fellow inmate told one of Brad's good friends that Brad was "eating with a fag" and that he was going to "smack the taste outta [Brad's] mouth." Brad felt that he had "no choice" but to fight him, because the harasser "forced his hand." That inmate was not the only one who noticed, leading to Brad getting "bled out" of the gang:

One of my friends, well, one of the [gang], he was the treasurer, and he called me out on it, like, "Why are you walkin' around with this fag all the time?" I'm like, "It's my dude's cousin." I lied to him at first. And then two days later, I was just like, whatever. And so I went up on the hill and told 'em, "I'm steppin' back, I'm not doin' this no more." So then, I stepped back, they let me have my patches [tattoos] still, and then after I stepped back, I wadn't fuckin' with the [gang] no more, cuz like, me and Reese was always together. So finally, like, a couple days later, I'm just like, whatever. Here it is. And it shook some eardrums. (chuckles) They didn't like that too well. So next, me and Reese's relationship just took off from there. I got my patches covered up, and then we had it where we were in the same block, same rack, just hangin' out.

I asked if he was ever concerned that they would target Reese for violent retaliation, since he was "the fag" who they did not approve of Brad spending time with. He replied that the gang wanted to hurt him, not Reese, because he "made them look bad" by being a gay man in such a high-ranking position in his group. I also asked if leaving the gang opened him up to anti-gay harassment from others. He reported that the "only people that cared was the fellas, cuz I basically made 'em all look stupid. That's how they felt, and I could see the way they felt." However, after he left the gang, he did encounter some trouble with possessions being stolen by his "bunkie," since it was known that he no longer had anyone to back him up. After another fight and a trip to administrative segregation, his problems lessened until his release.

For closeted participants, the fear of being discovered was linked with concerns about very serious consequences. These men feared alienation, ostracism, and expulsion from their gangs, but also physical assault, rape, and even death. Thus, the perceived benefits of coming out were judged to be few and far between. Although participants would be free to be themselves and might be able to ascertain who their true friends and allies were, these benefits did not outweigh the long list of potential risks.

"I Couldn't Even Trust My Own Family"

An undercurrent in many of the preceding narratives is the explicit comparison of the gang to their families, or of the link between their families and their gangs. Several men joined gangs because these groups provided them with benefits their families would not or could not provide for them. Men did not want to lose status either in their gangs or in their families of origin. To do so would have meant losing all of the few resources available to them. In light of the negative reactions from family members upon their coming out, such concerns held merit.

Darius's story helps to expand upon these themes. Recall that because he felt abandoned and not shielded from violence by his family, he joined a gang for protection. His mantra throughout the interview was,

"You gotta do wut chu gotta do!" During his time with the gang, Darius lived a hidden gay life, complete with secretly having sex with fellow in-the-closet gang members, as well as older men who were paying him. He believed that one of the reasons he got kicked out of the gang was because the group's members found out he was gay, though he never actually came out to them. Regarding his decision not to come out, he reported:

> Because I think, once you tell one person, it's like you told the world! Like, I couldn't trust nobody, I couldn't even trust my own family, so why I'ma go out here, and trust somebody else first? So, I felt like, if I woulda told this person, he woulda told that person, cuz you know, errybody connect with different people, errybody trust different people with different stuff, it ain't always that one person that's gonna hold a secret, you can always tell this person that you really trust this secret, but chu never know. . . . But they know, and you can feel it though, cuz they look atchu different. Like, they might act different, but you can always see them lookin' atchu more, you can feel the eyes on you more, and it's like, "What?"

Darius attributed the "big difference" in the way he would have been treated to factors such as his prior claim that the Black community is "very violent with gay people" and his displeasure with his mother telling his private business to others.

Indeed, for some other participants, the concerns regarding their families' reactions to their sexual identities were well-founded, as was detailed in chapter 1. Perhaps one of the strongest indicators of negativity or ambivalence regarding gay identity is to contrast it with lawbreaking, both of which are stigmatized and can cause familial conflict. Brad, Boog, and Brian all suggested that their parents were more hurt and angered by their gay sexual identity than their involvement in crime, gangs, and/or long-term incarcerations; at the time we spoke, Boog and Brian still had no closure regarding their parents' negative reactions to their sexual identities. In Boog's case, his mother let him stay in her home after he was released from his five-year prison stint, but stopped letting him stay over after he came out to her. As for Brian, his parents were supportive of him through the disposition phase of his juvenile justice processing for drug sales; however, they reacted poorly when he wrote a letter to them during his juvenile incarceration in which he disclosed his sexuality. So poorly, in fact, that he had not spoken to his parents in over 10 years since coming out. Although these are some of the more extreme examples of familial discord precipitated by participants' disclosures of their gay identities, previous chapters detail various ways that participants' families tried to patrol their gender presentation and sexual identity.

At the time of their interviews, several men, including DJ and Spiderman, were contemplating coming out to their gangs (whether or not they were still members), and hoped their longstanding relationships would prevent the members of these groups from reacting negatively. Take this exchange with Spiderman, for example:

> SPIDERMAN: I really don't know, but I think, I mean. (pause) All these years, I think hopefully we would still be cool. Some of 'em might talk shit, but no, hopefully we'd still be cool, if it ever happens like that. Cuz all these years, it shouldn't really matter now. All these years went by, so. (pause) But I think some of 'em might prolly talk shit, I think some of 'em might talk shit. Some of 'em might even come out, too, like, "Hey, me too!" (laughs) Cuz I'm pretty positive there might be a couple more people.
>
> VP: But why don't you think they're willing to come out?
>
> SPIDERMAN: My reason is cuz we don't know what each other gonna say, and how we gonna react. That's what I'm thinkin'.

Interestingly, although he vacillated with his language ("I think hopefully"; "might prolly") Spiderman seemed fairly confident that not all members of the gang would accept his identity, despite their longstanding relationships. But he also articulated how the dynamics could change as the ratio of straight to openly gay members changes: when one person comes out and shows that the gang can be a space for gay members, others may be more confident in their decision to come out as well. It is perhaps the uncertainty of the reaction that is most paralyzing for closeted gang members. Another example is this exchange with DJ:

> VP: Are you out to any of the people that you were in a gang with?
>
> DJ: No.

VP: No? Okay, so can you tell me a little bit about why you're not?

DJ: They just not my type, I guess. I mean, everybody that I know that's in it, no. Maybe different people that's in the gang, but not the people that I grew up wit and stuff.

VP: How do you think they would react if you told them?

DJ: They prolly could be real. They prolly—they prolly—umm—they'd prolly laugh. And say "Quit playin'," or somethin'. But, I don't know, really. . . . Might accept it, might not.

DJ's stuttering indicates that he had trouble even settling on how the group might react. I asked another question about the potential consequences for him:

VP: Do you think that they would ever try to hurt you if you came out to them?

DJ: No, cuz we grew up. We knew each other since, I wanna say sixth, seventh grade. Sixth and seventh. Yeah, seventh grade.

VP: Okay, but you just don't feel comfortable telling them?

DJ: Not yet. (laughs)

VP: Okay. And do you think you will eventually, or—

DJ: Yeah.

As with Spiderman, DJ's comments suggest a profound uncertainty with respect to how his gang peers would react, which is combined with a mistrust of these individuals, even though they've all known each other for a long time. DJ's assertion that his fellow gang members are "not his type" (in terms of developing close friendships) further reduced his incentive to tell them.

James, who had been involved with his gang for 12 years, was not out to them because, as he suggested, "It ain't they business." He was not concerned with any serious repercussions, but rather with simply being treated differently:

I mean, ain't nuttin' bad gon' happen, cuz I'm already past all that, I'm into it, I'm already ranked, I'm already in my spot, can't nobody take my spot. . . . So, no, I mean, nuttin' cain't happen to me, it's just, I don't want them to look at me different. You know? Like, "Aww, damn, this muh-

fucka, now I gotta watch the way I dress or somethin', he might—" You
know what I'm sayin'? I don't want nobody to think like that, like, "Aww,
now I gotta change up." Just still be the person you was. I ain't gonna
come on to you, or nuttin' like that.

I wondered if maybe the lack of physical repercussions was related to
James's "spot" in the gang, or his well-established status. I asked if other
members who were not as high-ranking would experience any negative
repercussions from fellow gang members. He replied, "They wouldn't do
nuttin'. I mean, they'd probly be distant from him, if anything. Distant
from him, like, not even fuck [hang out] wit 'em, cut 'em off on certain
shit, basically. For real." Again, he thought that a lower-ranking gay gang
member might lose trust from the gang, or be excluded from money-
making and status-conferring activities. These concerns hearken back
to images of the alleged sexually predatory behavior of gay men, coupled
with stigma more broadly and the risk of losing one's status, even if his
economic position is secure. All of James's adult life has been spent in
this gang. His narrative suggests that, while he might not lose the tangible benefits available to him in the gang, the reputation that has taken
so long to build would be at risk if he decided to come out—a risk he
was not inclined to take. The fact that intangible qualities such as reputation were deemed as critical as tangible benefits further reiterates the
importance of masculine status.

Despite all of these perceived risks, four men in straight gangs did still
come out to their gangs, including Brad, who was then "bled out" of the
gang by having to fight. The other three men who came out did so when
they were sure they would be insulated from negative repercussions.
Brian came out while in a juvenile facility, but asked his gang to "keep
the volume down on it" and relied on them to help defend him and his
friends. They did help him, primarily because they were loyal friends
of Brian's cousin, who died. Dollars utilized his familial relationships to
protect himself from physical violence:

DOLLARS: It was, if you're gay, you get beat up. But, for me, it was
different, because of my cousin. She was very protective of me. So,
it was, you mess wit her, you get beat up, because she knew how
to fight.

VP: Did anybody ever mess with you because you were gay?

DOLLARS: I've never got jumped out there, ever. And I used to walk all up and down through that place. I was always wit her, so nobody ever messed wit me. And then when I was by myself, nobody still never messed wit me. Because they'd be like, "Ay, who is you?" [I'd reply,] "Jackie's cousin." That's it.

Dollars said that his cousin was "known," "cool," and also in his gang. Raphael counted on the fact that because most of his fellow gang members were his biological relatives and they had known him literally for his entire life, they would (or *should*) take it better than most:

RAPHAEL: Well, I told 'em, and some of 'em didn't like it, and some of 'em were just cool about it. But then, the people that didn't like it, they got used to it, cuz they found out who I really am, like, I'm still the same person regardless, from when I was little, or from now, I'm still the same person, I'm not gon' change that person. So that's when they got used to it, and they just said forget it, like, this who he is, this what he like, I couldn't do nuttin' about it.

VP: Did they ever say anything to you about it?

RAPHAEL: Not really. It's, like. (pause) They never said nothin' to me, but I know I had doubts, they say stuff behind my back. So, that's why I have doubts, but if they did say somethin', they just never come up to me. They prolly say it to somebody else, but they just never come up to me.

VP: And do you think it's changed any of your relationships with them? Like, do they treat you differently?

RAPHAEL: It's the same. If I just be me, then it just be the same.

As with DJ and Spiderman, who were unsure of how their gangs would react and were fairly confident that at least some members would have negative reactions, this is reflected in Raphael's experience. Even after coming out and gaining acceptance (or at least tolerance) from other members who originally reacted negatively, there was still a considerable amount of mistrust regarding what those members really felt, what they were saying, and who they were saying it to. Although they outwardly treated him the same, his "doubts" persisted.

Why Composition Matters

These findings dialogue with an important theme in gang research: how various structures affect gang/gang member activities and experience. For instance, a gang's sex composition, or the ratio of males to females, creates particular gender dynamics that can then affect behavior. Females in majority-male gangs had the highest frequencies of offending, followed by females in sex-balanced gangs, and, finally, by females in majority- or all-female gangs.[33] In sex-balanced gangs, where males do not possess a strong majority, gang males may intentionally exclude females from serious (and status-conferring) violence to retain their dominance in the group.[34] Additionally, majority-male gangs with few token female members may perceive no threat to their dominance and do not feel it necessary to monitor girls' activities. However, token gang females who become "one of the guys" may do so at the expense of other girls by expressing traditional and negative views of females, especially those who had been sexed in to the gang (required to have sex with existing members).[35]

What organizational factors underlie these dynamics? In her ethnography of a large corporation, management scholar Rosabeth Kanter suggests that female tokens may react to pressures placed upon them by overachieving according to the group's standards, or by attempting to blend into the organization's male culture by minimizing their sexual attributes (i.e., their differences from the dominant group).[36] Sociologist Hubert Blalock suggests that in order to maintain dominance, the higher-status majority group (males) increases its control of the lower-status minority group (females) as the latter's proportion increases.[37] These theories help to explain the relative delinquency involvement of females in majority-male gangs and sex-balanced gangs, respectively.[38]

Although sexual orientation composition is not completely analogous to sex composition, the sex composition literature provides a useful framework from which to build. That is, gangs with different sexual orientation compositions did indeed provide varied environments for gang members due to the dynamics created within them. In straight gangs that had an overwhelming majority of heterosexual members, token gay gang members attempted to blend into the dominant culture and minimize their differences (e.g., their gay sexual identity) by remaining in the closet. Unlike the female tokens in the male-dominated work culture described by Kanter and the majority-male gangs described by criminologist Jody Miller,[39] token gay gang members can conceal their difference precisely because it is not inherently visible, as biological sex often is. They can date females publicly and decline to reveal their gay or bisexual identity.

Interestingly, and contrary to what the sex composition literature might suggest, I found that gay males in straight gangs did not achieve being "one of the guys" (a valued male member of the gang) at the expense of other gay males. Even though they did not appreciate some of the behaviors of "fags," they were not comfortable with gay bashing (especially involving violence) and demeaning language, because they recognized that those actions attacked an important part of their identities. In this way, my data do not support the finding in the limited research on gay male gang members in presumably straight gangs that such gang members commit anti-gay violence. Unlike the gay-bashing queer gang members in gang scholar Mark Totten's study,[40] my participants did not report engaging in any homophobic violence. However, they did have similar concerns as Totten's participants regarding the disclosure of their sexual identities and the negative repercussions they might face as a result.

Gays in the Game

In this chapter, I have discussed participants' reasons for and processes involved in gang joining, the activities they engaged in with their gangs, and how the decision to disclose or conceal their sexual orientation to the gang has shaped their experience. Participants joined their gangs, which were often neighborhood groups, for protection, resources, support, and belonging. Typically, these decisions were made within a context characterized by familial and neighborhood disorder. About half had to engage in a violent initiation ritual, such as being jumped in or committing a retaliatory offense, while the others were allowed in because of their longstanding familial, neighborhood, or romantic relationships. Once in the gangs, they engaged in regular social activities such as sports and hanging out, but also in illicit activities such as selling drugs and fighting other crews. They participated in public fights with rivals to defend their neighborhood, territory, or gang reputation.

On dimensions such as gang joining and activities, these data complement the traditional picture of male gang membership, and could suggest that gay and straight gang members aren't much different. While this is partially true, gay men's sexual identities played a major role in interpersonal interactions and the public negotiation of their identities, especially within these overwhelmingly straight gangs. They attempted to minimize the differences between themselves and their fellow gang members, and blend in with the dominant (heteronormative) culture. Most remained vigilant about their presentation of masculinity and chose not to come out, fearing threats to their reputation, status within the gang, or physical safety. As a result, only a handful of men in straight gangs came out to their crews, typically when they knew they would be insulated from negative consequences. Others who were seriously considering coming out were ambivalent about whether or not their gangs would accept them, though they were well aware their crews would not be thrilled about having openly gay members in the group.

The straight gangs may very well be projects of resistance to marginalization and exclusion of many forms, and they provide avenues through which young gay men can construct public heterosexual identities to avoid further marginalization. However, despite participants' discomfort with anti-gay sentiment, being in a straight gang arguably doesn't represent resistance to societal homophobia, but instead complicity through hiding and covering.

The perspectives and experiences of gay men in straight gangs are only beginning to be revealed. Only a few other sources can give any insight: an episode of a talk show from the mid-1990s that featured such gang members coming out to their peers and the world; a couple pieces of scholarship that discuss their reasons for hiding their sexuality from their gangs; and a 2012 documentary about the struggles of gay Latino gang members, within the context of their ethnic and gang cultures.[41] Before conducting my study, I had very little to guide me, besides the gang literature that was replete with stories of young people in ostensibly heterosexual gangs. However, moving forward, I would not be surprised if gang scholars and outreach workers are more likely to encounter openly LGBTQ gang members, and I strongly encourage them to see these identities as meaningful for understanding the gang experience. There is something about recent cultural history that has facilitated gay and bisexual gang members in straight gangs feeling comfortable enough to talk with media, documentarians, and researchers. Maybe it's evolving public opinion, or the gay equality movement broadly defined, or how social media has changed the nature of queer visibility. We would do well to recognize that gay men in straight gangs have probably always existed and are now coming forth to tell their stories, and we should be ready to listen.

5

Hybrid Gangs and Those That Could Have Been

I am almost to the end of my interview with Mini. We're at Greg's house, which he shares with his mother and younger sister. Greg and his mom have just reached an understanding after years of difficult interactions since he came out as gay: to avoid arguments, they simply don't talk like they used to.

Greg and Imani are in an adjoining room watching dance videos. Some are vogue videos on YouTube, and some are stripping videos on XTube. I see them shaking their booties for the mirror and I laugh, but quickly apologize so that Mini doesn't think I'm laughing about the interview. They come into the room when Greg's mother comes home—he greets her with a reserved "Hello, mother"—and upon my asking, he tells me that I can finish the interview. I say we're almost done and ask Mini my last question.

"So, do you have any other thoughts? Anything at all?" The reply surprises me:

"Why don't you have a girlfriend?"

"Me?!" I am caught totally off guard.

"Yes."

I start to laugh, and stammer "Well, I—" but Greg interrupts with his own laughing. Mini responds to him with an indignant, "What?" It seems fair that I should answer questions participants ask me as well. I'm asking them to lay bare their own lives, so why not reciprocate? I proceed to tell them all about my breakup a few months prior, right down to who got which cat. That leads us into a whole new discussion about the effort needed for long-term relationships, the pros and cons of having "friends with benefits," how to deal with being lonely or having a broken heart, what it's like dating as a lesbian or a gay man, and so on. I've been talking about this stuff too much recently, I realize.

Some time later I give Mini his payment for participating in my study. Reflecting on the subject of code names, he mentions that he's thinking of starting to go by the name "Hood."

Oh right, I think to myself. I am interviewing gang members.

* * *

Greg and Mini belonged to a small clique that had a majority of heterosexual members, but about one-third gay members. The sexual orientation composition of their gang meant that they were able to be out and to be close friends with other gay people such as Imani. It allowed for more freedom in their gender presentation (Mini, for instance, was very feminine) and the ability to conceive of their gang membership partially in emotive terms, and also had implications for the range of activities their gang was involved in.

Gangs such as theirs straddle the boundary between the straight and gay gangs: too many gay people to have a heterosexist environment, but not enough for the gang to be a formal part of the Columbus gay scene. Six participants were or had been members of hybrid gangs, and two of these men also had belonged to straight gangs in the past. Of the 38 total gangs that my participants had belonged to, five of them had a substantial proportion of GLB members (one-quarter to nearly one-half of total membership), though GLB members were still in the minority. I refer to the gangs with a critical mass of GLB members as hybrid gangs, in contrast to the overwhelmingly heterosexual gangs, which I call straight gangs. Such distinctions are not in name only; straight gangs had far more restrictive standards for presentations of masculinity and sexuality than hybrid gangs. This chapter is devoted to discussing how the experiences of men in hybrid gangs capture a mix of dynamics of both the gay gangs and the straight gangs. To best paint the comparative portrait, I analyze similar dimensions as in prior chapters, such as gang joining and activities, as well as how participants negotiated gay identity within hybrid gangs. I also discuss how there may indeed be other gangs of a similar (hybrid) composition represented in my sample, but men's attempts to determine the percentage of gay, lesbian, or bisexual people in their gangs are affected by the pressures to remain closeted.

Gang Formation and Activities

Half of the men in hybrid gangs said they helped form their gang, rather than joining an existing one. The three men who helped form a hybrid gang were each an original member of their gang, and had a hand in the creation of the group. Those who were present from their groups' origins reported fairly organic shifts from friendship groups to official crews.[1] As with all gangs, illegal activity was one of the defining characteristics of these new crews. Take Batman's description of how his gang formed: "It was just a group of close friends and we were all high as fuck one day and we were just like, 'Man, we're about to make a crew.' And we just started drawing and making our tag [graffiti signature], and that was that." When I asked Batman how someone else might join the group, he denied that they would have to partake in any formal initiation ritual: "Pretty much, what you have to do to join is just be cool as fuck, that's about it." His response highlights the interpersonal or relational aspects of the gang. As another example, take Greg's description of how his second clique, of which Mini was also a member, formed: "These is people that I've known throughout all my life, well not all my life, but since I been out here [in this neighborhood], and we been through a lot, like, arguments, not bein' friends, then bein' friends, fights and stuff, and we been through it all together. So, like, my real friends, I would say." Greg attributes time, experience, and sincerity to his gang by marking them as his "real friends." These two narratives are extremely similar to the narratives explaining how the gay gangs formed. Unsurprisingly, the gangs that developed organically from mixed friendship groups ended up having a sizable proportion of gay, lesbian, or bisexual gang members (about one-third, in these two cases) because their members chose to form a gang with close friends, instead of joining whichever neighborhood gang was present in their area.

These young men joined or helped form their hybrid gangs at an average age of about 15. No one except Brandon said he had to complete an initiation ritual to join or form a hybrid gang; Brandon's initiation involved fighting to prove he had skills and could be "down" (dependable) for the gang. Regarding the three men who joined an existing hybrid gang, a sexual relationship with an existing gang member was the method of entry for two of them, Juan and Marcus. This was sufficient for them to join without an initiation ritual, whether or not the gang knew the true nature of the relationship.[2] Marcus's gang knew about his same-sex relationship, while Juan's gang did not; Juan was the only man in a hybrid gang who was *not* out to them. I discuss both relationships at different points in this chapter. Other studies suggest that initiation rituals are not always necessary for a gang recruit, especially for those youth who are allowed to enter gangs as a result of their familial or other long-standing neighborhood relationships.[3] The hybrid gangs foster an environment that emphasizes relationships, so the general lack of formal initiation rituals is therefore unsurprising.

A clarification is necessary. The gang literature discusses the concept of "sexing in" (having sex with some or all of the existing male gang members), which seems to apply only to young women's entry, not young men's. Being "sexed in" to a gang confers considerably lower status than being jumped in; however, the extent to which this practice occurs is unclear.[4] As for the three men who gained entry to hybrid or straight gangs via a sexual relationship, it should not be assumed that this is similar to being "sexed in"; participants emphasized the relationship, not any particular sex act that earned their place in the gang, and it certainly did not involve other members of the gang. Additionally, they did not describe their introduction to gang life in different ways than the members of the gay gangs who were similarly dating or interested in a young man who was already involved with the crew. This process is thus quite different in effect from sexing in, which facilitates fellow gang members' abilities to other and control gang females in gendered and sexualized ways that primarily male and primarily heterosexual gangs would not seek to do with other males. None of the three types of gangs—gay, straight, or hybrid—sexed in male recruits.

As with both the gay and straight gangs, members of hybrid gangs were involved in all sorts of legal and illegal activities. However, they were also likely to downplay the seriousness of their gangs, just as the all-gay gangs were. Batman said of his gang, Blaze Crew, whose other members had also been involved with Crip sets, that it was not the same as a "real gang": "No, like, with real gangs, you got to get jumped in, and I'm not trying to get jumped in or like, shoot anybody to get affiliated or rob someone, you know, just like rob a store or something like that, and I'm not into all that. I have robbed a store once, but it was just a blackout, nobody was there. That was a good time though." Batman also mentioned that he didn't like having "bad blood with people," which he thought almost certainly happened in "real gangs."[5] Because Batman was involved in the creation of his crew, he did not have to engage in any violence to gain entry, but neither did anyone else, since they formed it together. But regardless of this, his crew was not involved in much violence at all. In fact, the only "robbing" he had done (mentioned above) was actually a burglary, as no one was there at the time. Other conversations with Batman about his group brought us back to similar boundary maintenance. For example, I wanted to better understand the dynamics of his gang, its members' interactions with each other, and their group solidarity. In light of the fact that this was his main friendship network, I asked him if being a member of Blaze Crew was important to him. He replied:

> BATMAN: It's not that important, but it's what keeps us a group pretty much like, if you're down with Blaze Crew, then you're down, pretty much. So it's sort of important. Not that important though, it's not like "oh, I live and die for Blaze Crew."
>
> VP: Do you think that other people in their gangs would say that they live and die for their group?
>
> BATMAN: Oh yeah. Like when you get into the Bloods or Crips or whatever gang, once you in it, the only way you gettin' out is in a box [coffin]. So that's why I'm just like, "Whoa, if I'm trying to retire, I'm not trying to die." . . . I've heard a lot of people that I know get shot because they're in a gang, and die. Some of my cousins are Bloods, they been in jail for gang violence, selling drugs. . . . But yeah, it's pretty much because I'm not trying to get shot, not trying to do stuff I don't want to do.

The contrast Batman presented was strong: for urban gangs that are well-known for their illegal activities like drug sales and violent conflicts, he saw associated risks as arrest, incarceration, serious injury, and even death. He was involved in some drug sales, but outside of his gang and not at their behest or in relation to violent activities. His comments clarify why he didn't join a traditional street gang, but instead, one that is less than a "real gang."

Other members of hybrid gangs also spoke about straight street gangs and their associated violence in contrast to their own groups. Greg, for example, sought to clarify his clique's very selective involvement in violence:

> It's kinda neutral. We move as a clique, like, if one move, we all move. We all walk together, if one of us fight, we all fight. If one of us have money, we all have money, like, we all support each other, it's like we're a family, so it's kinda like a gay thing, but we just don't go out there, you know, escort together, sell drugs together. (pause) Go out there just fightin' for no reason, robberies, we don't do none of that. I would say they're my supportive group. When I'm down, they're people I can hit up to get me up. Cuz they're a lot of them, they're in school, still in college, gettin' an education, on the right path. So that's the people I try to surround myself with. . . . Like, out here, there's a lot of gangs, and they're not thinkin' too clear. . . . Or no crazy get-rich-quick scheme, like, I'm not 'bout to walk up and bust someone's windows out, cuz I have a very different conscience, if I do somethin', I'm gonna have to spill it. Someone's gonna know! (laughs) Yeah, so, just stay on the clear path.

Greg's description of his group as a family unit whose members seek to support each other is very comparable to the narratives of the all-gay gangs' members. Evoking the chosen families of queer communities, he even likens this family to "kinda like a gay thing," but clarifies that they don't do things either gay gangs or straight gangs do together. That is, they don't escort together (gay gangs), and don't sell drugs together (straight gangs). They also avoid pointless violence, which he suggests straight gangs participate in. However, some of this also may be impression management on Greg's part, as he was interested in telling a narrative about his efforts to get his life back on track after previously being involved with a straight gang. He quipped, "I used to be a little homo thug, now I'm just homo." That is, he was still involved with gangs, but not with the straight gang engaging in gratuitous violence that he described in the previous chapter.

When I asked Mini, a fellow member of Greg's crew, if the group was similar to a gang or different, he replied in a way that did not exactly mirror Greg's remarks (despite them being able to hear each other's interviews): "Yeah, cuz when somebody wanna fight them, we all fight! Like my brother [Greg] said, we all fight. We don't go stealin' together. We look for boys together! . . . I'm not gonna say gang-related, but sometimes it's gang-related, cuz somebody might have weed, or whatever, our niggas find some weed, or maybe sell some weed off, or whatever, but other than that, like, shootin' and everything like that, and goin' around killin' people, we don't do that. (laughs) That's bad!" Clearly, this gang was not involved in serious violent crime (one of the markers of "real" or deeply entrenched gangs), but its members were involved in fighting, drug selling, drug using, and escorting, though sometimes not as a group (as specified by Greg). Mini acknowledged how they could be seen as a gang and had "gang-related" attributes, but again reiterated the communal aspects of the group, partially evidenced by their willingness to back each other up in a fight. Some members of hybrid gangs, such as Marcus, Brandon, and Juan, made little attempt to downplay the illegal activities of their gangs, but all three joined existing groups whom they knew were involved in such activities and, importantly, had since left these groups.

To better illustrate this contrast between men who formed gangs and those who joined existing ones, some of the activities of hybrid gangs that participants joined (instead of formed) look nearly identical to those of the straight gangs. I draw from comments made by Marcus and Juan about drug selling. After joining a Crip set (Uptown Cuzz) that his boyfriend belonged to, Marcus started selling Ecstasy pills and marijuana when he needed money. He carried a gun for protection, claiming it was "common sense" and "just a street-smart thing." He noted that his crew had "beef" with several Blood sets in the city. Members of the two groups "jumped" or otherwise assaulted each other in public places, such as nightclubs or in each other's neighborhoods, sometimes with serious consequences. He explained:

> MARCUS: It pretty much went back and forth, and it still goes on back and forth. Like, when I was home, I legit watched somebody [from Uptown Cuzz] get shot, and picked up. And he's still in critical condition as we speak. He got shot in his neck. . . . They were shootin' at him the day before, and I was drivin', and they were drivin', and the funny thing is, they were two cars in front of me, and they pulled out

they gun and pop-pop-pop and he was layin' there. . . . I knew who he was, so I pulled over and then everybody started runnin' out, and that's when they called the cops and all that.

VP: And what are these conflicts over?

MARCUS: Territory.

VP: Just over territory? Over neighborhoods in general, or over drug-dealing territory?

MARCUS: It's drug-dealin' territory, neighborhoods, it's definitely crazy. It's pretty bad [there].

Recall that straight gangs were largely organized around physical space, whether it was the neighborhood or drug territory; Marcus suggests these "back-and-forth" assaults were about both. Gang violence might occur as a result of someone committing a perceived wrong while in the other gang's territory, be it traveling through the area uninvited or moving in on a zone where gang members sold drugs, and retaliatory violence might follow. In this way, Marcus's hybrid gang looks very much like a typical straight gang, whether as described here in my study, in the previous gang literature, or even in popular culture.

And just as members of straight gangs like Brandon were concerned about messing up while selling drugs and being harmed, Juan's hybrid gang also would deal out violent consequences for "fucking up," which Juan described: "Losing it, or stealing, or like, when they give you a certain amount, and you don't bring back the amount that you were supposed to sell, or there's stuff missing, there's money missing, that's fucking up." He said that the penalty was typically being jumped and prevented from selling in the future, but even death was a possibility. Similar to Marcus's drug-dealing gang, on this dimension, Juan's gang seems very similar to a straight gang. However, the relational aspects of hybrid gangs—such as the ways their members interact with each other—certainly set them apart from most straight gangs.

"Free to Be Gay": Life in Hybrid Gangs

Having a critical mass of GLB members (about one-quarter or more) allows hybrid gangs to have fairly different climates and cultures than straight gangs. Perhaps unsurprisingly, men were more likely to come out to gangs with a larger proportion of gay, lesbian, or bisexual members, and on the whole, they reported relatively positive coming out experiences. Of the six men who had belonged to hybrid gangs, five of them were out to these gangs. Along with Kanter's and Blalock's, a third organizational perspective that has been used in analyses of gang sex composition dynamics comes from sociologist Peter Blau, who theorized that within diverse groups, sizable minority populations can alter the normative features of the group.[6] Although this theory has not been found to be effective in explaining the behavior of mixed-sex gangs, it does provide a useful framework for the intragroup relations of hybrid gangs.

A direct comparison of the experiences of the hybrid gangs' members to those in straight gangs is provided by Brandon, who had been a member of both types of gangs. Brandon went from a mostly male crew with no openly gay members to a mostly female group, of whom almost half of the members were gay, lesbian, or bisexual. Regarding Brandon's first crew, the Terrors, he said:

> They would say it all the time, like, "We don't mess with fags," and, "If you a fag, you cain't hang wit us," and stuff like that. . . . They didn't know I was gay, but they was just sayin' that. Because I wasn't even out the closet at that time. But, they would have their jokes, I'll be like, the clown of the night, they'd tell me, "Oh, he's a fag, he the one who get all the niggas," and I didn't like that. So, I feel like they wasn't claimin' me, and I stopped hangin' wit 'em, and started hangin' out wit a new crew that I was accepted.

He later reiterated: "My first group was males and females, and nobody in that clique was gay, that's why I particularly left the crew, because I was gay and they didn't accept it." In contrast, Brandon's second group, NorthStar, was predominantly female (80 percent) and provided him with the acceptance he sought, as well as a respite from behaviors he found to be questionable:

> [With NorthStar], I really felt accepted, I really felt loved, and we did more, we had more fun than doin' things I was really uncomfortable with. Like, sellin' drugs, I wasn't comfortable wit that, stealin', I kinda was com-

fortable wit it because I was gettin' all my stuff for free. But, sellin' drugs and tryna be this gangsta boy that I was when I was with the Terrors, I was tryna be somebody that I wasn't. I felt loved by NorthStar. And then once I got with NorthStar, I was free to be myself, free to be gay, and free to say and do what I wanna do. And, I used to enjoy fightin', so it was just like, I was in heaven with them.

Brandon noted that in NorthStar, his nickname was "Homo Thug." Not meant to be derogatory, it was a descriptive and somewhat playful moniker the group used for him. Interestingly, the reason he initially joined the Terrors was because, "I felt like I did it to prove a point to everybody that I can be gay and still be hard." That is, he expected that joining a traditional, straight gang would elevate his status, but instead he was marginalized within that group. It was not until he joined a gang with a substantial proportion of gay, lesbian, and bisexual members that he received the respect he desired. This presented quite a complex story, because he could still be involved in a gang and commit violent crimes, but viewed his involvement differently than being a "gangsta boy" with a straight gang that disparaged gay people, thus disparaging himself. It was therefore the relational and social aspects of the gang that set it apart, while still providing opportunities for violence and other delinquency.

Batman's ability to get along well with his very small crew of "hood" friends included a certain degree of impression management. Specifically, he characterized his gender presentation as not totally suggestive of his sexual identity, and made a point to tell his fellow crew members who were straight that he was not interested in them sexually:

I knew them, they're like hood niggas, they associate with the Crip gang, and so they're all straight and hood and shit. I came out to them, it wasn't like, "Hey everybody, I'm gay," it was just like one of their friends was a lesbian but she was like, a boy lesbian, so she acted like a guy pretty much, and she came to me and she was like, "Are you gay?" And I was like, "Yeah, I'm bi." And she was like, "Oh that's cool," she's like, "Finally someone like me in the crowd!" And I guess by my persona or how I talked, walked, acted or whatever, some people can tell and some people can't, but they could tell. And they didn't really care, they didn't even bring it up, I guess I'm a cool ass person. And the reason why a lot of straight people are sometimes afraid of gay people and are always trying to bash them or get away from them or whatever, is because they think that they're always trying to hit on them and like, I always come at people, like with guys mostly, I always come at guys just like, "Oh, I'm a guy too, I'm not really hitting on you, I don't like you like that, so we're just gonna be friends." And that's why I get a lot of respect from most of my straight friends.

With his subtle gender presentation and clear confrontation of homophobic stereotypes about gay men's alleged predatory behavior, Batman was able to navigate potentially tense interactions with straight males who were "hood niggas." Batman noted that his crew did occasionally refer to men who they disliked as "fags," but it did not bother him too much because of the way they treated him personally. His crew even hung out with a group of gay and transgender individuals in their neighborhood. He suggested that he could really be himself around the crew, not only because they had known each other for a long time and had developed into a gang from a friendship group, but because, "I already know they accept me for who I am, so it's just like, cool." He did not face intragang status challenges and thus his maintenance of a uniformly masculine presentation was much less relevant than it was for men in straight gangs.

Men in other crews with at least a quarter gay, lesbian, or bisexual members similarly reported being comfortable with the members of the group. Marcus explained that he and his boyfriend were completely open about their relationship and could be so primarily because his boyfriend controlled much of the group's drug sales, but also due to the substantial proportion of gay, lesbian, and bisexual members in his gang. Regarding his (now ex-)boyfriend, he said: "He was [closeted] at first, cuz he thought it was gon' matter, but clearly nobody's gon' care when you're one of the biggest drug dealers, cuz clearly you got money, you got drugs, so errybody's gonna want the hook-up and errybody's gonna wanna mess [hang out] wit chu. So, after [he came out], errybody was fine wit him, errybody treated him normal. Like, he didn't have to go through none of the gay problems, like, none of the 'fag,' no, he goes through none of that. He probably still doesn't go through none of that." Simply being the boyfriend of this top drug dealer was enough for Marcus to have "a big respect thing out on the street," meaning he and his boyfriend were never harassed because of their relationship. If anything, Marcus said their relationship troubles stemmed from his partner being a "sucky ass boyfriend" by cheating on him with anyone who wanted a piece of him or the action, including other gay members of their gang.

Mini noted that he grew up with the members of his crew, who always knew he was gay. Greg, a member of that same group, confirms his ability to be himself: "They know the real me, so I can be real around them." Greg suggested that the heterosexual members of the crew are "pretty cool" with his sexuality, even listening to him talk about his "boy problems" or excitedly recount his sexual conquests, because they are secure with their own identities. Such claims provided a complement to the belief expressed by others that the most publicly homophobic men may be struggling with or hiding their own sexuality.

In addition, only one man in a hybrid gang was not out to most members of his crew, though he was both sexually and financially involved with a fellow member; sometimes, they handled the gang's drugs or money together. Juan reported living a triple life, complete with school, gang, and gay lives. He suggested he and other gay gang members "have to put up this image" and keep their lives discreet, "because you don't want people to know how really fucked up you are." This exchange with Juan not only speaks to men being closeted, but also provides insight as to why Juan remained discreet himself, even though he said about one-quarter of the gang's members were gay:

VP: Now, does that [estimate of 25 percent] include you and your boy-friend, who were not out?

JUAN: Well, I guess, okay, 25 percent gay, and another 20 percent that were discreet, because like, there were some members of the gang that we would do stuff with, but that's when we'd be really drunk, like, we'd do stuff, but it never really like, left what happened never.

VP: So by doing stuff, you mean you'd have sex, or mess around? You and your boyfriend both?

JUAN: Yep. Some of the drug dealers were actually gay, but like I said, they would always just be really discreet about it. That's why we never really talked about anything, and that's another reason that I didn't come out, because if I were to come out, they would be like, "Hey,

what have you been doing," or something like that, you know what I
mean?

VP: Because it would look shady, because the four of you would be off
doing whatever—

JUAN: Yeah, because we would always be together, so just like, "Wait,
if *you're* gay, then *you* have to be" or something, so that's the main
reason we didn't come out or whatever.

By staying in the closet, Juan was not only able to keep a low profile, but
was able to keep other closeted members' lives discreet, and could avoid
any suspicions regarding his relationship with his boyfriend (which was
not known to the gang). Interestingly, he did not think the gang would
have mistrusted him simply for coming out: "I don't know, really. I think
they were kind of [accepting], because I knew there were some gay people, they were okay I guess, because most of the people that buy [drugs]
from them are gay too." However, for strategic reasons, to protect their
economic and social interests, Juan and his boyfriend decided to keep
their relationship a secret. Importantly, they probably could have been
out with little issue, at least as it pertains to them being gay and together.

In hybrid groups where gay gang members comprised a critical mass,
it was not necessary for gay gang members to minimize their differences from the dominant group. Indeed, within groups that were more
balanced in terms of sexual orientation, participants often referred to
their ability to be the "real me" in a way that members of straight gangs
typically could not. This finding, while logical in itself and consistent
with one organizational theory, directly opposes research on gang sex
composition that would predict gang members' attempts to devalue and
reduce the power of gay, lesbian, and bisexual gang members as their
proportion increases.[7] While hybrid gangs might sometimes prefer that
gay gang members avoid certain behavior (such as trying to engage fellow gang members in sexual activity), their members expressed no sentiments that their interactions or personalities were negatively impacted
by such expectations. In fact, they suggested that they were allowed leeway in their self-presentations.

In addition, these findings suggest there are significant gradations
in sexual orientation composition within straight gangs. An important
tipping point for straight gangs seemed to be at about 25 percent; when

a gang had an estimated one-quarter of gay, lesbian, or bisexual members, gay gang members were more likely to feel as though they could come out without serious repercussions. Compared to the proportion of gay persons in the American adult population, this is a very high figure. A recent nationwide study estimated that approximately 3.5 percent of American adults self-identify as lesbian, gay, or bisexual, while more than 8 percent of Americans report having engaged in same-sex sexual behavior.[8] Thus, a group made up of even one-quarter gay members still has a very high ratio, not only for what might be expected in the general population, but especially for what might be expected in the hypermasculine world of street gangs. This signals the importance of paying greater attention to the diversity within gangs, especially on dimensions of sexuality and gender expression, which is fundamental for contextualizing gang members' experiences.[9] However, even gang members' estimates of their own gangs' proportions of GLB members were complicated by the politics associated with being out.

Estimating Unknowns: Gang Sexual Orientation Composition as a Difficult Metric

The comparison that much of this book is based on rests on the proportion of LGB to straight gang members, resulting in three types of gangs: gay gangs, straight gangs, and hybrid gangs. They are made up, respectively, of nearly all or all gay members, an overwhelming majority of straight members, and a majority of straight people but with a critical mass of LGB members. In order to create these classifications, I asked participants to estimate what percentage of their gang was gay, lesbian, or bisexual; then I looked to see if clear clusters emerged; and then I validated the existence of these three groups as conceptually meaningful and distinct by considering material found elsewhere in participants' narratives. But one huge question exists: what about those gang members who are not out, or who engage in same-sex sexual activity, but who don't identify as gay, lesbian, or bisexual? Participants themselves explored how their estimates could be murky, and why.

Prohibitions against same-sex sexual activity pushed many participants' behaviors and identities underground, and likely did so among other gay or bisexual male gang members. This was more salient in straight gangs than in hybrid gangs, which may lead to a distorted picture regarding the "true" sexual orientation composition of gangs. That is, men who were not in all-gay gangs expressed difficulty in estimating the percentage of their gangs' members that were gay, lesbian, or bisexual.

Regarding participants in hybrid gangs, although there was a countable, critical mass of openly LGB members, they expressed some hesitation about the accuracy of their estimates of the total LGB share. Above, Juan talks about the possibility of about a fifth of his gang being gay but "discreet" for strategic reasons related to selling sex or drugs. For others, there still remained some ambiguity about whether or not men who had sex with men, but who still publicly identified as straight, should be counted in their estimates. For example, Marcus estimated that 25 to 30 percent of his gang was gay, lesbian, or bisexual, but also noted, "There definitely were a lot of trades." (Recall that "the trade" or "trades," like "DL" or "downlow" dudes, refers to masculine or straight-acting men who have sex with men.)

I now switch gears to the participants in straight gangs. Only a very few men, such as Elijah, were absolutely convinced that no other members of their straight gangs were gay or bisexual. When I asked if any of them were, he replied with: "Oh, hell no." It was much more likely for participants to clarify that they were *not aware of* any other gay or bisexual males in their gang (stating there were no other gay guys "that I knew of"). Some took it one step further and acknowledged that although they were not aware of any other gay members in their gangs, if they were able to hide their own sexual orientation, others could as well. Summing it up very concisely, M6 stated, "If they are, I know as much about them as they do about me." Brad said he didn't know if anyone else in his group was gay, and offered, "And if they were, they're hidin' it, just like I was. I don't believe so. But you can never tell, for real!"

However, some men *did* know about others, precisely because they had engaged in sexual activity with closeted members of the group, sometimes facilitated by the Internet. Imagine Spiderman's surprise at who showed up to dates he made online for sex:

VP: Do the members of your group know that you're gay?
SPIDERMAN: Two of 'em. It was by mistake that they know. I talked to 'em on the Internet, they didn't know who I was, I didn't know who

they was, and when we met up, it was them. Like, "Oh, wow. I can't believe it was y'all!" (laughs) So, basically, two of 'em knows; like, people that I haven't messed wit [sexually] really don't know.

One participant, M6, declared that Spiderman's gang had "fags in it," but it is unclear how he came to this conclusion. For example, did he also meet some of its closeted members while seeking secret sexual activity (and chose not to reveal that to me), or was it from rumor alone? Interestingly, men who had had sexual encounters with fellow gang members included Boog and Darius, who either feared or realized repercussions from their group due to their sexual orientation. This group also included D.C., who gained entry to his gang via a sexual relationship with a current member, of which the gang was not aware.

Finally, several men suggested that the most publicly homophobic men in their gangs or neighborhoods were probably covering up their own same-sex sexual interests simply because it was not socially acceptable in their communities:

RAPHAEL: [They'll say], "Look at this faggot, I'm 'bout to beat this faggot ass," and I'll just look at 'em, like, "Seriously?" . . . We just know who they are, why keep sayin' it? It do be gettin' me mad, cuz I be havin' doubts, like, "Are you one? Do you wanna become one? Do you wanna mess wit that person?" But, now, it's a lot out there that say, "Look at this faggot," or whatever, but when it's that person and that person in one room, and they're together, they gon' do somethin' wit 'em, so. Like, you can say all of that in front of your homeboys, but if you by that person, or alone, you doin' that person, so you might as well just call yourself a faggot! I saw a lot around these hoods, around there. (laughs)

ROCC: [If you come out], they'll deny you to your face and then secretly be like, "Hey, bro, come over here," because I know countless many people, from things I've heard, of people sneakin' around in the hood. And I guess there's still people who're gonna do what they're gonna do, of course, but everybody has skeletons in their closet, and people hide stuff that aren't socially acceptable.

Raphael and Rocc imply that these men's actions in "sneakin' around in the hood" are more like open secrets, but perhaps it is because they maintain the façade of heterosexuality that they are insulated from negative consequences (either for engaging in same-sex sexual behavior, or duplicitous behavior). Jayden suggested that he knew definitively some of these men were gay, because he had personally had sex with them: "I've had a couple of them that I came across that, 'Aww man, you a faggot,' not sayin' to me, like, talkin' to other people, cuz I wasn't out, and them be the ones! Like, that I'll be messin' wit 'em [sexually]. Like, 'Okay' (laughs)." I do not purport that these men identified as gay, or that same-sex sexual behavior entails gay sexual orientation,[10] but merely that participants perceived them to be. For example, after asking Joe if anyone else in his gang was gay or bisexual, including the older male who he said tried to rape him, he replied with a joke and then laughed: "Yeah, I know he is. He just got out of jail for three years, he is!" Thus, the implication was that based on this man's earlier sexually aggressive behavior and his isolation with men for years, he had now "become gay" (a trope often referred to in a number of contexts over the course of my study).

I explored these occurrences of clandestine sex among closeted gang members with nearly every participant. Although it was more common than not for gay men in straight gangs to have sex with other closeted gang members (even among men who feared repercussions from their gangs were their sexual identities to be discovered), not all men engaged in such behavior. Expanding on my earlier exchanges with Rocc, I dug deeper into these dynamics:

> VP: You mentioned that there are some guys in the hood who are [gay], and they mess around behind closed doors; have you ever messed with any of them?
> ROCC: No, uhh, not me. I think that's too close to home, you know? So I kinda stay away from that. If I go out and meet somebody, that's cool, or on the Internet meet somebody, we'll go out and hang, kick it, it's cool, but yeah. The hood's too close to home, (laughing) so, no.
> VP: Do you think anyone in [your gang] was gay or bisexual?
> ROCC: Yeah, I mean, I know a couple guys were, or are. This lady, [she's] a good friend of mine, but her brother's gay. And, he has

countless stories, countless stories of different people. (laughs) And these are all the people that are like, "Fag this," and "Fag that." And like, I'm not new to this, so I kinda see stuff for what it is. I think most people who are homophobic have internal issues. They're kinda bashin' this, but secretly, they're doin' that. And, I think part of that is them tryna distance themselves from that publicly, but personally, it's them same people that they're calling fags in front of everybody else, and then they fuckin' wit 'em.

Rocc laid the tension quite bare: publicly homophobic men who privately engage in same-sex sexual encounters are aiming for impression management, but instead display their own internalized homophobia and self-loathing. Important to clarify is that my research participants did not seem to be particularly critical about closeted gang members in general. For starters, they hardly had much room to be condemnatory about closeted members when they were or had been closeted themselves, as they recognized that they all likely shared the same misgivings. The distasteful part about gay bashing by closeted members was the hypocrisy involved, and the offensiveness of criticizing gay people who were more self-assured and willing to be out. This also created tension regarding participants' general desire to minimize the differences between themselves and fellow gang members, because they wanted to speak up and either confront the homophobe, defend the gay person in question, or both.

Because of these sexualized instances, which were assumed to occur even more often than participants could directly account for, there was some doubt as to their gang's "true" sexual orientation composition. Sexually charged behavior made participants especially suspicious of fellow gang members' sexual identities. Spiderman offered this about the number of gay people in his gang beyond himself and the two he connected with online: "I think it was more than that, I really do, just because of the comments they be makin'! (laughs) 'You got a fat ass,' talking to me. 'I'ma smack that ass.' Smacking my ass, and all that. Umm, so I think it's more than that, but we actually really didn't do nothin' other than them smackin' my ass or talkin' 'bout how I got a fat ass, or they wish their girl had a ass like mines, comments like that! Like, oh, okay." That is, Spiderman actually experienced unwanted sexual touch-

ing from allegedly heterosexual gang members. Indeed, they may identify as heterosexual, and still engage in this touching within all-male
spaces regardless.[11]

Darius and Raphael said that although they were not aware of any
other gay men in their gangs, the proportion of gay gang members *could
be* as high as 100 percent. Their suspicions were due to a variety of factors, including their sexual encounters behind closed doors, neighborhood gossip, and what they perceived to be changing social norms:

> VP: Did anybody in your gang know that you were gay?
>
> DARIUS: Mmm, yeah, . . . When you're gay, since you're attracted to
> dudes, you're gonna try some, and I tried a lot of 'em, and a lot of 'em
> went! And it's like, okay, then that means you're gay! But, I know if I
> woulda said somethin', they woulda been mad, but like, cuz I know
> how it is when you gay, like, you wanna come out on your own time,
> when you feel it's more convenient. So, it's a lot of people that say
> they're straight that I done messed wit, that a lotta people think [are]
> straight, when it's not that. They're gay.
>
> VP: So like, what percentage of your gang would you say was gay?
>
> DARIUS: Oh, I would say like, 80 percent!
>
> VP: 80 percent of them were gay?
>
> DARIUS: Yeah, like, 80 percent. Like, nowadays, I think like 95 percent
> of the boys that walk the streets period are gay. Cuz now, it's like, out
> there! Bein' gay is out there. Now, you can look at anybody and you
> neva know, that's why. And 9 times out of 10, they are. Or they are
> going! Even if they aren't, even if they wit a girl or whatever, that still
> doesn't justify the fact. I was wit a girl, and I was still talkin' to dudes.
> So, to me, it's like, (laughs) the world is gettin' mo' open-minded to
> the options. Errybody startin' to speak up fo theyself. That's good,
> but in the end, it's betta for you to stop playin' wit people heads, and
> doin' all that stuff.

Of course, Darius was saying "gay," but more likely was referring to engaging in same-sex sexual behavior and the increased willingness to explore
these options for romantic and sexual encounters. He acknowledged that
these men were on their own paths to discovering their identities or their
sexual interests, but he wished they would go about it differently, in a way

that was not damaging to other gay men. Raphael was even more extreme in his assessment, buttressed by Jayden's interjection:

> VP: So like, what percentage of that group would you say is gay, lesbian, or bisexual?
>
> RAPHAEL: I'd say the whole clique! . . . Nowadays? I think the whole clique. I'd say the group down there, the Terrors, half of, or all of them are! (laughing) Half of all of them! Jayden know! . . . (laughs) Yeah, half or all of 'em are. Just basically, the North Side.
>
> VP: The whole North Side? Just, the whole North Side is all gay.
>
> JAYDEN: Yeah, Columbus is.
>
> (all laughing)
>
> VP: What about your group specifically, do you think that there's other people in yours that are gay or bisexual?
>
> RAPHAEL: Like, my cousins and them?
>
> VP: Yeah.
>
> RAPHAEL: I really don't know. That's a good question, I really don't know. Cuz I never see it as, like that. I don't know. It might be. I just never asked.

Tellingly, to identify gay gang members, Raphael was looking outward to other cliques and to the part of town that he lived in, instead of into his own family and immediate social group. He found the whole conversation hilarious, in theorizing that, hypothetically, an entire side of town might be gay, and there was no real way to know. And paradoxically, while Brandon felt much homophobia from the Terrors while he was a member of the group, Raphael thought all or half of them were gay. This is further illustration of the theory that men who are quick to insult fags (as Brandon said they were) are doing so to deflect attention away from themselves.

And of course, time allowed for information to become public that was not known in the past, or for questions to be raised based on behavior. Toby told me about gossip he had heard since coming out and getting involved in Columbus's gay scene:

> VP: Do you think that anyone else in the gang was gay or lesbian?
>
> TOBY: Yeah. Well, now I know, but back then, I didn't suspect it, but now, since I know a lot of gay people, I hear stories, and I be like,

wow! All this time? But, yeah. It be some of the top people, like, the
top dogs, too. And I was like, whaaa, that's crazy.

VP: Have you ever asked those top dogs though, if they're gay, or—?

TOBY: No, I would never ask 'em. But I would definitely mess wit [have
sex with] one of them if that was to occur. (laughs)

Although my second question to Toby may have seemed naïve, Toby
suggested it was not totally off-base: he would not ask directly, for that
is against the mores of the gay community (and especially with closeted
men), but would allow steps to occur that would lead to them having
sex, were it possible. The passage of time also allowed for a reinterpreta-
tion of behavior stereotypically associated with women (and thus read
as gay):

VP: Do you think that anyone else in your group, like, just the group in
Columbus, do you think anyone else is gay—

JAMES: Probly.

VP:—or lesbian or bisexual?

JAMES: Probly.

VP: Probably? Do you know of anyone, though?

JAMES: No.

VP: Okay. But you think they probably are?

JAMES: Probly. I mean, I done seen different type of reactions in situations. I be thinkin', like, "Is he gay?" Like, certain things dudes don't
do, like scream or somethin', like, "Ahhhh!!" Like, in a high, girl-
pitched voice. Like, what the fuck? (laughs) You know, just different
situations that make you think.

Beyond questioning stereotypical behavior, James's comments reiterate
the main theme of this section: it is highly improbable that individual
gay gang members in large gangs where they know no other openly gay,
lesbian, or bisexual members are the only GLB members, but rather, factors prevent others from coming out.

Although not nearly to the same extent as gang sexual orientation
composition, I also explored sex composition, or the ratio of males to
females, within the context of straight gangs. Regarding straight gangs,
they were typically mixed-sex, but majority-male groups. My discussions

with participants provided insight into the gendered dynamics of these gangs that further speak to the issue of masculine and gay status. For example, Toby, DJ, and James all belonged to gangs that were about three-quarters male and one-quarter female, and suggested that the males and females engaged in similar gang activities, including fighting. When I asked if any of the females in the gang were lesbian or bisexual, Toby said that there were one or two and that the gang was okay with their sexuality, "Cuz they was like dudes! (laughs) They was one of the homies." DJ noted that the lesbian or bisexual females in his gang would openly tell others that they were gay. When I asked how the gang reacted to them, he replied, "They just treat 'em like a male, I guess. They wouldn't get no special privileges." All of this led him to conclude that, in his gang, it was easier for a girl to be gay than a boy, given his concerns (described in the previous chapter) about coming out to his gang and how they would react to him as a gay male. The assumption he articulates is that lesbian or bisexual female gang members take on the characteristics of male gang members, making them "one of the guys." As such, they provide no threat to the stability of the gang, since their sexuality is not accompanied by concerns of effeminacy/softness, or a preoccupation with gay males' alleged sexual interests in other male gang members.

In this vein, James also spoke to the sexual double standard among gang members: "I mean, if they are [lesbian or bisexual], then it's all good too. I mean, it wouldn't piss me off, I would love it! (laughs) I would love it, man. Then I'll let it be known. There it is! That's just a lot of sex goin' on right there (laughing)." Even though James had been in a long-term relationship with Spiderman and was struggling with his bisexuality in the context of the gang, he still regarded females' lesbianism or bisexuality as sexually exciting and potentially beneficial to the gang. Clearly, gay and bisexual male gang members do not engender the same eroticized feelings, nor the assumption of equality. If men express delight at men having sex with other men, they will get swept up in negative opinions of gay men; if they are adamant that gay guys are still "one of the guys," they risk alienating fellow gang members who vehemently disagree. Advocating for gay men within the context of straight gangs is precarious; advocating for lesbian or bisexual women is much less so.

It is likely that straight gangs' discouragement of same-sex sexual activity and gay identity, as well as implicit inattention to lesbian female members, prevent accurate estimations of whether or not specific gangs are truly overwhelmingly made up of heterosexual members. Gay members of straight gangs are discouraged from coming out, as my participants were; thus, they remain largely unknown to each other, unless they happen to engage in a covert sexual encounter. In contrast, men in hybrid gangs with a larger proportion of *openly* GLB people did not face the same opposition from fellow gang members.

Hybrid Gangs: A Foot in Both Worlds

Drawing explicit comparisons to the gay and straight gangs discussed in the previous chapters, I focused here on hybrid gangs, which had a critical mass of GLB members. In contrast to straight gangs and comparable to gay gangs, men in hybrid gangs had more freedom to say and do what they pleased. They didn't feel forced to blend in to a group culture that emphasized traditional masculinity and heterosexuality, because that simply wasn't the interpersonal context of their groups. All but one of the men in hybrid gangs came out to these groups, and the others often told their gangs details about their lives that included their sexual activities with males, though they were still vigilant about their gender presentation and self-conscious about their sexual identities depending on the scenario. The men who still belonged to hybrid gangs emphasized the group's significance as their main friendship and support network, rather than a place for illicit activities. As could be expected, hybrid gangs have commonalities with both gay and straight gangs: they engaged in a variety of activities associated with each type, their members were equally as likely to join existing crews or form new ones, and their gang environments entailed some impression management but virtually no concerns about being out.

Because my categorization of the gangs in my study is based on their sexual orientation compositions—the ratio of straight to GLB members—and the resulting organizational dynamics, I wanted to be more reflexive about how those estimates may have been influenced by both straight and hybrid gangs having a majority of heterosexual members. Members of hybrid gangs mostly felt confident in their estimates, since there weren't comparable pressures for them to stay hidden. The forces that encourage gay gang members to stay closeted meant that men in straight gangs found estimating their gangs' proportions of GLB members to be challenging. They suspected there were others, but often could not be sure, though they questioned the vocal homophobia of some men and suggested it was a front. Relatedly, their estimates were complicated by the fact that they found an underworld, even within their straight gangs, where they could have sex with men, including other closeted gang members. This is why I argue that some of the straight gangs are actually "hybrid gangs that could have been." The sheer numbers may be there, but the implications for gang experience have not been realized. Were more people to come out, this would likely change the dynamic, reducing the pressure for others to remain hidden, and relaxing the expectations for gender presentation and sexual identification.

PART III

Strategies for Resistance

6

"Not a Fag"

Resisting Anti-Gay Harassment by Fighting Back

In fall 2011, Imani told me a harrowing story from when he was younger. It took me a minute to realize that I had heard this same story years prior at the youth center, and was just as struck by it then:

> I was comin' from band practice, and one of the dudes was like, "Come here." I was like, "No!" He was like, "Come here!" I was like, "No, bitch, I don't know you! First off, you're on a dark porch, why would I come on a dark porch?" Like, no. I don't know what you think I am. So, he like, "You faggot ass nigga," this that and the fourth. I said, "See, that's why I wadn't finna come up there!" I said it like that, and I started walkin'. So he get off the porch, he said, "Bring yo gay ass here." I was like, "No!" And I started runnin'. But, they started chasin' me. Like, once he got off the porch and start runnin', it's like three other dudes come off the porch. So, I ran, like, "Y'all ain't finna jump me!"

He clarified that he didn't try to fight them and instead ran "because it was too many of them, and I was by myself." Imani figured that they must have seen him get off at his usual bus stop, as he did the day of and the days before that first interaction, so he began to get off at a different stop to avoid a confrontation. Some days later, however, he ended up passing by one of the guys, presumably on his way to the old stop to meet up with his friends. The other two then started walking toward him until they met. They started to beat him up, and he was able to fight back with the blade he carried for protection, and cut one of his attackers. That allowed him to get away again, and his mother picked him up from band practice until his family moved from the area shortly afterward. He refused to be an easy target for anti-gay harassment, saying definitively: "Bitch, don't try to attack me. Don't do that. Uhh-uhh, my life is too good, I don't need you to be tryna attack me. No. . . . They was callin' me a faggot and stuff. You're not finna get me, like, no. I don't know what y'all think this is, y'all are not finna get me."

They're not finna get him, indeed.

* * *

Imani's story of fighting back against anti-gay harassment is troubling: he was on his way home from an extracurricular activity at his school, and had to navigate through this difficult terrain, making a choice to avoid a particular part of the neighborhood but ultimately still being faced with the threat of violence. In stark contrast to many other men in this study, he was able to call on parental help to insulate him from anti-gay harassment, and strikingly compares anti-gay harassment to his life that is "too good" to be affected by homophobes and violence. Despite facing other challenges in his life, it is likely that Imani has framed his unwavering commitment to be openly gay and respected as precisely what makes his life "too good" for such attacks. This chapter is devoted to the methods of and meanings associated with fighting back, often as a way to construct masculine and gay identity.

For men across many racial, socioeconomic, and geographic communities, aggression and physical toughness confer masculine status,[1] especially when other opportunities to gain masculine status, such as employment, are blocked or absent.[2] Thus, violence can be enacted to address disrespect and to defend "masculine ideals" such as honor and reputation,[3] especially if one's masculinity is explicitly challenged by another male[4] through insults or intimidation. Furthermore, especially among urban populations, violence serves as a conflict resolution strategy when formal systems for recourse, such as police and schools, have failed.[5]

Self-defense, both of the physical body and of the reputation, is also served through the commission of violence, as is the defense of others. Perpetrators view targets of their defensive violence as appropriate or deserving victims for initiating the conflict, and themselves as morally superior and justified.[6] For example, in criminologist Lois Presser's study of men who had been convicted of violent crimes, the men avoided remorseful feelings and blamed their victims by casting them as disobedient, as individuals who had harmed the interviewee or others first, or as offenders themselves.[7] Although society views the defense of self or others from serious harm as a reasonable (and legally accepted) justification for violent behavior, self-defense is sometimes constructed broadly to include the defense of a person's character, reputation, or identity.[8]

Nearly all of my research participants have been involved in interpersonal violence, many with their gangs, but even those who reported little involvement in violence appreciated such justifications. For example, Kevin acknowledged that sometimes "lines are crossed, and you've gotta knock somebody out." According to participants, somebody especially needs to get "knocked out" when he engages in anti-gay harassment or violence, or places a gay, lesbian, bisexual, or transgender person's safety in jeopardy. The willingness to defend those deemed "fags" persisted despite all of the misgivings regarding what it meant to be recognized as gay in the larger society and what is signaled about someone who is insulted as a "fag" in public. On that note, participants believed that an anti-gay comment or threat of violence must be addressed as a matter of maintaining one's respect; violence became necessary to deal with the harassment when other responses (such as verbal retorts) did not quell the conflict. Violence also has face-saving functions, and these men used it to reclaim masculine status by rectifying the affronts to their masculinity implicit in harassers' anti-gay speech.

In order to investigate participants' responses to anti-gay harassment, I briefly outline the meanings of anti-gay harassment and patterns of fighting back. I then discuss the men's strategies for avoiding harassment, followed by the conditions that must be present for them to engage with their harassers. I detail the series of escalating steps that commonly occur before conflicts turn violent but also explore the role of threats, which can lead to fights very quickly. I specifically discuss fighting back in schools, considering the fact that my participants are young men. Throughout, I reflect on the significance of the *fag/faggot* insult, especially in light of cultural meanings associated with "fags," and the ways that participants turn homophobic harassment on its head by fighting back, such as through "fagging out." Fighting back against anti-gay harassment provided an additional mechanism for the construction of respectable gay and masculine identities. Such identity negotiation occurs, in the case of gay gangs' members, while being "known" for being gay; in the case of men in straight gangs, in having to defend a non-normative sexuality within a heteronormative context; and, for non-gang participants and members of hybrid gangs, in the presence of one or both of these factors.

"Not the Thing to Say to Me"

Over two-thirds of the men in my study physically fought with another person due to anti-gay harassment, threats of violence, and/or actual violence. Over three-quarters of the members of gay gangs had fought for these reasons, as compared to just over 60 percent of the members of primarily heterosexual (straight and hybrid) gangs; over a third of this latter group belonged to hybrid gangs. That is, five of six men who had belonged to hybrid gangs had fought back. Finally, four of the five non-gang men had fought for these reasons.[9] Just as there is a relationship between gang type and being out, there is a clear relationship between these fights and being out. Notably, only two of the men who had fought over being called a faggot were not out to their gangs and the majority of people in their lives, though this was partially due to the fact that several men fought after or because of being outed to their gangs.

As evidenced by the sizable 70 percent of my participants who had fought over anti-gay harassment, they were not always able to avoid anti-gay harassment, despite their efforts. In fact, they encountered harassment in multiple spheres, often starting early in school. Physical conflicts occurred in schools and schoolyards; public places, such as clubs or community festivals; and even in juvenile and adult correctional facilities. Some participants described lifelong battles against anti-gay bullying and harassment. When asked how many times he thought he had been in a fight because of his sexuality, Greg estimated over 10, Derrick estimated over 20, and Brandon estimated over 30.

Participants asserted that being called "punk," "bitch," or "sissy" did not bother them nearly as much being called "fag" or "faggot." For example, Brandon noted that "faggot hurt the most" out of all the names he had been called, and it was the only insult he would fight over. An assault on one's masculinity implied in the use of "bitch" or "punk" was offensive, but the assault on one's masculinity *and* sexual orientation implied in the use of "faggot" could rarely be ignored. Because of its explicit attack on identity, the use of "fag" as an insult was considered to be "derogatory," "offensive," "hurtful," and a "low blow"; Casper suggested that only "lowlifes" use it. Jeremiah explained: "So, you could call me a bitch, you can call me out my name, I don't care, but when you call me a faggot, I know wut chu mean by that, and that's just as bad as calling me a nigger, or, that's the lowest you could go. That's you resortin' to your bottom pit, so I feel like once you call me that, I'ma resort to my bottom, and my bottom is wit my hands." Max similarly explained, "I don't like the word 'fag.' Like, I think that is such a derogatory term, it's not cute, it's just not the thing to say to me. . . . I'm not a talker, like I'll argue, I can say some rude stuff, but I'd rather punch you." For Johnny, being frequently addressed as a "fag" was intolerable: "Sometimes I'll ignore it, but it's like, after so long, it just gets so old, you get tired of people saying stuff about you, and calling you 'fags' and stuff like that, that shit get old, and then you gon' wanna say somethin'." Indeed, an active response to anti-gay comments was often deemed necessary, both to address disrespect and to curtail future harassment. However, participants first took steps to avoid anti-gay harassment.

Avoiding Anti-Gay Harassment

The members of gay and hybrid gangs and non-gang participants, who were more likely to be openly gay, recounted the ways they negotiated this safely in their communities. Especially in their neighborhoods, some participants felt insulated from anti-gay harassment simply because they had lived in the area a long time, or they were prepared to defend themselves. After coming out, Greg said he felt "safe now" because "errybody got to know me, people know who I am, and a lot of people are cool with who I am, now." Similarly, Josh felt "comfortable" because "I been out here forever, basically everybody knows me, so it's not no conflict. Errybody knows I'm gay." He also added that his best friends, Casper and Derrick, lived close by, so he felt he had allies in the area. Jeremy had very few issues in his neighborhood because "errybody knows me, and I dare somebody [to say/do something]! (laughs) And I always say that." He added, "the boys [there] love me for some reason," and call him to hang out. Being open and proud of their identities was a way participants tried to head off harassment. Among more extreme measures to ensure safety, Ricky mentioned carrying large kitchen knives (his favorite one was eight inches long) and interestingly noted that being gay allows him to carry it easily and keep it hidden: "I have a wonderful purse! That's one thing about being gay. I can go anywhere with a purse, and nobody should say anything, because, hello, I'm gay! It's my bag! I'm used to it." Batman also said that he carried a knife because, "People are crazy nowadays, so you gotta be crazy wit 'em!"

Other conditions that gave participants peace of mind were their neighborhood demographics—Casper and Rashad, for instance, each described being surrounded primarily by "older people." Rashad explained that his neighbors were older and that they still speak to him and wave to him, but he wanted to move further out because he felt unsafe as he approached a corner store that served as a boundary line between his housing community and the larger neighborhood. And Javier reported feeling safe in his apartment complex partially because he and his boyfriend had seen other gay people in their community. Juan lived in the Ohio State University campus area, so he was surrounded by younger people and had never experienced neighborhood trouble for being gay, but added that if someone was being a "complete flamer," then "anywhere they go, they would be kinda weird," but would only be harassed in his neighborhood by people who were drunk—he did not specify whether by college students or non-students.

Some participants had actually been harassed in their neighborhood; however, an anti-gay incident didn't necessarily cause participants to feel unsafe, but sometimes only more aware. Reese said that although his rainbow magnet on his car was stolen and he overheard some neighborhood boys say that "faggots" lived in his house, he felt safe because, "Everyone around here knows I'm gay. I make sure that it's known." Aga said the times that made him nervous in his neighborhood were when "it be a lot of boys around here and I be by myself." He remembered a time when he and a group of friends were walking down the street and were verbally harassed for being gay by a group of guys who lived there. Aga said it didn't bother him, though: "They never put their hands on us, [and] because it didn't matter, y'all waited for us to pass y'all for y'all to talk stuff about us." That is, the boys were cowardly in their harassment, so Aga shrugged it off at the time, but remained vigilant against other incidents. And perhaps fatalistically, Elijah said that in his neighborhood, "I walk down the street, people call me faggot. All the time. I'm used to it!" He had also been jumped around the corner from his home; however, he was not interested in remaining closeted to avoid such conflicts: "I like to let people know, just because I'm gay don't mean that I cain't do the same thing you do. It's not a sickness." Importantly, Elijah used to fight back against being called a faggot, but has relaxed his standards for responding violently. He stated that if he were called a fag by someone today, he could let it go: "I'd just brush it off. Obviously you noticed me, so I'm doin' somethin' right. I don't really get too mad over the word."

A specific strategy to avoid anti-gay harassment and violence was simply to steer clear of parts of town that they judged to be dangerous for gay men, or to modify their gender presentation when walking through those areas. They perceived that if they presented as more masculine or neutral, they wouldn't be visible as gay, and thus wouldn't attract attention. Silas explained he would not feel safe in his neighborhood were he to be openly gay or visible. He said, "I think I can hide it [my sexuality] pretty well, so as long as I walk with my head down, and don't talk, or say anything to anybody, I'm fine." He added, "I wouldn't hang a gay flag on my porch." That is, he is out to anyone who wants to know, but he doesn't want to be overly visible by speaking, enacting exaggerated gestures, or utilizing gay symbolism, since it might cause problems for him. In contrast, when in the gay parts of town, which his neighborhood bordered, he said, "I'd be more comfortable. I'd walk however I wanted to, talk however I wanted to, do whatever kind of hand gestures I like."

One day, after sitting outside on Imani's porch for a bit, we walked halfway down the block for him to show me the boundary line of where he lets his little sister ride her bike. He said that further up his street, it was "mayhem," the people were "ghetto," they would "shoot you," and it's "much worse." He explained of his block, "This is suburban compared to what's down there! Down there, there ain't no grass, there's just dirt, gurl, they got dogs in the front of they house, like, child [oh my]!" Even when his friends would try to get him to go to a party in that area, he told them they could come to his house to party instead. He said, "You don't know what's gonna happen." Part of his hesitation was due to the boys down there who harassed people for being gay. He remembered a time where he was walking through that part of the neighborhood with his gay crew: "They [my posse] wanna be real hood, and be real gay and walk down [my street], and this one dude, I heard him on the phone, he was like, 'Bro, he gay as fuck.' I heard it, I started cracking up. They was like, 'Bro, he a fag.' I was like oooh! They finna beat y'all up. (laughing) It's no shade, but they finna beat y'all up. I feel sorry for you, gurl. I feel so sorry." The "gurl" Imani was addressing was the member of his posse who was called a fag. It was common for participants to call their gay male friends "she" or "gurl," but it is hardly coincidental that they tended to do this more with their visibly gay friends. No one got beat up that day, but such incidents are why Imani does not like to go down there and tells his friends to stay away as well. Though he also alleged that "half of the boys down there like dudes! They're just gay." Since he thinks this is illogical and traveling through that area is mostly unnecessary, he'd rather stay away.

Outside of the neighborhoods where participants lived, they also wanted to preempt any possible harassment by keeping a low profile. The majority of my participants were involved in gangs, but they were unwilling to confront other groups of men by themselves. Of a neighborhood in Chicago where he planned to move to, Johnny said:

[It] really is a bad area, but I just mind my own business. . . . When I walk past a group of boys, or like, gangbangers and stuff, I just walk past them and I just don't say nothin'. . . . You have some gay people that walk past the group and try to switch [swish their hips] extra hard, and talk loud, and be extra gay so they can be noticed, and then that's what gets you beat up or talked about, laughed at, because you wanna be extra flamboyant. . . . It's stuff that comes along with that. . . . It really ain't that bad for me because I just mind my own business.

Johnny later noted that he did occasionally get "extra flamboyant," but certainly not "in public" or "in the ghetto." That is, were there to be heteronormative gangs in rough neighborhoods, he knew that being flamboyant could invite challenges. The "bad attention" and "trouble" this type of behavior caused was not worth the risk to his personal safety. Likewise, even though he was an androgynous man, Bird said he could "switch up" his "act" to not be insulted for being gay. He explained, "I can't hide my gayness, but I can switch up my energy as far as not being called a fag." Imani asserted, "I can be straight if I have to." He said that he would be the least flamboyant "when I'm somewhere I'm not from." He explained: "If I'm on the North Side of Columbus, Ohio, I am a whole man. I don't know nobody out there. Y'all don't need to clock my Ts [tell me what you think of me], especially when I be on the bus! And I'm not from here, y'all don't need to know if I'm gay or not, so y'all can attack me. Hell no! I be quiet." It is important to note that actions such as changing one's body language and avoiding walking alone through particular areas of town are risk-avoidance strategies used by other urban young men of color, gay identity notwithstanding.[10] The forms of self-presentation taken by other young men are obviously not meant to obscure gay identity, but other salient statuses.

At times when anti-gay harassment cannot be avoided, another option was to exit the scenario without responding at all to the harasser, in order to avoid further or escalating harassment. Despite "fiercely" defending himself against anti-gay harassment in school, Jordan and his friends left a gas station when a "big, thugged-out" guy confused one of Jordan's friends for a woman and threatened to kill them for being "faggots" and "sissies." Jordan said he and his friends chose to leave the scene because, "You never know, people might pull out a gun or something." Being hyperaware of the potential for anti-gay harassment was informed by prior instances, such as those discussed above and in previous chapters. Some men, like Rashad, always felt a cloud of doubt when in public places, including businesses. This exchange with Rashad and Max is illustrative:

RASHAD: So that's why I said, like, bein' gay sometimes is scary. You never know what situation you'll walk into. Bein' in stores, people give you looks and stuff, I've even experienced that. Some of the women like it, but you can tell there's a few that give you that look, like, alright. It's overwhelming, cuz you be like, "Uhh, why'd I walk in here?" Because everybody just looked over like (pause) and a lot of gays get that, it's dangerous bein' gay sometimes. And some people, they pick on you just because of that aspect—

MAX: We have friends that have had guns pulled on 'em—

RASHAD: So, I be sayin' to some young ones, be careful.

> MAX: One of our friends got a gun pulled on him at a gas station.
>
> RASHAD: Don't put yourself in a situation, always follow your first instinct and get up outta there! (laughs) Cuz people will pick wit chu.

Rashad and Max didn't feel unsafe everywhere, but they interpreted uncomfortable interpersonal interactions as evidence that these incidents, such as disapproving glances, could morph into more serious altercations. Thus, their advice to gay men was to exit any potentially explosive public scenario if one is unsure of what will happen. Being alone, outnumbered, or outgunned factored into several other participants' decisions to exit scenarios rather than engage with harassers. Thus, even for those who saw fighting back as a worthwhile endeavor, careful assessment was required to determine whether a fight was indeed in a man's best interest (i.e., if the status pursuit entailed a perceived low risk of serious injury). In service of self-preservation, individuals are more likely to choose "fight" over "flight" when the opponents are known persons, there is an audience, the location is familiar, friends are present to help, and/or the groups of combatants are equally matched in numbers.[11] Otherwise, serious injury is more likely to occur, and a devastating loss is more likely to erode masculine status.

"Taking It to the Next Level": Conflict De-escalation and Escalation

Although violent retaliation was usually an option to respond to anti-gay harassment, it was not always the first option. Participants described a series of escalating events that could occur before violence was deemed necessary to solve these conflicts. While some participants defended only their own behavior and identity, others chose to also defend members of the larger gay community, whether it was their romantic partners, their friends, or even patrons of a gay bar whom they knew little about. The gay community became a "higher loyalty"[12] whose needs must be met, even if that required violence.

When insulted with an anti-gay slur or comment, the most common response was to say something back to the offending individual. Strategies included asking the person to repeat the comment, clarify it, or to say it "to my face." All of these strategies were intended to cause the aggressor to capitulate and essentially withdraw the insult. Capitulation was taken as evidence of the harasser's underlying cowardice, and could end the conflict. If the harasser maintained the insult or responded with additional slurs or threats, this served to escalate the conflict into one where violence was necessary to settle the dispute. With each successive step of sustaining or strengthening the comment, participants found increased incentive to respond violently to the harasser. As the harasser had now engaged in a series of behaviors intended to challenge their masculine status, action was needed to secure it.

Despite Max saying he was "really serious" about "defending my honor," he said that he never had to fight to defend himself against antigay harassment for two reasons: he is tall and muscular, and he lets everyone know he will respond to inappropriate comments in a way that communicates his seriousness. He explained:

> It never got to the fight, because they would be scared. . . . Once they see that you're not a punk, that you're gonna say somethin' back, they back off, they do. People do. It happens that way a lot. Like, they'll be talking to somebody else about you, you'll be in the store or something, you know, "What the fuck you just say?" . . . [They reply,] "Oh, I didn't say anything." [I say,] "Oh, I didn't think so." Like that. I go through that a lot, I do. . . . Because most people when you say something to 'em, they back down. . . . I'm gonna stay and defend myself until it's over. Because I'm not a fag, your dad is!

When a conflict ended before any physical measures needed to be taken, my participants were convinced of the aggressor's lack of fortitude and masculinity. For example, Elijah recounted what he said when a man withdrew from a verbal confrontation with him: "I'd be like, 'You just got punked by a fag. So who's the fag?' And I'll leave it there, and then they'll feel stupid, because you just called me so many fags, look at chu now! You just got punked by the fag."

Of course, such exchanges were meant to maintain participants' self-respect, and in some cases, to demonstrate to those viewing the conflict that they were not to be harassed. Johnny recounted a story from his summer job at a theme park:

When I first started working [at a theme park], there was this one boy, during training, I just knew that he was sayin' little comments and stuff like that, but I had went off on him at work . . . I had told him, "You not gon' disrespect me because you think I'm gay," I was like, "I will fight you like I'm straight." Ever since that, I had my respect from him, and from everybody else that worked there that was there . . . everybody treated me good after that. Sometimes you gotta let everybody know that chu not weak. Just because I'm gay, that doesn't mean that I'm weak. Because they take a lot of gay people for being weak, and that's not the case. . . . Just cuz we're gay doesn't mean we can't fight or doesn't mean that we can't defend ourselves or say anything back to you if you say somethin' towards us, don't just think that we're gonna be quiet because we're gay. A lot of straight people typically think we're soft and all of that, and that's not the case.

Perhaps more so than any other participant, Johnny repeatedly denounced stereotypes of gay men (and gay people more generally) as unwilling or unable to defend themselves. One of my favorite sound bites of the entire study, "I will fight you like I'm straight," effectively references and challenges all of the assumptions about gay males' lack of nerve and fighting dexterity to make Johnny's point clear.

Despite the fact that "fag" was routinely referred to by my participants as "disrespectful," "offensive," or "hurtful," an anti-gay insult was usually insufficient to spark a physical altercation (especially among friends or family members) unless it was coupled with an aggressive delivery or another wrong. In the following exchange, Reese and I discussed an incident with a straight patron at a gay bar. It was not uncommon for Reese to get into fights at his local gay bar, the only one of its kind in his small town north of Columbus. Disrespectful interactions, such as flirting with another man's boyfriend, could easily spark a fight. Despite fighting with other gay men there, Reese still thought of the bar as a "safe" space. He made clear distinctions between patrons who were deserving of violent retaliation for specific transgressions against him and any particular patron of the bar who might be harassed by an outsider. He was willing to defend the rights of the harassed patrons and himself with violence, as described below:

REESE: I fought with a couple of people, like the [gay] bar would get crowded or whatever, we seem to have a lot of straight people come in there, and they thought they was running the show, because we actually have lesbians and gays in there, kissing or whatever, and that pissed them off. Well if we pissed you off, get the fuck out! . . . He came in our bar, where we can be comfortable, you can get comfortable or you can leave, and he was like, "Shut the fuck up you little faggot," so that instantly puts me off and we started fighting. . . . He disrespected me!

VP: And he called you a faggot right on your turf?

REESE: Yeah, yeah, I could see if I was on his turf, but he was on mine.

VP: Okay so let's imagine that scenario. If you went to a straight bar—

REESE: (rolls his eyes and starts shaking his head)

VP: I know, but let's say you did. You went to a straight bar and he called you a faggot there, would you have fought him at the straight bar?

REESE: Most likely. . . . If I get that, it will not even really be if they call me a faggot, because if you're just like, "Yeah whatever, fag," I'm fine, but if you're doing it as being disrespectful, then that will piss me off and if I can, I'm gonna fight you, and if I can't, then I'll be pissed off and leave.

VP: So would you ever fight with someone [when] you knew you weren't gonna win?

REESE: Yeah, I have. . . . It's more about the respect, like if I give you respect, I demand respect back.

In this exchange, Reese identifies the local gay bar as a sacred space for a marginalized community. There, gay and lesbian people should be able to express aspects of their identity that are regarded unfavorably in the larger society without the fear of being harassed for this behavior. Visitors from the larger society have no right to bother patrons in one of the few semi-public places they feel they can really be themselves. Reese's narrative also suggests that a heterosexual man in society may have the right to object to same-sex displays of affection on "his turf," and presumably, anywhere that is not a gay establishment could be "his turf." The limited space that gay and lesbian people have to call their own creates pressure to maintain that space, a pressure that Reese is willing to shoulder. Although displeased with the straight patron's behavior, it was not until the patron aggressively used an anti-gay slur that Reese felt it necessary to respond with violence. The disrespect, both to himself as a gay man and to the gay community, gave Reese the justification to respond violently. This scenario of gay patrons fighting back against those who seek to control them at a queer bar also evokes images of well-known acts of resistance. Although Reese beating up an unruly patron is not quite the same as gay, lesbian, and transgender people resisting police violence at the Stonewall Inn, the motivations are similar: an unwillingness to be affronted by straight people in queer space.

As with Reese, the willingness among other participants to defend gay individuals extended beyond defending one's self from harassment, threats, and violence. Several men in my study had formed identities around their commitment to the defense of others, especially those who could not properly defend themselves, were outnumbered, or were at risk of serious injury (as evidenced by threats or acts of violence in progress). This also allowed for justification from a moral standpoint: fighting back against cruel bullies was a source of pride. Brian told me that he started fighting while in a juvenile facility to defend "the mentally challenged," "younger gays," and anyone who was otherwise "vulnerable" or "weak." Because he had been bullied his entire life, he said that he "just can't stand to see someone getting picked on." Max was "really serious" about defending his own honor, but also the honor of others who might be unwilling or unprepared to fight for themselves. He claimed that some friends even referred to him as their "order of protection." He reported a history of fighting on behalf of boys who were smaller than their attackers or were outnumbered, but his unwavering defense of gay individuals was directly linked to their treatment in society. I asked Max to elaborate on who he defends:

> MAX: They don't have to be gay, but I don't like for people to fuck with the downtrodden. If they're already down, why keep putting them further down, you know?
> VP: Do you feel that gay people are more often downtrodden than—
> MAX: (interrupting) Yeah, because of the outlook on it. It's "not right," you know? So that's why.

Undoubtedly, the cultural messages regarding the alleged immorality of being gay frame the beliefs of participants like Max and Brian that gay people are deserving of enhanced protection from their peers. A common theme in these narratives, remarks to that effect suggest that the harassment of other members of the gay community is regarded, on some level, as a personal attack.

An anti-gay slur coupled with another wrong, in which someone else needed to be defended, could also escalate to a fight. Batman described his encounter with an acquaintance who, after stealing money from both an older woman and his friend's young child, started to disparage Batman around the neighborhood. Batman used words and fists to let him know that these transgressions had not gone unnoticed:

> This one kid, this was like maybe a couple weeks ago, he was talking shit about me, calling me all types of "fag" and "dick-suckin nigga" and all this type of stuff. And so I just beat his ass. I only hit him like six times, he didn't fight back, so that's why I stopped hitting him. I was like, "Well, I'm not gonna continue hitting somebody if they're not gonna fight back, but you deserve to get your ass beat." . . . He doesn't know me like that. I got really offended. . . . And then I explained the reason why I was beating his ass, and he was like, "Man, I don't even know you man" and I was like, "Yeah, you don't know me, don't talk shit! Cuz you don't." . . . I was always raised to not throw the first punch, so I really never threw the first punch. . . . He was just a punk. All he did was talk mess and couldn't back it up, he was just a punk. . . . I don't like just beating someone, just bullying. I wanted him to fight back. And that's why I stopped hitting him, because he wouldn't fight back. I was telling him to fight back, too. "Fight back!" [He replied,] "I don't even know you!" . . . I just felt like he needed to get hit a couple of times so he could realize what the fuck he's doing. [If he would have fought back,] I woulda done way more damage than I did to him. . . . He did [deserve it]. I don't even feel bad.

Although not proud of initiating the fight, and not wanting to be a "bully," Batman felt he was justified due to the other man's misdeeds: to steal from parties unable to defend themselves was bad enough, but when he denigrated Batman's sexual identity, he clearly crossed a line. He was not even in a position to discuss Batman's personal life, as the two did not know each other well. And, although an age contemporary, Batman never refers to the other party as a "man," but rather, as a "kid" and then as a "punk." Fittingly, it seems, Batman's self-selected pseudonym references an avenger.

Most participants were willing to engage in tit-for-tat exchanges where respect was on the line. Men who were hesitant to initiate a physical fight still acknowledged the potential for the confrontation to escalate from exchanging disrespectful words, to invading someone else's personal space, and ultimately, if the need arose, to fighting. Above, we saw Johnny's willingness to verbally respond to harassment, but sometimes his motives were to incite further action:

> No, I wouldn't fight over [being called a faggot], I would probably say something back that would probably lead them to want to fight me. (laughs) . . . I'm not gon' start a fight, I'm not like an initial fight-starter, but if they say something to me like that, it will make me mad and I will say somethin'. . . . I'm not gon' fight. If it leads to it, if I have to, yes. I might get in yo face, because that's disrespectful, at the end of the day. . . . I'm real argumentative. I'll argue with you before I'll try to fight you. . . . If you try to disrespect me, then I'm gonna try to disrespect you.

Specific comments intended to escalate scenarios included insulting the harasser or his father, as suggested by Max calling the harasser's dad a fag; Marcus responding with "Your dad likes me"; Ali saying, "And I'm fuckin' your dad"; and Jayden quipping, "It takes one to know one." Hurricane, also determined to defend his honor, described a series of steps where he gave peers who harassed him for his effeminacy the opportunity to avoid a conflict by declining his challenge to fight:

> I've never been able to handle [people talking about me]. That's why I call myself the Hurricane, I will flip out. . . . I don't care if you don't know me, if I think you're talking about me, I'm going to approach you and ask you about it. (laughs) If you give me the answers that I'm looking for, then we'll go to the next level. But I've never been the type to just beat somebody up for nothing, though. . . . I was always picked with, growin' up through school because like I said, people saw my feminine side. . . . The reasons that I fought is because I was defending my honor. And you

will never try to hurt my pride walking in school. . . . I'm here to get an education just like you, so if you don't [like that], you can go on to the next person or we can go ahead and fight and get it over with. And most of the time, because I was challenging, (laughs) they wanna fight. So, I fought. . . . People teased me a lot, and I didn't like it, and it came a point in time, I felt, if you didn't like what I said or what I'm about, do somethin' about it. . . . I've never been the type to pick the fight. I mean, I even gave a little bit of lip back. . . . After I started getting taunted enough, I opened up my mouth and started speakin' up for myself, like, "No, you got me fucked up!"

Hurricane's narrative is especially revealing because, although he claims he has "never been the type to pick the fight," he implies that he was "looking for" the answers that would spark a fight when he confronted those who were gossiping about him. Additionally, he was the one who often challenged his opponents to fight. Elsewhere in the interview, Hurricane told me that he would throw punches before it was clear that the other party was ready to engage in a physical fight and would continue hitting his opponents after they fell to the ground. Even his chosen pseudonym refers to his fighting style. The reliance on this identity of not being "the type to pick the fight" while engaging in escalatory behaviors suggests that he believes whoever initiated the harassment (the true start of the *conflict*) to be the one who picked the fight. In this way, Hurricane can maintain that he was the one being bullied because he was defending himself, rather than the one doing the bullying. Another example of this sort of strategic arguing was reported by Elijah, who was very explicit about his desire to egg on the harassing party: "I would just try to get them hyped, so they could get me more hyped, so I could just punch 'em and not have no feeling behind it, you know?"

Bird's narrative is illustrative of many of the themes already described here. He said he would attempt to avoid a situation that could lead to violence and did not consider himself to be "a violent person," but if he was disrespected or if his space was invaded, he would escalate the conflict first by verbally confronting the offending party and then by continuing to "take it to the next level" depending on the harasser's behavior:

I've been called every name out the book, and most likely I try to avoid the situation, but if someone gets in my face, and is finger-pointin' and callin' you out, yeah. . . . I was really, really rowdy, and I had a mouth, and if someone look at me the wrong way, I would say something. . . . A few years ago I was going out with some friends, and a guy bumped into me as I was walking, . . . and I was like, "Excuse me, watch where tha fuck you goin'," and he's like, "Oh you fuckin' fag, you better watch where the fuck YOU goin'," and I was like, "Excuse me? Say that shit to my face." And he got in my face, I pushed him, he pushed me, I tried to hit him, and he kept shovin' me. . . . My friends just pulled me away. I'm not really a violent person, but I can take it there to protect myself. Cuz I know what to expect out of those type of situations, you know? So I try to avoid it, but if they put their hands on me or if they make any type of threats, then that's when I take it to the next level of handling it. Sometimes I won't feel like speaking, I'll just handle it with my hands. . . . I won't stop until I see blood, or [loss of] consciousness. But I haven't really been that physical in such a long time.

Ten participants explicitly mentioned occasions when arguing before fighting was simply not worth the hassle, so they skipped right to fighting. The fight became inevitable because the offending party had angered them to the point that they were ready to throw the first punch. However, as in Bird's case, intervention by third parties can prevent conflicts from escalating into physical violence.[13] Intervention can also end fights before serious injury occurs. After Ali exchanged insults with a harasser, the harasser got in his personal space, which led Ali to throw a punch because, in his words, "You're not 'bout to get in my space, because you not about to hit me first!" It was only a "30-second fight" because Ali's friends pulled him away.

Steve was also willing to engage verbally with a harasser until his opponent tried to assault him. After that, Steve held little back:

I was walking in the gay district, and this guy was like, "Oh, you faggot." And it kinda pissed me off, so I showed him how big of a faggot I was. . . . I don't really look gay, not most of the time, but if I'm walking with a guy, I'll hold his hand or whatever, and [if] someone says something, I'll pretty much, just cuss them out. And if they wanna come at me, it happens, but not really. I wouldn't say it happens a lot. . . . I walked out of the gay bar, and I used to wear a necklace that was a rainbow, and he called me a faggot, so it kinda upset me, so I just told him, "Faggots can do whatever, it's a free world." . . . He swung on me first. I dodged it, and beat him up. And I didn't stop until I felt I was comfortable with it, until I seen enough blood [coming out of his] nose, eye, ear. And I kicked him a couple of times until I seen blood, and then I finished beating him until I was happy. Made sure he never called one of us a faggot again. [Maybe] he just didn't feel comfortable around gay people. I don't know, maybe he was gay hisself, and he was just upset because he couldn't walk around, go to a gay bar.

Making the case much more strongly than other participants, Steve actively claimed the identity of fag when he fought back. In fact, he was ready to show what a "faggot" is capable of doing; namely, severely beating another man who has offended him. Several other men, including Elijah and Jayden, temporarily welcomed the identity of "fag" while on the path toward reducing their harassers to "punks," either with words, fists, or both. During a verbal conflict that eventually escalated into a physical fight which he knew he would win, Jayden warned his harasser, "I'm gonna show you what this faggot can do!" Steve also explicitly called his attacker's masculinity *and* sexual identity into question. He simultaneously denigrated his attacker's masculinity and reified his own by indicating that he chooses to frequent gay bars, wear rainbow jewelry, and hold hands with another man, all of which could communicate his gay sexual identity to outsiders. Steve asserts he is proud of his identity, while his attacker is not secure or confident enough to be himself.[14] Regardless of their initial impressions of their attacker's masculinity, Steve and others felt justified in responding to anti-gay harassment with violence once they perceived the harasser to have escalated the conflict with aggressive language or actions. Furthermore, as psychologist Albert Bandura argues, when men are successful in their aggressive pursuits, the benefits of aggression are reinforced because the preservation of reputation creates a sense of pride and self-satisfaction for those committing the violence.[15]

As reflected here, threats of violence and actual physical contact required no additional escalating factors to precipitate a physical fight;

they were triggering events in themselves that tipped the scales in favor of violent retaliation. Recall, for example, that Bird would only "take it to the next level" if someone touched him aggressively or threatened him. Once a harasser promised harm or began to engage in violent conduct, a physical conflict was imminent. As declining to fight can result in a loss of masculine status, participants felt it necessary to respond to the explicit challenge of their masculinity, which was combined with the insult to their sexuality *and* masculinity. JD responded to the threat "You faggot this, faggot that, don't step outside" by defying the aggressor and stepping outside, where a fight ensued. Jayden fought his own brother after being told, "I'll beat your faggot ass," while Dollars fought his sister when she put her finger in his face and told him, "You're nothin', you're [just] gonna be gay."

An example of how anti-gay insults, threats, and violence combine to result in reactive violence is illustrative. Imani did not belong to his gay gang until after he participated in a violent conflict against a group of "college kids." It was not an official initiation, but rather a chance encounter that convinced the gang of Imani's fortitude:

> You know how those college kids get drunk, and they were [in the gay bar district] just being reckless, saying "fag this" and "fag that," and [my posse] just had to tear 'em up. And I was there, so I had to help. . . . [T]hey was up on a balcony and they was like, throwin' stuff down, so me, I gets mad, I'm like, "Bitch, don't be throwin' stuff down the thing," I swear to God, I started throwin' rocks up there. . . . So they come down the stairs. They started followin' us, callin' us fags and stuff. . . . We just took it upon ourselves to attack 'em. . . . They thought they was gonna get us! I don't know why they think gay people cain't fight. We was beatin' them up. That was crazy.

Although gangs often respond violently to actual or perceived threats from other groups, the threat of anti-gay violence was especially offensive to Imani's posse, because they are an all-gay gang. The conflict served not only to increase the group's solidarity, but gained them a new member. According to Imani, when they saw he was a skilled fighter who was willing to fight to defend his gay identity even though he was not officially a member of the posse, they asked him if he wanted to join the group. It is unsurprising Imani felt the all-gay posse "had to" fight the college kids: they initiated violence, utilized anti-gay insults, and presented a real physical threat to his posse's safety.

"Building a Reputation": Combating Anti-Gay Harassment in Schools

While all of the men in my study who responded to anti-gay harassment with violence did so to punish someone whom they perceived to be harassing one or more gay people, another goal was to prevent their own and others' future harassment. This was especially evident in the narratives of the participants who fought back to prevent future anti-gay harassment in schools. Although such instances were years in the past for some participants, the fact that they occurred during the formative period of adolescence reflects the ways that advocating for oneself can be integral to identity development and negotiation.

LGBTQ youth report high levels of verbal and physical homophobic harassment in schools, as well as low levels of teacher intervention in these incidents.[16] Participants discussed their efforts to address disrespect in terms of "building a reputation" as someone who would fight back, and was not to be messed with. In an attempt to prevent future disrespect and violence, retaliatory fighting can aid in building a reputation for toughness, especially when agents of formal intervention, such as police officers and school administrators, have failed.[17] Psychologist Arnold Grossman and his colleagues' research on a sample of sexual minority youth of color who attended New York City schools validates this: in light of the lack of official intervention in their victimization, some youth resorted to violence to respond to victimization and to prevent future harassment.[18]

The men in my study reported a general dislike of school not because of the work, but because of classmates who constantly teased them. Concerns about being a target of homophobic bullying were amplified when participants moved schools or moved up in grade. For example, when Jeremiah was asked how many times he thought he had fought over someone calling him a fag, he suggested seven times, which directly corresponded to the number of schools he had attended. He added: "But once you fight one person at the school over it, they don't do it no more.

Like, not wit me, anyway, they didn't. They left me alone. So it always takes, like, every time I switched schools, it took for me to fight at least one person." Notably, frequent school transitions are a predictor of youth violence.[19]

Hurricane's narrative (presented above) indicated improvement over his school career. Although he initially did not fight despite "always being picked with" and instead endured the teasing until it became intolerable, he attributed his respite from homophobic teasing in high school to his constant fighting in middle school: "It didn't get better until I got into high school, because by the time I had got into high school, sixth, seventh, and eighth grade, I had built my reputation, so everybody that I was in middle school with transferred to the high school that I went to or whatnot." For Nate, school was "good," with the exception of the teasing he faced. He said his last fight occurred during his sophomore year of high school after incremental improvements in his interactions with classmates:

> My worst I had growin' up would probably be elementary school, cuz I wasn't out, but I was like, iffy about it, and I guess people seen that, and you know, the names, the f word [fag], the g bomb [gay], name-callin', stuff like that. But like, middle school, I gained more [confidence], and still the name callin', here and there. But high school was pretty much cool, cuz I guess more people knew me, and they was like, "Aww, yeah, he's already gay, we know that," and I knew people, so it was really nothin'. . . . Like, in elementary school, or middle school, it was just like, a bad word, and I just felt [it was like] callin' a girl a b word. I just felt like I had to get them back, and it hurt my feelings, so I had to fight 'em. You're not gon' call me that word. It's rude and disrespectful. But in high school, I really didn't hear the word too much, and if I did, it'd probly be an outsider, like, somebody changed schools, or after a week, they prolly never said it again cuz they knew me.

Nate's comments illustrate the emotionally charged nature of retaliatory violence: he felt he "had to" personally "get them back" for their disrespect by fighting and inflicting physical pain, instead of seeking the formal sanctions school officials could provide. Sanctions they could provide, that is, if teachers were willing to intervene. Recounting his own experience with a very serious incident of anti-gay sexual harassment perpetrated by a new student, against which he eventually fought back, Darius described his teacher as "a real nice white lady" who remained immobile during the sexually explicit comments and resultant fight.[20] This lack of intervention may also be representative of larger patterns of interaction between white teachers and Black students,[21] with gay identity and/or same-sex sexual harassment complicating the (un)willingness to intervene.[22] Darius recalled that he did not experience additional anti-gay harassment from anyone after he defeated his opponent by injuring him with a stapler.

Participants directly addressed how they thought "building a reputation" functioned, specifically in reference to homophobic bullying. After besting his own opponent, Jeremy suggested that losing a fight should give pause to perpetrators of anti-gay harassment in the future: "If you get yo ass whooped, now you gon' be lookin' like, 'Okay. I just got my ass whooped by a fag, so maybe I should think about it!'" He asserted, "Just cuz you're straight, I'm not gonna back down." Several other men discussed the misconception that gay males would not advocate for themselves, let alone fight, when threatened with physical harm. ATL asserted that only after gay people defied existing stereotypes and fought back would they be taken seriously: straight classmates will learn that "Faggots fight too, they'll defend theyself too." Drawing from his own experience with homophobic bullying in schools, Darius summed it up: "They don't respect gay people, cuz they think gay people are not gonna take up for theirself, but when you take up for yourself and do stuff for yourself, then you see the respect."

These assertions are consistent with urban sociologist Elijah Anderson's claims regarding inner-city violence management strategies: "repeated displays of 'nerve' and 'heart' build or reinforce a credible reputation for vengeance that works to deter aggression and disrespect."[23] Not only was a response necessary for them to prevent future harassment, it was necessary to maintain their self-conceptions as gay men worthy of respect. Such concerns may also be particularly salient within school settings, since peer opinions are critically important during adolescence. Even Joe, whose harassment continued after he fought back, was motivated by the desire to maintain self-respect. He stated that he had been teased so mercilessly by classmates that he brought an aerosol can and lighter to school and started spraying (for which he was arrested, placed in juvenile detention for one day, and beaten up by his father), and had fought back against anti-gay harassment five or six times. He said he could let the laughing and name-calling (such as "fag" or "fruit") by groups of classmates roll off his back, but he felt the need to fight back if it was done continuously. Recalling one instance, he said, "I'll just get real angry, and wanna throw a textbook at 'em. And then they just wanna all come over here and jump me, I fight the biggest one, and unfortunately, me being so miniature and little, I lost. But still! I fought." Even in losing, Joe maintained some self-respect by demonstrating his willingness to fight. Of course, a win would certainly confer more masculine status than a loss.

Participants were well aware of cultural stereotypes regarding gay men—that they were weak, passive, and would not defend themselves. Both within school and outside of school, they were pleased to defy these negative stereotypes: Derrick proudly proclaimed, "I'm not scared of no straight person, if you gon' come at me, I'm still a boy at the end of the day. It don't matter how gay I am, how gay I might be, I can still fight a straight dude." Marcus mentioned being able to get the upper hand due to these stereotypes: "They wouldn't expect it [me hitting them], cuz they'd be like, 'Oh, he's gay.' Underestimatin' me, forgettin' that I *am* still a boy. And then they're shocked, like, 'Oh!'" In essence, participants used markers of masculinity such as physical toughness and fighting dexterity to defend stigmatized sexual identity. Criminologist James Messerschmidt notes that normative masculine resources such as fighting can be marshaled to "correct" scenarios where a man has been subordinated by another.[24] These resources become especially salient when men have little social support or avenues for recourse. Repeated homophobic bullying, which attacks an individual's masculinity and sexuality, coupled with low institutional support and a lack of teacher intervention, produces additional, direct motivation for gay youth to fight back in schools.[25]

Fagging Out

The aforementioned descriptions of "fighting back" demonstrate the value participants placed on an honor-based, aggressive (or at least reactive) masculinity. The analyses in this book even make it tempting to assume that gay gang- and crime-involved men (especially those in straight gangs) would prefer to be read as straight, and visibility as a "fag" was never acceptable. However, as is evident from Steve's, Jayden's, and Elijah's temporary reclamation of the term during such conflicts, referring to oneself as a "fag" when winning a confrontation was a way to challenge a heteronormative slur.

This also suggests some of the nuanced possibilities for gender fluidity that exist within the context of fighting back. One such possibility discussed by participants was "fagging out." When he was called a fag as an adult, Ricky said,

> I'd just fag out. Which is, you know, the typical word of getting really loud, acting really gay out of nowhere. . . . "You wanna call me something that I know I'm not, but, hey, I'm a punk? No, I'm far from that. I'm gonna fag out on you, so everyone can know that you're the punk." That's basically what you do when you fag out. You scare somebody. They get scared, automatically. Like, "O-kay. This person's really—something's wrong with him." . . . When you fag out, you just click. It's like, say we were talking right now, and somebody was to come in the room and say somethin' real stupid, I would literally stop this whole conversation, and go off. And the head'll be bobbin', and noddin', and the neck'll start goin', and the hand work'll start doin', and I'll be cussin' every other word! (laughs) Every other word out of my mouth would be a cuss word. Basically, that's fagging out. And that's when you start walkin' towards the person, that's when you fag out. I've fagged out at Burger King, McDonald's, Wendy's, it doesn't matter.

As described, "fagging out" is acting stereotypically gay (flamboyant) in overt and aggressive ways, to show that being flamboyant can also mean being fierce to defend oneself. It transforms being flamboyant from something that connotes weakness into something threatening and fear-inducing. Ricky also suggested that he and members of his gay crew would all "fag out" at the same time to deal with heterosexual cliques, in response to which their opponents would "get scared" and "just run off."

Further reiterating the gendered aspects of fagging out, Imani explained, "People already know I'm gay when they see me. And then when

I do get masculine, they don't know what to be with theirselves, cuz it's like, 'Huh?' I am everything! I'm like a whole man sometimes, but I don't know! Some days, I be faggin' out! That's what be gettin' me together [making me confront someone/speak candidly]. Somebody'll say somethin', and I'll be like, 'Uhhh-uhhhhh!' You know, somethin' like that, like, 'Oh, gurl, no she didn't!' I be lookin' like a whole man, and then I fag out." Imani's language suggests that regardless of his self-presentation at the moment before he reacts, "fagging out" then renders him as recognizably gay, and therefore he is perceived to be less of a man, instead of the "whole man" (stereotypically masculine) image he was enacting. However, a man's underlying goal in "fagging out" is to display a propensity to physically protect himself from anti-gay harassment *because he is a man*, and is therefore unwilling to tolerate disrespect, even if his gender presentation is feminine-leaning. This particular aspect of "fagging out" is predicated on a refrain I often heard to justify fighting back, which was "I'm still a boy/man," discussed above.

Because being called a fag was often linked to atypical masculine gender presentation, "fagging out" was a strategy to incorporate the gender-atypical behavior that the insult addresses into a man's response to the insult. By magnifying the behavior, adding aggressive actions, and scaring the instigator, study participants essentially inverted the insult and reduced their *harassers* to punks and "fags" (in the derogatory way that the harasser meant). Thus, participants' meaning system is complex and challenges static understandings of homophobic harassment.

While "fagging out" has underpinnings similar to criminology's well-documented masculine justifications for violence (such as fighting to address disrespect), it is unique in that it draws on gay cultural resources to achieve these ends. Associating aggressive and potentially serious violent demeanor with "fags" and flamboyant behavior is certainly not theoretically realized elsewhere in the criminological literature. And indeed, even among participants' talk (described here and in chapter 2), *fag/faggot* could be used as a noun, an adjective, and even a verb, with varying positive or negative connotations depending on context. Perhaps the activities marked as "faggot shit"—being flamboyant, loud, colorful, and importantly, visible—were themselves forms of gay resistance to anticipated heterosexist harassment and violence. Fagging out becomes a way for men to reconcile societal rejection with personal affirmation, recuperate from violence and exclusion, and create personal myths as gay men who are not to be messed with.

Fighting Back: Proclaiming the Right to Be Gay

Most participants felt that being called a fag was insulting to them on many levels. It attacked a primary aspect of their identity (one for which they already faced rejection), and lumped them into a category of gay men to which they did not want to belong. Participants were more than willing to explain who a "fag" was, and their descriptions often hinged on feminine grooming and personal style, in addition to other social behavior such as being "loud" and "flamboyant," which drew attention to themselves. Although some might enact sexual stigma verbally by calling flamboyant gay men fags, suggesting some level of internalized homophobia, no participants appeared to exhibit homophobic behavior in violent ways. Quite the contrary: even while constructing boundaries between themselves and unacceptably feminine gay men, participants simultaneously defended themselves or other members of the gay community and their rights to be gay, out, and proud.

In these scenarios, violent retaliation functioned as a performance of traditional masculinity that was necessary to successfully defend their non-traditional sexuality. Specifically, anti-gay harassers determine gay men to be of lower status because they perceive certain markers of masculinity, such as a propensity for aggression or possession of fighting dexterity, to be absent for gay men by virtue of their same-sex sexuality or feminine-leaning gender presentation. The willingness to fight and the ability to win secured the masculine status in question and could even elevate the harassed man's normally subordinated masculine status above the harasser's status.[26] For example, when my participants were called "fags" and "punks" by other men, their narratives suggest that they did not feel vindicated until they effectively made a "punk" out of the perpetrator of the harassment.

What is especially striking is that the group of participants who were willing to utilize violence for these reasons included men who otherwise reported little involvement in violent behavior. For example, Kevin attempted to fight a man who called him a "fag" and then assaulted his lesbian sister, and Silas beat up a boy who outed him to several classmates at a new school because of his assumption that he would face negative consequences as a result of his sexuality. These examples underscore some of the themes present in the narratives of other participants who have histories of violence. These themes include a refusal to allow others to disrespect them or their family members, to talk about them behind their backs, or to expose their private lives. More importantly, these examples speak to the perceived seriousness of threats to a man's safety based on his sexual identity; for men who are otherwise non-violent, the willingness to use violence to defend themselves or others from anti-gay harassment or violence is a testament to the gravity of these threats. Finally, this chapter illustrates the wide breadth of places where anti-gay harassment can occur, such as school, work, home, retail establishments, and participants' neighborhoods. Identity negotiation as an interactional process knows no bounds regarding public or private space.

It is not surprising that these participants, even those with little involvement in violence, chose to respond violently when harassed because of their sexual identity, considering the high number of gay men who have experienced an anti-gay bias crime—nearly 40 percent, according to a recent national probability sample.[27] The specter of victimization is always present for gay men, who have to continually negotiate an unpopular sexual identity. There is no indication from the literature that gay men who are not members of gangs or involved in regular criminal activity would react in a similar way, but it may be that the necessary questions have not been asked. As has been discussed, gay victims' resistance strategies or responses to attackers have not yet been analyzed, perhaps because of heteronormative assumptions about gay men's non-involvement in violence.[28] My findings illustrate how gay men can enact violence to respond to victimization, to prevent future victimization, or to construct identity through the conferral of status that such violence can bring.

Additionally, as all of my participants are "out" to some degree, their sexual orientation is a part of their identity they believe is worth publicly defending. The responses of gay men who are not out may differ, and indeed, the participants in my sample who were more fully out were more likely to defend themselves against anti-gay harassment. The same is true for men in gay gangs, who were not only more likely to be out than those in straight gangs, but were more likely to fight back. Furthermore, because most of the participants in my study who decided to come out either found some acceptance within their gangs or left those groups, these factors likely explain the stark contrast between gang scholar Mark Totten's findings and mine, as his gay gang members were involved in gay-bashing incidents partially to prevent their sexual identities from being revealed.[29]

My findings challenge the criminological literature's discussion of masculinity and its representations of gay men in several important ways. First and foremost, there has been little investigation into how gay men use and justify violence, as well as the ways violence contributes to their identity construction. The inattention to gay men's presentations of masculinity (and lack of research on gay men in general) has left ambiguity as to whether they share heterosexual men's "masculine norms," particularly with regard to violence. The men in my study *do* value the honor-based masculinity valued by other men; however, they must do additional "identity work" not only because their sexuality is in opposition to the traditional masculine ideal, but because the exclusion of gay males is a feature of traditional masculinity. My findings push our theoretical boundaries by suggesting that gay men who are members of gangs and/or involved in criminal activity *can and do* use violence as a way to address anti-gay harassment. These men are not passive victims, as the literature might suggest. They find motivation for violence in anti-gay disrespect, and construct masculine and gay identities partially through their willingness to defend themselves. Indeed, participants were determined not to be ready victims; they vigorously defended their gay identities, sometimes with violence. The willingness to use violence allowed each man to emerge from these conflicts with most of his status and dignity intact. The threat of violence due to his sexuality looms large, and a response to this threat is deemed necessary to protect his safety, his masculine status, and his self-respect as a gay man.

How to Fight Back

The scenarios described by the men in my study suggest that a response to anti-gay harassment and threats of violence is necessary to maintain masculine status and to prevent future harassment. The men described ways to preempt harassment, such as through strategic gender presentation in order to not be read as gay. When harassment did happen, violence might not have to be used as the first line of defense, but a willingness to use violence was deemed necessary to deal with the harassment when other responses (such as verbal retorts) did not quell matters and the conflict escalated. In these narratives, participants cast the perpetrators of the harassment as deserving victims of retaliation for initiating the trouble and, occasionally, for forcing them to "take it to the next level." Verbal comebacks and violence served as vehicles to reclaim the masculine status that was at risk when a man was harassed for being gay. While an anti-gay slur alone was typically insufficient to spark a fight, being *repeatedly* referred to as a "fag" by outsiders was too offensive to ignore, and necessitated a violent response when it was combined with a threat, another wrong, or an aggressive delivery. This suggests that identity work in the form of violence is not necessary until the insult is part of a series of behaviors designed to degrade another's masculine status.

The majority of participants had fought at least once because they or another gay person were called a fag or other anti-gay epithet; some fought many times. Sometimes, entire gay gangs fought straight crews because of this sort of harassment, leading to increased solidarity and group cohesion among the gay gangs. Although participants typically utilized idealized markers of masculinity, such as physical toughness and fighting dexterity, to defend their stigmatized sexual identity, some even described "fagging out," or acting in aggressive and flamboyant ways simultaneously. Because being called a fag was often linked to gender atypicality, "fagging out" was a strategy that reconceptualized the insult by inverting it. Thus, these men could derive status from being a fag, even though the word is meant by harassers to be anything but empowering.

Participants' sexual identities and loyalty to the gay community arose as key factors in justifying these behaviors, as the targets of their aggression had perpetrated some wrong against them or against other members of the gay community. They maintained claims to traditional masculinity through the inclusion (and defense) of other gay individuals, rather than their exclusion. In so doing, they also responded to their own exclusion by the larger society, especially by normatively gendered male peers. In this way, part of being a respectable gay man meant defending his own and others' right to be gay, and even to be a "fag."

7

"Tired of Being Stereotyped"

Urban Gay Men in Underground Economies

"Come here, Vanessa. You gotta see this."

Silas leads me to the computer that's in his bedroom. Steve and Jordan are sitting around it as well. They are all watching YouTube videos and presumably have found a funny one. They've shown me some pretty good ones before, so I'm hoping for a treat.

It was decidedly not what I would consider a treat.

The title of the clip is "Prostitute Confesses to Incest." It's a video filmed by a white man in a truck who sees an older, somewhat heavyset Black woman in a low-cut tight black outfit and calls her over, telling her he'll give her some money. The video is from his point of view. She is missing some teeth, her hair is disheveled, and her outfit is dirty and damaged. She first says that she's a prostitute, that she started stripping at 16, she used to have a career in porn, and she'll now "suck dick" for "whatever you want me to suck it for." He has handed her a dollar or two by this point, and he asks her if she wants more money. She offers, "Hell yeah. I'll show you my pussy." He asks her to show it to him. She bends over, moves the crotch of her outfit out of the way, revealing her labia, but he asks her to do it again because he couldn't see the first time. "Oh yeahhhh," he says when he can see better. He asks her four explicit questions and she answers three of them; her answers reveal that she has sex with her son.

"Wow," is all I can say. The cameraman sure seems to be having a good time, as are the laughing Silas, Steve, and Jordan. Silas and Steve are white and have sold sex before, while Jordan is of African descent and has had a "sugar daddy."

More conversation between the man and the woman, including his request to see her breasts, which she complies with. She eventually asks if he's "done yet" and "done paying" so she can go buy some cigarettes.

He continues by describing how he'd like to have anal sex with her. She replies, "I know you would, but you'd have to pay me."

"Here it is, here it is," Silas says.

She repeats herself because the man didn't hear her: "You'd have to pay me, nigga!"

Raucous laughter from Silas, Steve, and Jordan.

The driver continues asking extremely explicit questions about what he could do with her sexually, and she answers yes to all of them. I am overwhelmed with sadness and disgust. "This dude is gross," I say out loud, but don't say anything about the woman. I wonder if any of my research participants have ever been involved in exchanges like this, with them in either role, and if this is any more exploitative than other exchanges, such as sex for drugs (or even sex for money). The majority have sold sex acts for money, and although they say they can make more that way than at any of the legal jobs they hold, they were sometimes grossed out by their clients' bodies, requests, or mannerisms.

The driver has more to ask her, especially about sex acts with her son, and hands her more money as she answers. I have mostly tuned out by this point, but Silas, Steve, and Jordan start laughing again when the driver asks her if he can come to her room and do all of the things they talked about, to which she replies, "You have to pay me, nigga!" She then asks him several more times if she can go, and he asks for one more look at her "ass and titties." She shows them, grabs the last of her money, and walks off. He chuckles to himself as he stops taping.

"Yikes," I say, shaking my head and hanging it down.

Still laughing, Steve offers, "I used to be that bad. I just wasn't that ghetto."

* * *

Silas, Steve, and Jordan are not unique to my sample, as nearly 60 percent of my participants had sold sex for money, and others had engaged in paid activities that bordered on sex work, such as dating someone in exchange for money or gifts. Thus, the reactions to this video by Silas, Steve, and Jordan illuminate some of the concerns that gay men have when engaging in illicit economies more generally, and sex work specifically. Walking the streets, looking disheveled, engaging in sexualized behavior for low sums of money, and having little or no boundaries regarding what behavior was allowed were all things to be disdainful of. For gay men involved in illicit economies, there was an expressed need to construct images of themselves as *respectable* gay men. Any behavior that gave up too much control to the client or debased one's self, especially without appropriate compensation, resulted in damage to participants' senses of self-worth. Such exchanges mirror other concerns of gay men regarding their acceptable masculinity and gayness in other social settings, such as with family, friends, fellow gang members, and in public. All of this is foregrounded by structural inequality (e.g., a white man initiating an economically exploitative scenario with a Black woman) and the ways it has played out in participants' lives.

The clip and participants' reactions also indicate a number of other disturbing realities, including a patriarchal social structure that sets up women's sexuality as a cultural resource or commodity, racist stereotypes regarding Black people's hypersexuality, and the dearth of quality employment for urban people. And, while it was one of my few white participants who marked this behavior as "ghetto," which is imbued with racial, socioeconomic, and behavioral connotations, participants of color (who comprised almost 90 percent of my sample) were concerned with an overlapping racialized stereotype—of being "deadbeats" unable to provide for themselves financially. Social pressure exists for men to be economically independent, while women have greater leeway in how they meet their financial obligations, also setting up a system where men who need help or dabble in illicit pursuits can lose masculine status, unless they are successful in achieving independence.

Research suggests that both monetary and status returns are important when deciding if illegal work is preferable to legal work.[1] Jobs available to inner-city residents—particularly men of color—are often low-paying, low-status, and unstable, where every shift is a possible source of degradation and humiliation.[2] In general, "hustles" and criminal activities can provide greater autonomy and professional satisfaction because they are less structured, less time-limited, require less discipline and formal control than regular employment does, and can even be fun and exciting.[3] Additionally, external factors (such as limited time or education) complicate individuals' decisions, which sometimes results in income-generating strategies that are "just enough," even if they are undesirable.[4] For example, in the case of sex work, workers may appreciate the autonomy and sense of self-worth that the profession brings them; however, they may also experience exploitation,[5] as well as risks to their safety, health, and freedom. While there are risks specific to sex work, some of the "downsides," such as the unreliable nature of the business, can also happen in minimum-wage, shift-based service work, where workers are at the whim of those in management.[6]

Logically, money is a key motivating factor for involvement in underground economies. Illegal work is almost always more profitable than legal work in unskilled professions.[7] Selling sex, drugs, or stolen goods also produces immediate cash, sometimes referred to as "easy" or "fast" money.[8] Ultimately, any combination of licit and illicit activities is meant to bring economic self-sufficiency. Cultural anthropologist Bettylou Valentine argued that the American dream of economic success, although difficult to achieve in the ghetto, is what keeps urban people hustling.[9] Sociologist Sudhir Venkatesh echoed this argument, suggesting that poor individuals struggle to "bridge the possible with the probable" by "continually hoping for long-term solutions—often framed in dreams and diffuse aspirations—while taking refuge in immediate adaptive strategies."[10] Criminologist John Hagedorn concluded that his gang-involved, drug-dealing research participants held conventional aspirations, such as the American Dream, and also held "conventional ethical beliefs about the immorality of drug dealing."[11] They wanted to "settle down" with careers and families but doubted they would ever succeed, partially because of the prison time they had served.

Thus, a way to gain masculine status is through employment,[12] but this is not a particularly viable avenue for inner-city men, where access to legitimate employment is blocked or absent.[13] Accordingly, economic self-sufficiency obtained through a variety of licit and illicit means can also confer masculine status. Consistent with what might be expected, nearly every participant in my study described what a "real man" is by alluding to fulfilling financial responsibilities, stating that a real man is independent, works, provides for his children, or something similar. Although I heard many other words often, such as "honest," the notion of "taking care of yourself" or "making it happen" was central to these "real man" narratives. Referring to the similarity of his description of a "real man" to his boyfriend's answer, Max stated, "That's almost everybody's definition of it, because there's no other way to really put it. I mean, if you can't take care of yourself, you're not a man, you know?"

Max was right—other men's responses were very similar. They discussed the importance of being a working man in constructing a masculine identity as they moved into adulthood, and all of the social meanings associated with holding legal employment. Participants made moral and conceptual distinctions between money generated from illicit and licit pursuits, and detailed their motivations for seeking employment, but especially legal employment. However, when legal employment was sometimes out of reach, their narratives reflected attempts to reconcile their actions with ideal behavior. These men's narratives also reflected themes in the criminological literature on crime as work, as well as the lackluster conditions of urban employment prospects and the factors that motivated individuals to participate in underground economies. However, other scholars' analyses are often framed in the context of men's adherence to heterosexual norms, while my findings suggest a complex interplay in which expectations of masculinity and status-conferring economic activity are affected by gay sexual identity.

Accordingly, in this chapter, I discuss my participants' involvement in making money by engaging in illegal work. I first briefly discuss the patterns of such involvement, and how they got involved. Next, I explore their reactions to cultural representations of men like themselves, as they resisted stereotypical depictions of how gay men, Black men, and gang members make money. This was especially salient since their gangs, gay friendship networks, and other social groupings allowed them access to illegal behavior that they thought effectively made them into a "stereotype." Some also had to deal with personal obstacles to legal employment, such as criminal records. I then discuss the ways they conceptualize "easy money," or money from illegal acts, and focus on illegal sales of both drugs and sex. I describe two characterizations they developed to deal with the stigma of these acts: the good drug dealer, and the escort.

Sex Work and Drug Sales

Although I will focus on illicit work in this chapter, it is important to first note the employment patterns among the participants. Nearly half were employed, most of them legally, but with a few working off the books (though off-the-books work was relatively unreliable). Just over half were unemployed, including a small number who were drawing SSI benefits for reasons of physical or mental health. Because of their frequency in the sample and their conceptual significance, I have chosen to highlight involvement in selling sex (either by selling one's own sex acts or pimping others) and selling drugs (including direct sales, but also being a courier, holder, or lookout).[14] Nearly 60 percent of participants had sold drugs, and nearly 60 percent had sold sex; over a third of the sample had done both, while nearly a fifth had done neither. Among the gang members, those who had sold drugs were more likely to have belonged to heterosexual (straight or hybrid) gangs (about a three-to-two ratio), while those who had sold sex were more likely to have belonged to gay gangs (about a two-to-one ratio). However, it should be clear that there was much overlap among the gang and illegal-activity types.[15]

I asked participants to tell me about when and how they got involved in selling sex or drugs. Take Ricky's explanation of how he started escorting:

> It was a few years ago, it was like I stumbled onto it. It wasn't like, "I'm gonna make my mind up, I need to go and sell my body," it wasn't like that. It was like, everybody that I knew was escorting, and I was kind of like, "Are you serious? Y'all are really—?" . . . And then it got to the point where it was like, I need money in my pocket, my paycheck's not due for another week, my bills are paid, I need a little bit of money. So, that's when I started it. Someone else introduced me to it.

Similarly, on his own decision to become involved in escorting, Aga remarked, "I went out there one day and saw how good the cash was, so honey, I had to get it!" When I asked Ali how he got involved in escorting, which he called turning dates, he replied: "Bein' around somebody who does it, like, you know how they say, you're gonna fall into what your friends do? Bein' around somebody who does it, you seein' their money come in, and you seein' what they doin', and at the time, none of us had jobs, so basically damn near everybody was doin' it, so it was like, why wouldn't you do it, it's easy." Money was thus the motivating factor for participating in escorting, and typically was facilitated at least initially by other people they knew.

Making money was also the primary reason participants entered drug sales, and was usually determined by access, but there was a much wider range of reasons why and ways into drug selling. For example, Darius and Brandon felt forced to sell drugs by their straight gangs; DJ and Joe were involved in secondary roles such as lookout or holder because those were the roles their straight gangs wanted them to play; Marcus and Juan were introduced to it by their boyfriends; Steve and Eric (who were not gang members) started as a way to support and facilitate their own habits. However, just as with escorting, seeing the fast money that could be made was attractive. Brian said, "My cousin and his set turned me on to it, and I just picked up on it, because I saw there was a lot of money in it," while Johnny said that he wanted some extra money in his pocket. Sometimes their reasons crossed over: Hurricane explained that because he smoked weed and always had it on him and people wanted to smoke with him, he decided he should start making money off of it. In participants' narratives, drug sales were not as tied to gay culture as escorting, but both figured heavily in gay identity negotiation.

Hittin' the Stereotypes: What Gay Men "Do"

Gay identity and gay social networks produced additional opportunities in or motivations toward underground economies, especially when combined with the conditions of inner-city employment. As mentioned, men in gay gangs were more likely to participate in sex work and crafting (economic crimes like fraud) than men in straight gangs, likely because they learned these survival skills from other young gay men. Interestingly, crafting and escorting were seen as endemic to gay culture and their place within gay peer groups and gay gangs was thus perceived to be completely understandable. Take Ali's explanation: "[I started stealing] when I started kickin' it wit gay people, honestly. . . . It's just what they do! Most gay people, they turn dates, or they mess with trades [have sex with closeted men]. Gay people just steal! They crafty, they use credit cards, stuff like that. That's in a gay person's life. Like, if you look at gay people, that's in their history." The following exchange about Ricky's gang's activities further underscores these themes:

> VP: Did anybody in your group craft, like with credit cards, or checks, or—
>
> RICKY: Yes, some of us have, of course we have. (laughs)
>
> VP: Why do you say "of course we have"?
>
> RICKY: Because I think most gay people do. To be honest, most gay people eventually either buy something that's crafted, for half of the price, or like, just 10 percent of the price, or have crafted themselves. . . . I will buy something that has been crafted.

Just as Ricky stated that "of course" his crew members had crafted,[16] he also offered that "gay people are prone to doing coke."[17] Also called powder, Ricky said that to obtain coke, people will "suck dick. Get fucked. For like 20, 30 dollars." These stereotypes were particularly salient of men in the ballroom scene, with Javier alleging that people traveling for balls are "escorting there . . . most of them, I would say 80 percent of them do, so it's a lot, or then they do checks or craft." Similarly, Rashad said, "Most [ballroom-involved] people I know are either coke addicts or they're 30 years old, livin' in a house full of gays with no career." Stories regarding sex work, crafting, and/or cocaine occurred repeatedly, often without prompting. Participants were well aware that these were stereotypes of the gay male community, and would describe them as such. For example, after I asked him about escorting, crafting, and drug sales, Tony exclaimed with a laugh, "Ooh, gurl, you hittin' all these stereotypes!"

These were not only stereotypes; they formed a constellation of behaviors that became the stigmatized identity and ready-made punchline. In specific reference to such stereotypes, the members of the Royal Family had a running gag making fun of people whom they knew were engaged in these behaviors. On some occasions when certain people "known" for selling sex for drugs/drug money came up in conversation, they would lean forward and stick their butt in the air, put one index finger on their nose, wave their other arm, and say loudly (with a particular tone and cadence) while swinging their body from side to side: "I *suck dick* for MO-NEY, and I'm COKED *out*."

Participants sometimes identified the people in their lives who first relayed these stereotypes to them. For Silas, it was his brother: "I remember one time he told me, because he knew gay people escorted, I guess that's the thing that goes around, that gay people escort, and he's like, 'You better never escort, because you'll get AIDS.'" For Eric, it was his father, who also believed this stereotype because he had been solicited with sex-for-money propositions by other men in truck stops. Eric reported this exchange upon coming out to his father: "The first thing that he told me was like, 'Well, I hope you're not doing it for the money.' And I was like, (laughing loudly) 'Oh wait, I could be making money being gay?'" With this reaction, Eric's father indicated that he could not separate gay identity from same-sex sexual activity for money—a testament to this trope's prolific reach.

Such stereotypes have traditionally been at the center of research on gay men's involvement in crime. Research on gay-identified males who sell sex has typically focused on street-based prostitution; specifically, on the dynamics of poverty and street-level violence that face street sex workers, sexual behaviors engaged in with clients, and sexual abuse as a causal factor of sex work.[18] In fact, depictions of street sex workers in both scholarly works and the media from the 1970s through today commonly portray them as runaways and homeless youth who are desperate for money and a place to stay, and often as abuse survivors.[19] The emergence of HIV provided the impetus for scholars to focus more specifically on gay- and bisexual-identified male sex workers; some researchers regarded them as "vector[s] for transmission of HIV infection into the heterosexual world."[20] However, recent studies suggest that gay-identified male sex workers who contract HIV do so through their risky behavior outside of sex work by engaging in casual sex and intravenous drug use.[21] Additionally, the literature on gay male sex workers makes connections between sex work and drug use, but also suggests that they began to use drugs before they entered sex work. Public health researchers have investigated the relationships between drug use and risky sexual behavior among gay men in order to provide policy and program recommendations that could help quell the spread of HIV/AIDS.[22]

Tropes such as the gay male sex worker also have their beginnings in beliefs about gay men as "sexually degraded predators," and the cast of characters is recognizable in historical analyses and in popular culture.

For example, gay men have been depicted as child molesters, prison rapists, sexual aggressors (particularly as it relates to queer people of color), promiscuous disease-spreaders, and more. Gay people's sexual practices have been reviled as dirty and degenerate.[23] Of course, such stereotypes also intersect with myths about Black men's hypersexuality, insatiable sexual appetites, and predatory natures[24] to construct damaging assumptions about gay Black men specifically. These concerns about gay men—even regarding participants' gay friends—have been seen throughout this book.

Unsurprisingly, then, sometimes the stereotypes discussed by participants captured intersectional concerns of race, gender, and sexual orientation. Max reported that he "can't" sell drugs because he feels like he'd "be falling into a stereotype." He went on: "You know how people talk about, like, 'Well, Black gay people,' a lot of people think that Black gay dudes always take credit cards, always take people's identity, they always sell coke or snort it, you know, it's just the things that people say, I feel like I'd be proving that right if I was to start doing things like that." He added that escorting is also a stereotyped activity of gay men, but he didn't know about the stereotype when he got involved in it. King describes these stereotypes and tensions more explicitly:

VP: So why is it so important for you to keep up this clean [legal] job?
KING: Yeah, being a Black male, because I'm already stereotyped, like if you a Black male, then you gonna be a [professional] basketball player, and I'm studying to become a nurse, I don't wanna be a basketball player, . . . or that you gonna be in jail, I'm not going to be a gangbanger, I mean, I guess you could call me a gangbanger, but I really don't know.
VP: So you don't want to be known as a gangbanger?
KING: I don't want to be known as a gangbanger, and I don't want to be known as a deadbeat dad, . . . I don't wanna be stereotyped, I'm already tired of being stereotyped as a Black man period, and then to add on being gay, talking about, "Gurrrl," [being flamboyant] and that you gonna contract HIV, and all that, and I don't want to conform to that stereotype, and I'm not gonna be that stereotype.
VP: How does the clean [legal] job fit into that?

KING: The clean job fits into that because I can be something other than what the gay stereotype is for the Black dude, like they not gonna do nothing, all they do is rap, bounce checks, they trick, they go out there and sell themselves, . . . and doing fraud, and I said, this is not a gay Black man, that has a stable mind, that's levelheaded, that don't do nothing, I mean, I do got the crazy friends, but they don't do that crazy lifestyle, and they be real family oriented, and just normal, you know, levelheaded, and normal. Now don't get me wrong, some of them are a little "Girl" [feminine-acting] but they not saying all that, they keep a good, clean, gay, normal life.

King does not restrict his comments to his identity as a Black gay man, as he speaks to negative stereotypes about Black men as criminals and even as "deadbeat dads," despite elsewhere suggesting that he has no interest in women sexually. Rashad, who escorts, said, "Y'all can say whatever about me, but I'm not out here sellin' drugs, I'm not out here robbing people, I'm not out here having kids with different girls, bein' a deadbeat dad." The negative cultural messages about Black men as absent fathers are simply so strong that my participants felt the need to repudiate them, even if they do not have any desire to engage in sexual behaviors that could result in pregnancy. These comments were variations on another intersectional theme: the stereotypes regarding Black men in general. Kevin said, "[I work so] I can't be categorized as a Black man who has no job, you know what I mean? I like being a Black man with a job, even though if it's flipping burgers, or if it's sitting in a office, I want to, I need to have a job." Because participants perceived the "deadbeat" to have been racialized in these ways, the threat of being seen as one is strong motivation to seek out work, even for Kevin, who earlier admitted that he "hates working."

This was not the only "deadbeat" stereotype that participants rejected; their narratives suggest that gay men, Black men, men from poor families, and gang members all risk being labeled as deadbeats for their lack of total concurrence with expectations of society's ruling class. Johnny explained, "With Black gay males, it's easy to get sidetracked with drugs, and stuff like that. You know, the typical Black male grows up, 9 times out of 10, in a rough area, and strugglin', and stuff like that, and that's what kinda get 'em sidetracked"—sidetracked, he clarified, from "being on their business" in ways that he viewed white gay men as being capable of. These intersectional concerns mirror those discussed elsewhere in this book, particularly as they relate to participants being respected as gay men trying to make ends meet within particular racial or socioeconomic communities. And of course, thinking about intersections in context, some statuses may be more or less salient in particular scenarios; the fact that participants look to construct respectable gay identities may sometimes come secondary to overarching concerns about being a productive and successful urban Black man. On the subject of being an adult man with no job, Rashad asked, "How can you be a gay man, or a man period, and not want more for yourself?"

Self-esteem and masculine status are derived from the ability to be a provider, but especially in legitimate ways. While participants' networks may provide opportunities for illicit profit, they did not want to capitalize on these opportunities precisely because of how they arise and how they are perceived by mainstream society. Participants are pulled in different directions by complicated expectations: succeeding economically, especially using the "honest" and not the "easy" way, but also by avoiding the "gay" way of making money. However, when earning clean money is not an option, and the only money to be had is "easy," these patterns of behavior remain present for participants to fall back into.

"You Gotta Do What You Gotta Do"

Unsurprisingly, to "make it happen," my participants suggested that often, "you gotta do what you gotta do." This phrase could communicate a willingness to engage in demeaning work, but it was typically code for engaging in illegal work. They preferred legal work, but sometimes issues such as their criminal records presented challenges to gainful employment. Money from illegal pursuits was described as "easy" and "dirty"; the opposite of the "clean" or "honest" money obtained from legitimate employment. Although my participants by and large expressed a preference for legal work, describing themselves in ways such as "a workin' type of dude," they articulated—and appreciated—the positive outcomes of hustling. However, illicit opportunities had to be conceptualized in such a way that they didn't seriously damage a man's claim to respectable gay masculinity.

Structural factors such as racism and changing employment land-scapes after industrial restructuring have resulted in many inner-city residents remaining chronically jobless.[25] In a striking example of how race and criminal records affect applicants' chances, sociologist Devah Pager found that employers were less likely to hire either white or Black applicants who possessed a criminal record compared to those who did not, but were equally as likely to hire a white applicant with a criminal record as a Black applicant without one.[26] Pager's findings suggest that criminal records have particularly strong and negative effects for Black applicants, and race remains a factor in hiring decisions.[27]

Over three-quarters of my participants had been arrested and over half had been incarcerated, and their criminal records or incarcerations affected their chances of being hired. Eric said, "Before I got arrested, it was so easy for me to find a job, and now it's like, really hard." Ali also said he was "lookin' for a job, but my background won't allow me to get one yet." His "background" consisted of a very recent misdemeanor charge for petty theft. And, although Brad's felony conviction for rob-bery didn't directly harm his job prospects because it was more than seven years in the past, the seven years in prison that he served for the offense left a gaping hole in his employment and reference history. Hur-ricane directly attributed his ongoing illicit involvement to his criminal record: "I sell weed, I sell (pause) I sell ass, I sell dick. (laughs) . . . I am all out there. Any way I can get it, I'm gon' get it. Because I have no other opportunities or chances that I can do it. I can't go out and just find a job. I have a felony record." Collateral consequences of felony convic-tions can entail the denial of public housing and/or assistance, college admittance, employment, and voting rights, along with dozens of other restrictions.[28]

The threat and impact of a criminal record was so overwhelming that these same participants refused to call the cops on romantic partners, even those who had done them serious harm. While we were at a house party, Eric described an extended altercation between him and his most recent ex-boyfriend, in which the boyfriend had kicked him in the head, knocking him unconscious. Eric did not call the police "just for the sim-ple fact of how my domestic violence conviction totally fucked up my life, I decided to be nice and not fuck up his." Ali relayed to me that despite the fact his boyfriend "all the way stabbed" him in his arm and caused him to get six staples, "That woulda been a felony! (laughing) That woulda messed him up, that's why I ain't [call the cops]." He lied to the emergency room and said he "got into a fight with random people." Ali's friends were within earshot of the interview, and interestingly, it was their insistence that they would have "called the police chief" which prompted him to offer his reasons for not prosecuting his ex. For a man to survive such actions and not seek official intervention likely speaks to other structural factors (such as a historically grounded distrust of police),[29] but also to the realization that criminal records have long-lasting and severely detrimental consequences. These consequences include chronic under- or unemployment, which can motivate men to pursue "easy money."

Easy Money

Describing illicit money as "easy," "fast," and "quick" perhaps does not capture the relative temporal lengths of the exchanges involved. Indeed, illegal transactions produce a fairly immediate source of cash, are much less time-structured than formal employment,[30] and nearly always yield more money per hour, even when measured in yearly "salaries."[31] An example from my study is illustrative. During fall 2011, Aga was employed by a dollar store, and was even able to pick up extra shifts with some regularity. These occasionally came up without warning; I once drove him to an extra shift immediately after an interview we conducted in his house on a day when he thought he was available all afternoon. He also received "food assistance," which he often shared with friends. I did not think to ask Aga how much he made at work, but it was likely $8 or less per hour, as the minimum wage in Ohio was $7.40 per hour at the time.[32] However, I did learn how much he typically charged for various sex acts. He reported being paid between $200 and $250 for the highest-paid sex act reported by almost every participant who had escorted, which was being penetrated anally. Thus, Aga would have to work at least 25 hours to equal the non-taxed, cash payment he could earn by engaging in one sex act, and the untraceable cash would not count against his public assistance. Although he reported at that time that he was no longer escorting, these vastly disparate totals suggest why participants might find illicit economic pursuits to be so attractive. Some participants reported receiving equal or higher sums for other sex acts and drug transactions, making the relative economic gain of illegal versus legal work vastly disproportionate in favor of illegal work.

Although masculine status can be derived from being financially independent, and status on the street can be derived from being a successful hustler, there was not much personal pride to be derived from these illicit exchanges. This is perhaps best illustrated by JD's comments, where he struggles with how to describe his involvement in escorting (selling sex): "Like, if I'm not working a nine-to-five, then [I'll escort]. (pause) And I don't, you know, I don't have any money in my pocket, then I, you know, I dress up [as a woman], it's time to make money [by selling sex]. I'm, like—It's—I don't—Whooo! I just feel like it's. (pause) It's a easy way of makin' money, you know? It might be wrong, but it's an easy way." JD's multiple false starts and pauses communicate his hesitation and conflicted feelings regarding sex work. Illegal work can be dangerous, but typically the men did not perceive it to be difficult. Selling drugs or sex provided "easy money," but was still to be avoided if possible. For example, Boog explained, "I don't want to go in too deep to what I used to do [by selling drugs], but you know, I still wiggle and do certain things to get money." Boog's "wiggling" was selling weed, but not "hard drugs." Ricky said he was "tryna get out of" escorting, while Greg exclaimed, "I try to leave that escortin' alone, as much as I can!"

Easy money carried additional, serious risks to those who engaged in these street games. For example, Oz said that when working at a job, he didn't have to worry about "getting hurt, catchin' anything." Although Oz was likely referring to "catching" a sexually transmitted infection, there were very real concerns of "catching" charges as a result of illegal street activity. When I asked if he considered the guys in his family of origin to be real men, Jeremy responded with: "No! They some hustlers! Don't nobody have no nine-to-five. They got money, don't get me wrong, they got they own place, but it's not an honest way of livin', it's not. I got some uncles that's in the business world, and yeah, I look up to them. But like, the drug game, and trappin' [selling drugs], no, I don't have time for that. . . . They got nice stuff, but it's not honest money, so. . . . They one-sided. Like, they do stupid shit, and then they go to jail, get out, and they go right back for the same shit." Even if drug selling provided status-generating money, possessions, and housing, it was logical to voice the negative outcomes associated with it, such as incarceration. Batman thought that when life goals included activities that carried serious risks of arrest, this was a problem:

> BATMAN: Yeah, [goals can define a man] if they're not like, outrageous goals, you know what I'm saying? They're like legit goals that will just help you live a healthy life, pretty much.
>
> VP: What would you consider an outrageous goal?
>
> BATMAN: Like, an outrageous goal? Like, trying to be the top drug dealer in the world, or some shit like that. You know, trying to make easy money. Like, you can't expect to keep on making easy money and not get caught for what you're doing, you know what I'm saying?

In his estimation, "outrageous goals" for easy money communicated a lack of seriousness about mature masculinity.

Illicit work can entail psychic risks as well, as described by Bird:

> I know that it's just easy money but that's not the route that I wanna take because it makes me feel disgusting as a person and I'm tired of feeling disgusting. I have no reason to feel disgust. Especially when you love yourself you shouldn't have to feel disgust. So, that's one thing you have to change and that's one thing I did so now if I don't have any money, I'll try to work for it in the good way or sell some of my stuff that I made or sell some of the stuff that I bought, or whatever as far as like, helping people. You know, moving things around the house and stuff like that. My mind doesn't think like that anymore as far as taking the easy way out, because it's the easy way out and it's dirty money, so I don't really think like that anymore cuz now I train my mind not to think that type of way so that would be the last option for me if I had to make money again. But if it comes to a desperate time or a desperate moment to do it, then yeah. . . . I never did it to buy drugs. But I did it so I can feed myself and take care of myself. I never got caught into it like that's the life to live. No, I just do it cuz it was easy cash, easy money. It's not like I can donate blood [because gay men are banned from doing so] or pawn my TV or do normal things. It's not like I can take a loan out or something like that. It's just easy cash.

Selling sex is perhaps unique in that it is one of the most personal hustles, as there is often (but not always) nudity and/or direct physical contact, and it may entail penetration of one's body. Although participants generally acknowledged that they could derive pleasure at least occasionally from such encounters, the majority were displeased with what they felt was "resorting" to selling sex. For example, Rashad said that selling sex is "not something I like to talk about"; Hurricane said "it degrades my life"; Dollars said it was "uncomfortable"; and Oz said it made him feel "nasty and trashy."

On this note, Darius explained that his escorting was "embarrassing" to him, and added, "I can change, and be on my reputation, but I ain't got no job, so it's like, I'm gonna be doin' this until somethin' betta comes along!" Because of its role in bringing him necessary money, Darius even seemed to suggest that his escorting was legal: "That's why I escort, wouldn't no job take me, so that's the other way, that's the loop around the job. It's like a job, but it's like, it's not a legal job. Well, it's legal, but you know what I'm sayin', it's like, not worth it." It should be noted that Darius and most other participants who escort treat their sex work as a "business," but Darius apparently has mentally transformed his illicit sex-for-money exchanges into legal work. M6 described "selling weed, selling dope" as "borderline illegal." These ideas about sex work and selling weed are likely linked to moral determinations that these crimes do not harm anyone, but also speak to a certain level of "professionalism" regarding crime not only as work, but as a *business* that must be treated as such to succeed. They also are arguably linked to efforts to destigmatize their activities, as sex workers and drug dealers both represent perceived threats to the moral order of society. Because study participants knew the negative perceptions of their behavior, they were apt to construct boundaries which communicated that their activities were somehow less harmful than those of other sex workers and drug sellers.

Indeed, the most disliked folk devil in the escorting world was the drug-addicted, streetwalking sex worker, as suggested by Bird's comments and the YouTube video that had Jordan, Steve, and Silas laughing hysterically; the most disliked folk devil in the drug-selling world was the "hard drug" (typically crack or heroin) seller, as suggested by Boog. The morality work undertaken by participants regarding these folk devils illustrates that they did not view all dirty/easy money as equally dirty.

Participants took solace in the fact that although they might earn dirty money every once in a while, it wasn't the *filthiest* money. That designation was reserved for hustles such as trading sex for drugs or selling hard drugs to people who were obviously addicted.

The "Good" Drug Dealer

The drug-pushing gang member is a cultural trope, an urban boogeyman in some ways. To avoid negative perceptions that hinge on drug dealing as an enactment of "thuggish" behavior, participants who sold drugs made efforts to construct images of themselves as the "good" drug dealer, or one who's not just out for the money and would prefer not to hurt people. Unsurprisingly, the mantra of the men in my study seemed to be that weed is not a drug and is not serious. As described above, some even initially denied they sold drugs on the basis of their fervent denial that weed qualified. Take, for example, Boog's response to whether he sold drugs: "Naw, I wouldn't sell drugs, you know, sometimes I might sell weed, yeah, okay, I do sell drugs." He added, "I won't sell no harsh drugs or nothing, nothing that I don't do, I ain't gonna try to promote." Jayden said, "I don't like seein' people on crack. I really don't. Now, weed is not bad at all . . . so that's why I sell it." Regarding marijuana, participants have told me that no one gets violent on weed, no one overdoses on it, rarely does someone get addicted to it, and above all, it's a plant that God made. Others made similar and imminently reasonable arguments about prescription pills: how is it bad to sell prescription drugs when they have legitimate medicinal uses? Drug sellers in other studies similarly resisted the "dealer" label, instead preferring to see themselves as "doing people right" or "doing a service" by selling drugs with therapeutic value.[33]

Overall, the self-identified dealers that I interviewed expressed a bias against so-called "hardcore drugs" such as heroin, cocaine, crack, and crystal meth, or "tina" as it's called on the street. However, for those who did not refrain from selling coke and tina, they mostly paid lip service to the dangerousness of these drugs. For example, Eric told me that crystal meth is the gay crack. Despite its perceived disparate negative impact on the gay community, Eric still sold crystal meth because, quite simply, it fetched a higher price than crack or weed, and Eric knew plenty of gay men who used it and were willing to buy it, including himself. When Juan was selling with his hybrid gang, they primarily targeted cocaine users in gay clubs, since "a lot of people that would buy coke are gay." Dollars also intentionally sold to the gay community, not just because he said "in the gay life, there's a lot of people who do coke" and thus he'd "be rich" if he was still selling it, but because he preferred to sell to gay people over straight people. He stated, "with gay people, you know how much their body can take when you sell." Juan also constructed himself as a "responsible" and "good" drug dealer, explaining how he avoided selling to people who were "addicted" or had an "addictive personality":

> If it's gonna hurt somebody, I won't do it, because I have told people I know that want to buy stuff from me, like coke for example, which I don't really sell coke anymore, but if I knew they . . . have an addictive personality, I just will be like, "I won't sell it to you, buy it from somebody else." So I'm not really a bad, I would say I'm like, a good drug dealer. Because I do care about people that I know, like my friends or somebody, I just won't sell to them or get them stuff, because sometimes they'll ask for something, and I'm just like, "I'm not gonna get you that," but if they're okay, if I've done it with them before and I see that they're okay with it, and they're not addicted, then I'll sell it to them, because I know that they wouldn't abuse it. . . . I wouldn't give somebody something that they'll get addicted to, and then I'd be responsible for it.

Additionally, Juan noted, coke in Ohio sucks, and he wasn't interested in selling a shitty product.

Silas also argued that he was a good drug dealer. Even though he had sold coke and mushrooms in the past and sold pills and weed at the time of the interview, he said that he was not and has never been a "hardcore drug dealer." He described a "hardcore drug dealer" as someone who sells crack, tina, or heroin, and who is "a big scary Black man." Remember that my sample is racially diverse, but about 90 percent non-white. Silas is a white, formerly gang-involved drug seller, who made sure to make the requisite "I'm not racist" caveat after that comment. Silas argued that hardcore drug dealers "don't care about you. They [wouldn't] give a fuck if you went out there and fucking shot up and died. They would not care, as long as they made their money off of you. And I'm not like that. . . . I wouldn't sell anything that I know would fucking kill somebody." He didn't sell coke to people he didn't know, but later acknowledged that it was not because he was afraid someone else would get hurt in the deal. He said, "Well no, it wasn't about them hurting themselves, I just didn't want to get caught. Especially with shrooms and coke, it's a lot worse than marijuana. Coke is actually prison time." Tellingly, when explaining why they wouldn't sell hard drugs, some participants gave the short answer of "time," a well-known reference to formal consequences. And indeed, the risk of "years in the county [jail]" is what deterred Dollars from continuing to sell coke and others such as Casper from taking the "risk," since hard drugs are "taken more seriously than marijuana." Importantly, such concerns kept some from selling drugs altogether; for example, even though Greg acknowledged that both escorting and drug selling entailed risks of being caught and incarcerated, going to prison for drugs would be for "who knows how long."

For others such as King and Boog, the resistance to selling "hard drugs" was directly related to their experience growing up in drug-ridden neighborhoods. Although they know there is money to be made, they argued that they did not want to contribute to the downfall of the neighborhood. Narratives of desistance, or cessation of offending, also play a role in these changing standards of decency.[34] A reduction in drug selling was related to one's own declining drug use; as participants tried to clean up their own acts, they did not feel right selling to others with serious drug problems. They provided descriptions of drug addicts to me that included terms such as "dirty," "bummy," "nasty," "run-down," "clothes lookin' demolished," "black eyes," and "strung out." Addicts will "fiend," "jones," and "geek" for a fix, and may harm or steal from others in their quest for drugs. Steve reflected on his past of selling "hard drugs." Although he did not feel bad about it at the time, looking back, he said he felt guilty about his actions:

> [I feel bad now because] it's killin' people, hurtin' people, messin' their lives up. Maybe they have kids at home, and I sold them a drug with their, maybe they gave me their kids' money to eat on that night, and now that I look back on that, there's been a few cases where I've traded drugs for food stamps. . . . I knew that there was probably a kid not going to be able to eat, because their parents are hooked on drugs. But back then, I really

didn't care, and I didn't really look at that picture. I looked at the picture as money in my pocket. But now I look back on it, like, that's kinda wrong. So maybe their kid's starving now, because I sold them drugs.

He specified that he now sells weed instead of cocaine, pills, or crystal meth, and doesn't see anything wrong with it, because he didn't think anyone could overdose on or be severely addicted to weed.

Bob's comments viscerally illustrated these concerns. He said his mom was "on crack" and his father had also been on drugs, but he chose not to sell them, though his brother did:

I could have done it [sold drugs], cuz my brother is into it, . . . but I thought about it and I said, I don't like people who sell that to my mother, because to me I just feel like [they] just want a quick dollar but they're not thinking about the outcome of it, or the consequences for the other person, which they really don't care because it's not them of course, but I don't wanna be selling to someone else, it's no telling how they get this money, they probably stealin' it from their kids, no tellin' what they're doing, so I said I don't wanna feel bad. . . . I been through it and I know how it is to have a parent that's on drugs, and it's not easy at all, so I don't wanna see no other peoples like that. . . . I don't like him [my brother] doing it either, cuz it's dangerous, it's very dangerous. Risky, and not only that, but it's traffic through the house, you know what I'm sayin', that's disrespectful to me. You don't bring that stuff into here. And there's other kids here and altercations have broke out in our house, and shootins and stuff like that.

Bob illustrates the ways families can be hurt by drug use, including spending money on drugs instead of food or other needs, and the increased chaos and risk of violence in their homes. Some of the literature on gang members' drug sales describes sellers who have rules against certain sales, such as to those pregnant women, kids, or in exchange for food stamps,[35] whereas other sources suggest no such rules exist among gang members.[36]

The narratives presented here suggest that participants do not view drug sales as a victimless crime, in that someone is likely hurt from these transactions. Thus, the identity work that must be done when selling drugs focuses on how the seller can minimize risks to others in order to be the "good" drug dealer. This stands in stark contrast to sex work, which participants did conceptualize as a victimless crime, and in which their focus was more likely on how to reduce risks to their own health/safety and to maintain boundaries not only between themselves and their clients, but between themselves and other, less respectable sex workers.

Escorting: A "High Class" Hustle

Regarding participants' identity work via their involvement in sex work, "escorts" are able to make appointments and earn more for their services than street sex workers and thus have greater control over their work.[37] Working independently, without pimps or brothels, the "owner-operated" nature of the market allows for upward mobility in addition to increased control.[38] The advent of the Internet has introduced new opportunities for control over sex work, as both escort service websites and personal websites exist for sex workers to advertise and only respond to clients of their choosing, instead of whomever walks or drives by, as is the case with street prostitution (though, street sex workers are also able to exercise decision-making in selecting clients).

The use of the Internet and the autonomy it brings was evidenced in the ways that members of gay gangs used it dexterously, while members of straight gangs used it to ensure greater confidentiality. Internet escorts can make appointments that they deem to be financially acceptable and safe, and can choose not to attend an appointment if they are worried about getting arrested or hurt. They also emphasize being "professional" and treating the work as an occupation.[39] There were "tricks of the trade" involved in creating Internet ads, usually learned from others. Ricky said: "Normally I don't come up with the stuff [for the online ads], I have someone else, like my PR, you know, to take care of that kind of stuff. . . . It's just, coming up with the ads and stuff, I can't do that part. It's like, if I come up wit it, they flag me [for removal]. So, I let someone else who's been in the game longer than I have come up with a name." Max described how he attempted to post his own pictures in his ads, but that his friends stopped him from doing so. Not only did it increase the risk of getting caught, but in the event that he wanted to cancel the date, the client would know what he looked like. He said he was "taught" such strategies, which also included not drinking when on dates to avoid spiked beverages. Participants also agreed that the client should make the first contact, and ads should never mention prices, but instead include words such as "generous" and specific substitutes for "money" such as "roses." The guidelines changed depending on what site they were using; e.g., they might post slightly different ads to Black Gay Chat, Craigslist, Backpage, and Facebook.

The preferred demographic to sell sex to was white men over 30, because participants claimed that these men had more money, they were easy to "get over" on, and they were less likely to haggle or stray from the plan. Casper also suggested that he was taught to look for cues that a would-be client was "the police." Some men even expressed the belief that asking a date if he was a police officer would give them protection from prosecution (as if it would allow an entrapment defense were the date to actually be a policeman).

Most participants reported a mix of Internet and street sex work; only one had sold sex exclusively on the street, while several said they would "never walk the street." Of those who had done both, only ATL preferred street sex sales to the Internet (being a "street ho" instead of an "Internet ho"), because he thought he had a lower chance of being seen by his boyfriend or people he knew if he was on the street, instead of posting his picture online. However, this is informed by the fact that he was a very recent transplant to Columbus, and thus did not know many people in the area. Everyone else who had been involved in both forms (as well as those who had never solicited on the street) preferred escorting via the Internet. In general, this was related to having more control over client selection and the transaction, being able to earn more money, increased perceived safety, and issues related to better self-perception. Specifically, selling sex on the street entailed lower status.

Participants often articulated a conceptual difference between the two forms. Only several saw no difference. JD said that selling sex on the streets or over the Internet was "being a ho," while Oz declared that having sex for money was prostituting, whether it was on the streets, in a car, or at a hotel, and he preferred to call his sex sales "hustling." Greg reasoned that he didn't want to sell sex on the streets because he didn't want to be seen by people who knew him, but that ultimately it was all the same: "It don't matter if you're online, [or] on the street, you have the same mentality: please a man to get money." Other than these few exceptions, escorting was more highly regarded than "prostituting," which was done on the streets, according to participants. These were also identity categories, but fluid in that participants saw themselves as prostitutes when they were doing what prostitutes do, and escorts when they were acting as such. For example, when Steve and Dollars sold sex on the streets, they called it prostituting, but called their other sex work tricking and escorting (respectively).

These shifts also could happen chronologically. Silas said he started selling sex by walking the streets to gain clients, but then became an escort by changing his strategy: "I was a professional, I guess, if you could call it a professional. I was an escort, not a prostitute. I was a prostitute at first, and then I became an escort where I would make appointments with people, and I would go to their house, or to their hotel [to sell sexual services]." He also added that escorts make more than $10–20, which is what he claimed street sex workers made. When I asked a question to confirm that "prostitutes" walked the streets and got into cars, he corrected me again using his own terminology: "That's a hustler." Hustlers, he said, "will do anything, for any amount of money. And they're usually on major drugs, like heroin and other intravenous drugs. Escorts, from what I've seen, and learned, they usually aren't on needles, and they have values on what they will and will not do." When I asked if he knew any hustlers, he said, "Not now. I used to know one, and he was pretty nasty, pretty dirty, and he was always on the street, and he never made any money, because he'd let somebody fuck him for five bucks, and I'm not gonna let anybody fuck me for under 200 bucks, seriously. So escorting, you're gonna make more money, you can be able to get ahead a lot more faster than hustling. Hustling you're making five bucks. You can't buy a Happy Meal for five bucks." Important to note is that Silas was one of two participants who admitted to engaging in unprotected sex for money, but did so after negotiation and getting his price met.[40] Silas was the only one in the sample to use the word "hustler" to refer to the unselective streetwalking sex worker, and his usage was conceptually similar to "prostitute." Regardless of the term, it was perceived that streetwalking sex workers drove down the price for escorts.

As with Silas's comments, the appraisals of prostitutes versus escorts were often strongly worded and richly descriptive, the former categorization hinging on low prices, indiscriminate client selection, drug use/addiction, HIV-positive serostatus, and/or unprotected sex. Mini explained:

> I think escorts is more high class than prostitutes. And, a prostitute walks the street. Regardless if it's snowin', rainin', hot, cold outside. Most of them do crack, just like, hard drugs, hardcore drugs, stuff other than weed, they have sex wit anybody and have unprotected sex with anybody, they get in anybody's car. (pause) It's a real difference between a prostitute and an escort, because an escort, you get to see that person, you get to know that person or whatever, and it's just more high class than a prostitute. . . . Probably some [escorts] walk around, but most of 'em be at hotels, or out of town, in a hotel, somewhere really nice! So, it's a big difference to me. . . . When I see a prostitute, I'm like, oh my God, that's a ho! Like, that's a nasty ho. But when I see an escort, I'm just like, well, she just tryna make her money safely.

Mini's descriptions of high class, high life, and high safety essentially romanticize the Internet escort, but also acknowledge the control over the work that being inside and traveling (or not) to an appointment provides. Rashad also expounded on this:

> I'd rather escort and do it behind closed doors, as in, over Internet. I meet you at your hotel room than actually stand out on a corner the whole night, or a street, a block, a radius, for 10 and 20 dollars. It's like. (pause) No. It's dangerous. . . . They [street sex workers] walk up to whoever pulls up! On the computer, it's kinda the same, but it's more money involved. I'm not getting in your car for 20 dollars, and we're goin' around the corner, and you're doin' all this to me, and we're doin' it raw [no condom], and no! No! (laughs) Not for 20 dollars! Like, this is your life at the end of the day!

Regarding Rashad's claim that it's "kinda the same" in that it's unclear who is on the other end of the computer screen, this risk was referred to by participants as "the Craigslist killer." They were referring to the man alleged to have murdered and robbed women he met via erotic services ads on the site in April 2009. On this note of risk, Casper suggested that on the streets, "Anyone can pick you up, and take you to anywhere they wanna go, and harm you in any type of way." When they did walk the streets, strategies to stay safe included not allowing a client to drive them across town in his car, not taking the client to their own home, and not giving the client any of their personal information.

These status and safety concerns were recurrent themes, which communicated "standards," professionalism, and self-respect. Ali said that the term "escort" not only "sounds more professional," but that escorting was preferable for a number of reasons:

> It's more professional, so people that are on the Internet and stuff probably have a lil bit more money than somebody goin' and tryin' to pick up a prostitute on the street. . . . I think an escort's probably more open to different things, like, I don't think a prostitute's havin' too many dates come and want just like, a massage. A prostitute is off the street. But, somebody who works online, they might just have somebody that wants to just come take them out to eat, wine and dine them, and get paid for it.

With these comments, Ali suggests that clients of escorts are also interested in discretion, have selective tastes, and have the money to pay for them. Escorting allowed for more "high class" opportunities, including erotic services like massages. A participant in another research study on the stigma associated with gay male sex workers astutely asserted, "Nobody's ever gonna make a fag *Pretty Woman.*"[41] Although that speaker was not talking about real-life possibilities, my participants were convinced that no gorgeous rich man was going to pick up a street-walking male sex worker and change his life for the better. If anything, the street was more expedient, but cheaper as a result. Of the streets in Columbus, Aga claimed, "The cheap girls be out there, and they take it down to 10 dollars, 12 dollars, 5 dollars. Whatever, not me! That's why I had to stop. You're not makin' no money out there."

Ricky also said that he preferred to use the Internet, and the only time he'd sold sex on the streets was when he lived nearby the stroll "where most gay people go and whore." Accordingly, he said that "seeing me on the street made me feel like a real whore." When I asked him why, he replied,

Cuz I'm walking up and down the street in a pair of six inch pumps, talkin' 'bout some "Hey, baybee," and bending over for cars, and shaking, you know, trying to shake my socks in my bra, to make it seem like I had real tits, and they would really pull over. So, I felt like a real prostitute in Las Vegas, just in Columbus, Ohio. . . . If you really think about it, when you're on the street, that's not escorting. That's prostituting. Escorting is when you really have to sit down, and, "Well, how about we try this. You give me 175 and we can do this and this," or, "We can do 150, and we can just do this and that." That way I'm in control. On the street, I'm not in control, because they can pull a gun out on me anytime. I've had a gun pulled on me before. Escorting is not as scary as it is prostituting.

Again, elements of professionalism such as negotiation arise, as well as safety concerns. The prostitute was coded not only as streetwalking, drug-using, cheap, and HIV-positive, but as a woman (cisgender or transgender) or at least presenting as one. Some of them said this explicitly, in connection with those other claims. Casper said, "I just feel like prostitution is like a downgrade or a low name, like, (pause) a prostitute is a woman that walks the streets. . . . Mostly the walk-the-streets [method] is for women and transvestites, you know? Transsexuals and stuff." Indeed, participants knew the exact cross streets of the "tranny stroll" or the "beat," which could in fact suggest far more about the nature of niche markets than about the proportion of streetwalking versus Internet-using female and transgender sex workers. To this effect, participants and their friends had used the Internet to arrange dates while presenting as female, but the folk devil remained.

Almost all who had sold sex or erotic services also told me about making money from clients without having to sell sex. Typically, they also called this "escorting" since it was part of the "business," but some called it "clean escorting," or "tipping." Clean escorting included conversation, such as via text or on the phone; in-person company, such as going out to dinner or to a family reunion; spending the night in the same bed but not having sex; being taken on shopping trips; and acts that are sexualized for clients, but not necessarily sex acts as they are legally defined, ranging from massages to fetishes (like watersports, adult baby play, and bondage). Participants also told me about times where they were able to collect their money without going through with a planned sex act, either by saying they didn't feel well and/or had to leave, otherwise deceiving the client, or demanding partial payment when the client tried to change the arrangement. Such money was not exactly clean money, and still sometimes carried feelings of disgust (particularly the fetish-related money), but could be legal money and thus less risky. Although being able to "clean escort" instead of engaging in oral or anal sex was preferable to participants, clean escorting could be combined with sex acts to produce additional cash, at their discretion.

Participants' linguistic and psychological boundary maintenance techniques were designed to retain self-respect, even if symbolic, since even most of the Internet escorts reported feeling "nasty" or "dirty" for selling sexual activity for money. The use of the term "escort" itself is designed to avoid much of the stigma associated with prostitution and especially street sex work. In this meaning system, a man can engage in sex acts because he is desperate for money, but he cannot *behave* like he is desperate for money by engaging in certain stigmatized behaviors, such as trading sex for drugs or low sums of money. To do so would suggest that he is out of control, a decidedly unmasculine trait.

How to Make It Happen

Using similar narrative techniques as they have when speaking about other topics, participants made conceptual distinctions between money generated from illicit and licit pursuits, but ultimately agreed that economic self-sufficiency was necessary to stake a claim to full manhood. They were displeased to be involved in stereotypically "gay" illicit activities, and wanted to defy negative stereotypes of both gay and Black men and what they "do." However, participants also derived status from achieving financial goals by engaging in those illicit pursuits. In this way, some men were able to defy one stereotype (that of the gay and/or Black deadbeat) with easy money, but simultaneously "fell into" other stereotypes, such as being a drug seller or an escort. They wanted to stake claims to respectable gay identity by illustrating how they sold drugs or sex in ways that were ethical, smart, and professional. In doing so, they continued to construct who they are, or hope to be: "real" men.

There are several possible interpretations of these findings. One focuses purely on boundary maintenance, in which participants aim to create social distance between themselves and others by demarcating lines of acceptability. Urban ethnographer Elijah Anderson argues, "By successfully singling out people who 'fail,' the person making the charges may be better able to cover his own shortcomings and to see himself as upholding certain standards of conduct."[42] Another interpretation is that, despite obstacles, making money means that participants ultimately do subvert negative stereotypes about themselves. Indeed, the reality of the men's experience probably involves a combination of the two: resisting social and economic marginalization through achieving financial independence, while simultaneously needing to clarify how their illicit sales prove their adaptability and resilience, instead of weakness.

Conclusion

Queer, Here and Now

"Did you hear about this?"

Several emails in March 2015 from friends and colleagues let me know that a new documentary was being produced, which focused on "how three bullied DC teens started the only documented all-gay or transgender gang in America."[1] Although subsequent news stories were much less definitive about it being the "only," there's obviously a reason that this documentary and gang, both called "Check It," garnered much attention in popular media: the belief that it was indeed the only queer gang in America. I'm sure people thought, let's be real, how could it not be? However, while my book is proof that Check It is far from the "only" gay gang, notably, its members' experiences are quite similar to those of my participants. Law enforcement definitions marked Check It as a gang, though they called themselves a family; its members wanted to have a reputation in D.C.; they weren't organized around geographic space; and they engaged in retaliatory violence if their members were affronted, which sometimes insulated them from further victimization and anti-gay harassment.[2]

My initial reaction to this documentary was that I felt a bit scooped, but still, I was pleased to see that these dynamics and experiences seem to be similar among gay gangs in other urban areas. Although qualitative research is often critiqued for its low generalizability, the existence of other gay gangs with strikingly similar challenges and behaviors helps assure me that I'm not telling a story of unique happenings in my hometown. It's not something exotic that I stumbled upon. It's something more structural, spurred by gay marginalization that is replicated wherever queer people are ostracized and excluded. Spoiler alert: it could be anywhere.

In fact, recently I received an email from another friend saying he has met members of an all-gay gang in the Southern city he now calls home, and more often I'm hearing from scholars who have met LGBTQ members of gangs. I'm happy to be "known" as the gay gangs scholar. I fully believe this is important work that is both about gangs and not, but always about being gay.

I set out to complete this book with several goals, one of which was to challenge existing heterosexist assumptions in criminology, beginning with questions as basic as who can be a gang member, and how crime, violence, and gang membership produce avenues through which to construct gay identity. Similarly, my analyses have focused primarily on the impact of the social contexts of masculine and gay identities in shaping the gang and crime experiences of urban young gay men. Throughout, I have examined a complex meaning system whose boundaries are proclaimed and enforced, but also are simultaneously blurred and challenged. Although some boundaries *seemed* impermeable, they often were not. Much of this book discussed participants' identity formation, disclosure, and performance, which are interactional processes set within a context of pervasive societal heterosexism and misogyny. A common theme was participants' efforts to construct a respectable gay identity by balancing negative opinions of stereotypically gay or feminine behavior with an appropriate time, place, or situation to explore gender fluidity and being out. Occasions where these balancing acts were particularly salient tended to be times spent with their families and around their peers, whether they were in gay, straight, or hybrid gangs.

Participants' narratives illustrated ways that they fended off negative portrayals of themselves as either folk devils or men of stereotypically disparaged status: the fag, the thug, the gangbanger, the drug dealer, the prostitute, the deadbeat. However, even when participants thought they embodied these characters, these statuses were typically not seen as master statuses; furthermore, participants' presentations and negotiations of identity were highly socially situated and dependent on context. Take for instance, the example of fagging out, or acting in aggressive and flamboyant ways simultaneously. Often when a participant was called a fag it was an attempt to patrol and insult feminine gender presentation, and "fagging out" was a strategy that reconceptualized the insult by first *claiming it* and then *inverting it*, or in the words of one participant, "showing what this faggot can do."

It is tempting to say that these analyses center on identity negotiation that is primarily related to concealment. There are many examples of this. In their young lives, it was "cover-ups" in the form of unwanted girlfriends; in straight gangs, it was controlling information about their sexual identity and the obfuscation of their male partners; in public, it might be vigilance against engaging in any mannerisms that might expose their gay identity; and regarding their illicit employment, it was being discreet about sales of drugs or sex. However, it is a far more complex issue than that, as participants also detailed how they found same-sex sexual partners in the criminal underworld while remaining closeted to their gangs, most were out to their families and/or friends, and even in gay gangs where they were able to be out and experienced less rigid standards of gender presentation, they still were held to certain standards of loyalty, toughness, and being in control. Just as important were the ways they negotiated identity by actively constructing gay and masculine identities: joining gay crews and attempting to become known, fighting back against homophobic harassment, and resisting harmful stereotypes of gay men. Complex and contested, participants' meanings illustrate the nuanced challenges facing urban gay men who are involved in gangs and crime, but more generally exemplify pressing concerns for many young queer people intent on constructing respectable identities.

Pursuits in Criminological Realness

A related goal of this book was to show how much can be gained, both empirically and theoretically, when issues of sexual orientation and gender presentation are made salient. I have situated this book primarily within criminology, focusing on topics such as gang membership, violence, and crime as work. But to claim that criminology has all of the tools to accurately contextualize and analyze these young men's lives would be inaccurate. Rather, integrating diverse disciplinary perspectives into criminological analyses is necessary to add richness, and similarly, criminological research can aid in various interdisciplinary projects. In terms of gay identity formation, for example, criminology has virtually nothing to offer us, but queer studies similarly has had little theorizing on gangs and interpersonal violence outside of situating gender and sexual nonconformity as motivation for conflicts. Disciplinary boundaries are of course useful in that they help us determine appropriate scopes for our scholarship, but to be able to do intersectional and nuanced work, we must look beyond single-discipline explanations.

My remarks are also explicitly in reference to the exclusion of LGBTQ people from mainstream criminological consideration. Queer criminology is gaining ground,[3] though still is seen by many as a niche or fringe topic. At several points in this book, I reference the notion of "realness," or convincingly exuding a particular persona. In my estimation, criminologists themselves have been involved in a realness project: determining which populations' actions truly fall within our disciplinary boundaries, and therefore who/what we think our audience will approve of as appropriate subjects of study. Virtually none of the articles published in our discipline's flagship journals have LGBTQ people or heterosexist social forces as foci.[4] This work is thought to fit better elsewhere: within another social science that has a longer history of queer work, in an LGBTQ-focused specialty journal, or in some other place, however vaguely defined. For many, it may seem like it's happening anywhere but here.

Blanket exclusions such as these will ultimately slow the advancement of our field. Queer liberation as a social movement has progressed rapidly since the turn of the century, resulting in a cultural shift where marriage equality is the law of the land, household names include those of openly queer people, and the political activity of millennials (who hold fewer homophobic ideals than any other generation) is overwhelmingly visible. So I ask: are we as criminologists sure who our audience is or what they're interested in? Especially considering the increasing diversity of our field, exclusionary tactics based on dated assumptions or on criminology's status quo seem ill-advised.

Within criminology and criminal justice, there is also the issue of how to extrapolate information for prevention and intervention purposes, but we must first try to unearth the mechanisms at play. The situation with gay gang members is no different, and although they may have similarities to other populations better covered in the literature, our discipline alone hardly has the tools to make sense of their experiences. I am reminded of an etiological issue raised in the gang literature about girls. Studies find that some girls join gangs for protection, just as boys do, but protection from what? Protection means something very different in a context of neighborhood volatility versus a history of experiencing familial physical or sexual abuse, or even the interaction of the two. Similarly, gay men's claims of joining gangs for belonging fall well within the "typical" reasons that young people join gangs, but may hold particular meaning in light of misogynistic and heterosexist expectations imposed on young men who exhibit gender atypicality and/or identify as gay. Indeed, its significance can hold true for men joining either a straight gang or a gay gang depending on other elements underlying their motivation: a straight gang would provide a way to construct a stereotypical masculine identity for outside observers, whereas a gay gang not only provides a gay support system, but also serves as a buffer for them to explore gender fluidity and still exhibit some markers of traditional masculinity. With just a bit of assistance from other disciplines regarding a set of theoretical tools, we can make meaningful sense of LGBTQ people's motivations and techniques in the gang or crime contexts.

On the subject of realness, I return to an issue I have lamented elsewhere: repeated questions about whether or not my participants are "real" gang members and/or members of "real gangs." I admit to being exasperated about this line of questioning, for I am often defensive about what I interpret it to be: an assumption that queer people have fundamentally different capacities, interests, and values than heterosexual people. I often liken this to a challenge of their agency, where LGBTQ people are perceived to have little choice or power in interpersonal interactions. I hear my inner voice shouting, "Of course they can be gang members! What kind of question is that?" Though, being neither a queer assimilationist nor a queer apologist, I am hesitant to claim, "We're just like you," because—if this book is any indication—we're not, at least not in some significant ways. However, I am also very sensitive to claims that exposing gay men's gang membership, violence, drug/sex sales, and so forth gives fuel to the anti-equality movement's fire. Still I insist, here as I have elsewhere,[5] that discussing queer people as capable of the full range of human behavior is the only appropriate model for moving forward. Despite this, as I near the end of this book, I must ask myself one final time, as even my manuscript reviewers have: are these groups, especially the gay gangs, real gangs?

I shudder when it occurs to me: perhaps they are not. Maybe in the context of urban young gay men, a gang is the closest cultural referent for a group that provides social activities as well as illicit economic opportunities. Indeed, even as participants stated that their all-gay groups fit the definition of gangs as they understood it in their social worlds and would claim this identity were there to be intergroup conflict, they also expressed hesitancy regarding what being a member of a "real gang" meant for their identity. The gay gangs also fit with reigning criminological definitions of gangs, and even with law enforcement definitions. But their characteristics that have to do with shared sexual identity and gay culture gave participants pause. For example, in my first interview of the study, when I asked Kevin if he was in a gang, he answered, "If you see a [vogue] house as a gang, then yeah. But, other than that, no, not as I go shoot people and rob people for fun, no." These perceived characteristics of "real gangs," such as engaging in serious violent crime, were discussed earlier, and when asked, Kevin stated that not everyone in his vogue house commits crime, and it's not part of their group's regular activities. In this way, Kevin's vogue house is not a gang as they are traditionally defined, and he is included here as one of the non-gang members of the study, but why the ambiguity for him? Probably for one of the same reasons that people find gay gangs incredible: they straddle a conceptual boundary between youth street gangs and friendship networks who just happen to engage in crime and intergroup conflict as a result of their claims to turf and status around town.

Acknowledging the tenuous boundaries between gay gangs and gay friendship networks is also centrally related to queer criminology and the issue of LGBTQ invisibility in criminology and criminal justice. To call them gangs is to engage in some amount of othering and stigmatization of already-vulnerable populations, when members are arguably engaging in theft and prostitution as survival strategies, as evidenced by the fact that some started selling sex and stealing daily necessities in their teens. Sociologist David Brotherton argues that we must move beyond pathologizing and stigmatizing discourses about gangs and gang members if we ever hope to understand and accurately represent their experiences, lives, and meanings.[6] Indeed, I do not seek to demonize these young men, but rather to highlight the ways that they respond to marginalization, inequality, and victimization—what Brotherton might deem "bringing resistance back in" to gang research.[7]

It is hard to let go of the nagging issue of gay-gangs-as-real-gangs. I wonder about what it means for the gay gangs to call themselves gangs and not something else. In a different generation, or perhaps among people from different racial/ethnic or class backgrounds, a group whose members fight back against anti-gay harassment, use underground economies to meet their needs, and share a common meaning system might call themselves a radical political group, not a gang. Is being in a "gang" actually my participants' means of contributing to a social movement in the ways they know how? Or take the recent political activity of young people of color that responds to institutionalized violence, partially through public (though typically non-violent) resistance. If I had spoken to these young men in gay gangs after the growth and expansion of the Black Lives Matter movement, would they instead categorize themselves as part of a similar movement? These gangs and friendships networks emerged when they did for a reason. There must be something about the moment in time in which I spoke to them, which was far enough along in history for them to be visible and vocal, but perhaps not far enough along for them to have other recognizable modes of resistance they could draw from to make sense of their experiences.

I find it most fascinating that scholars engaged in queer criminological research—some who identify as LGBTQ, and some who do not—have also challenged me on this issue of whether the gay gangs are real gangs. I suppose it is not just a matter of the political implications and issues of representation that I have alluded to above, but of fundamentally upholding heteronormativity by framing these young gay men's experiences within an existing scholarly framework, instead of conceptualizing it in a new way. Ultimately, the question is whether we do our participants and our data a disservice. Are we comparing apples to oranges, or, at the very least, decontextualizing our participants' experiences by using normative and dominant theoretical frames or analytic lenses to make sense of what is happening? Based on my interviews and fieldwork, it does seem that the gay gangs have essentially "settled" on the idea that their groups are gangs, mainly because that is the closest available cultural referent for their chosen families who also engage in crime and violence together. However, this example provides a careful lesson in using existing frameworks to make sense of queer people's lives and experiences, when these frameworks have almost completely ignored those same lives and experiences.

For these reasons, I encourage scholars engaging in research with LGBTQ populations to seek out participants' indigenous meanings about their identities, attitudes, groups, and behaviors. Only secondarily should attempts be made to reconcile key concepts or meanings with a dominant and/or normative framework, though this is likely necessary if one wishes to have a definable audience and scholarly outlets for this work. I argue that, much like my participants' fluid boundaries around acceptable behavior for gay males, the boundaries of the discipline and its theoretical frameworks should become more flexible by allowing for the recognition that gay identity is an important contextual influence.

In case it has not become clear by now, I feel emboldened by these young men's determination to be included and regarded with respect. They face countless obstacles, but are able to "make it happen" daily: they form community, create their own paths, and carve out respectable lives. They're not running away from their marginalization. Undoubtedly, they are resisting racist, classist, and heterosexist forces that exclude and devalue them. These gay lives are legitimate, and these authentic voices need to be heard.

APPENDIX

Summary of Participant Characteristics and Experiences

Pseudonym	Age	Race	Gang type(s)	Ever fought back?	Job status	Ever sold sex?	Ever sold drugs?
Adidas	19	Black	Straight	No	Unemployed	No	No
Aga	22	Black	Gay	No	Employed legally	Yes	Yes
Ali	22	Black	Gay	Yes	Unemployed	Yes	No
ATL	22	Black	Gay	Yes	Unemployed	Yes	No
Baby	22	Black	Gay	No	Employed legally	Yes	No
Batman	19	Black	Hybrid	Yes	Unemployed	No	Yes
Bird	23	Black/Latino	None	Yes	Employed off the books	Yes	No
Bob	20	Black	Gay	No	Employed legally	No	No
Boog	27	Black	Straight	No	Unemployed	Yes	Yes
Boss	20	Black	Gay	No	Employed legally	No	Yes
Brad	28	White	Straight	Yes	Unemployed	No	Yes
Brandon	18	Black	Straight/Hybrid	Yes	Employed legally	No	Yes
Brian	25	White	Straight	Yes	Unemployed	Yes	Yes
Casper	21	Black	Gay	Yes	Employed legally	Yes	Yes
D.C.	18	Black	Straight	No	Employed legally	No	No
Darius	19	Black	Straight	Yes	Unemployed	Yes	Yes
Derrick	18	Black	Gay	Yes	Unemployed	Yes	No
DJ	20	Black	Straight	No	Unemployed	No	Yes
Dollars	22	Black	Straight	Yes	Employed legally	Yes	Yes
Elijah	18	Black	Straight/Gay	Yes	Employed off the books	No	No
Eric	24	Black/White	None	No	Unemployed	Yes	Yes
Greg	19	Black	Straight/Hybrid	Yes	Unemployed	Yes	No

Pseudonym	Age	Race	Gang type(s)	Ever fought back?	Job status	Ever sold sex?	Ever sold drugs?
Hurricane	23	Black	Gay	Yes	Unemployed/SSI	Yes	Yes
Imani	21	Black	Gay	Yes	Unemployed	Yes	Yes
James	28	Black	Straight	No	Unemployed	No	Yes
Javier	24	Black	Gay	No	Employed legally	No	No
Jayden	19	Black/White	Straight	Yes	Unemployed	No	Yes
JD	21	Black	Gay	Yes	Unemployed	Yes	Yes
Jeremiah	27	Black	Gay	Yes	Employed legally	Yes	No
Jeremy	22	Black	Gay	Yes	Unemployed	No	Yes
Joe	18	Black	Straight	Yes	Employed legally	No	Yes
Johnny	21	Black	Gay	Yes	Unemployed	Yes	Yes
Jordan	21	Black	None	Yes	Unemployed	No	Yes
Josh	18	Black	Gay	Yes	Unemployed	No	No
Juan	21	Latino	Hybrid	No	Employed legally	Yes	Yes
Kevin	21	Black	None	Yes	Unemployed	Yes	Yes
King	21	Black	Gay	Yes	Employed legally	Yes	Yes
M6	25	White	Straight	No	Employed legally	Yes	Yes
Marcus	19	Black/White	Hybrid	Yes	Employed off the books	No	Yes
Max	22	Black	Gay	Yes	Employed legally	Yes	No
Mini	18	Black	Hybrid	Yes	Unemployed	Yes	No
Nate	20	Black/White	Gay	Yes	Unemployed	No	No
Oz	18	Black	Gay	No	Unemployed	Yes	Yes
Raphael	19	Black	Straight	Yes	Employed legally	No	No
Rashad	23	Black	Gay	Yes	Employed legally	Yes	No
Reese	26	White	Gay	Yes	Employed legally	No	No
Ricky	24	Black	Gay	Yes	Unemployed	Yes	No
Rocc	21	Black	Straight	No	Employed legally	No	Yes
Silas	27	White	Gay	Yes	Unemployed/SSI	Yes	Yes
Spiderman	23	Black	Straight	Yes	Unemployed/SSI	Yes	Yes
Steve	25	White	None	Yes	Employed legally	Yes	Yes
Toby	19	Black	Straight	No	Unemployed	No	No
Tony	20	Black	Gay	Yes	Employed legally	Yes	No

METHODS APPENDIX

"Best of Luck in Your Research, Dear"

I began this research in late 2009, with an original goal of 20 participants. Although I had some leads, I really had no idea how long it would take me to complete the study and if I could even make it to 20. I made a contingency plan with my graduate school advisors about what to do if I couldn't reach my sampling goal. I wanted to make it happen, so I used many strategies to try to attract participants. Most people were shocked when I was able to interview 48 gang-involved participants and 53 men overall. They often ask me how I was able to do this. How did I find gay gang members? What did I do to gather such revealing data? How did our differences play out during data collection? In answering these questions, I am able to explore some of the misgivings about gay gang members, responding to which was one of the guiding forces of my study.

RECRUITMENT AND SAMPLE

I primarily recruited participants by utilizing a snowball sampling design—a method commonly used to access underground populations—in which willing participants refer additional participants to the researcher.[1] I obtained the initial group of eligible participants by contacting men previously known to me when I lived in Columbus and volunteered for and used the services of several LGBTQ organizations. I reconnected with the men on social media, or used phone numbers or email addresses I already had for them. My social ties in Columbus, as well as previous gang research conducted there to build from, made it an ideal study site. It also didn't hurt that I could stay with family and friends whenever I visited.

I also asked non-eligible (queer, but not gang/crime-involved) individuals who told me they had connections to eligible participants to speak to their friends on my behalf in the same manner that I asked eligible participants to refer friends. I placed flyers in several LGBTQ community centers and gathering places, and spoke to folks at those organizations to encourage referrals. I even utilized social networking websites (both MySpace and Facebook were popular at the time) to view user profiles and then contact men whose profiles suggested gang membership or involvement in criminal activity. All of these strategies, with the exception of the flyers, produced eligible participants who completed an interview.

There were some hiccups in my recruitment process. Early on, I attempted to seek referrals for participants from youth violence prevention groups in central Ohio, but I was told by an affiliate of one coalition that some members of Columbus's youth anti-violence task forces were "pretty homophobic" and would not respond positively to my referral requests for gay gang members. Additionally, she expressed concern that acting as a bridge between me and the coalition could put her own professional reputation at risk. Another member of the coalition relayed to me, "Many of the youth violence prevention folks are pretty conservative, in every sense of the word." Among those organizations, a request for help gaining access to gang members would have been deemed much more reasonable than my request, which was geared toward gay men involved in similar activities. This was discouraging, but clearly didn't stop me. Although other gang researchers have found eligible participants by "hanging around" an area and gaining rapport with the gangs and gang members who occupy that space,[2] that would have been difficult for this study. Indeed, many of the members of straight gangs were not out to their gangs, and the gay gangs were not organized by geography.

Other hiccups were more laughable, but still captured the issues I was facing with my project being taken seriously. At the end of 2009, I posted an ad for my study to the "Queer Forum" on the Columbus Craigslist webpage, in case that might drum up interest of any kind. It couldn't hurt, I figured. One person questioned why I hadn't posted my IRB approval number, implying my study was illegitimate, but didn't have anything constructive to offer me after I posted it. What better way to ring in the new year on January 1, 2010, than with an email from Craigslist Forums telling me I had a reply to my post from someone else:

Vanessa darlin', save your pennies and watch TV shows such as the cable channels TruTV, History and others. Trust me, you will get enough stories from guys in the age group you mentioned on these shows. These jail/prison reality shows, including America's Most Wanted, Gangland, COPS, Bait Car and many others already have these young jail/prison inmates revealing so many of the details of their gang associations, sex, hustling, assault including their lives in jail and prison and other information you have expressed in your query. Not only that Vanessa, trust me, many of their stories are explicit, raunchy and hot. You will throw down your writing tablet and wallow in the sheer wanton masculine natural tales spoken by these guys. You could also use your money and simply pick up DVD copies of the HBO tv series OZ. You can't get any more real than that semi-fictionalized tv show. Vanessa, today's street gang members will most likely listen to your $15.00 offer for an interview and simply give you a smile. The gang members in the hood today will demand a lot more green just to sit down at your table for 1 to 3 hours. Best of luck in your research, dear.

I should have known better than to get worked up by an Internet troll, but this post had me so irritated. It effectively crystallized the issues I saw with existing representations of gay gang- and crime-involved men: that they are dramatized and sensationalized. I didn't want to conduct a voyeuristic study of people and their behaviors that are "explicit, raunchy and hot," but rather gain a better understanding of marginalized young men's social worlds and identity negotiation. The reply was also oozing with condescension, assuming that the only reason "gang members in the hood" would participate in research was for my money, and implying my paltry graduate school offering wouldn't do the trick. I suppose what got me so worked up was the fact that the comments made in that post mirrored many of the ones I had heard in my daily life that questioned my study's success. I was more determined than ever. Thank you, Internet troll.

Back on the subject of methods that worked, the varied strategies I used to recruit participants allowed me to tap into different friendship networks and gangs in order to interview a diverse group of participants. They were current or former members of 38 different gangs, spanning three types of gangs (gay, straight, and hybrid). The gay friendship networks were also diverse: participants referred members of not only different gangs, but of rival gangs, as well. The networks were also interconnected: Darius was officially referred to the study by Baby, even though he had moved to Columbus very recently in light of dating Johnny. Ali, ATL, Ricky, and Spiderman were all living together at the time of their interviews. And several participants were in gangs together previously, before their most recent gang affiliation. Because the men would refer close friends or boyfriends to the study, I also sometimes ended up in the middle of a falling-out, a breakup, or a reconciliation.

The chain of referrals also meant that I was more likely to spend time with the key players in my sample recruitment, who included Silas, Imani, Oz, Spiderman, and Elijah. Their social positioning was reflected in their referrals. For example, all of the white men in the study can somehow be traced back to Silas, who is white, and only one of the five non-gang participants (Eric) was able to refer a gang-involved participant. And Elijah, though he belonged to a gay gang at the time of his interview, only referred members of straight or hybrid gangs to the study, as he had formerly been a member of a straight gang. The chain also illustrates how well-connected people like Imani and Oz are, as evidenced by the wide variety of men they were able to refer: 11 and 13 participants, respectively. Most of Imani's referrals were to other members of gay gangs, while Oz's referrals were evenly split between members of gay and of straight/hybrid gangs. While there are respondent-driven sampling methods that reduce the extent to which the original referring party dictates the entire sample, such as allowing only three referrals from each participant,[3] the restrictive nature of my sample criteria precluded those methods. This is another reason that I focused on starting from an initial sample of several men, from various points of contact, instead of just one.

It took dozens of requests for interviews or referrals to generate the first 15 or so participants. Recruitment picked up substantially in October 2011 after I interviewed Imani, and even more so in November 2011, after I interviewed Oz. I began interviews in November 2009 and fieldwork in March 2010, and continued with both until January 2012.[4]

I was living in Albany, New York, when I collected the data, so I would travel to Columbus every 6–12 weeks to conduct interviews and fieldwork. This meant that I sometimes had multi-month dry spells, but I just kept at it.

In getting participants to agree to be interviewed, I did encounter some of the issues that others thought I might. Before and even during periods of recruitment success, some potential interviewees were leery of speaking to an outsider about their criminal activity, even when a friend of theirs vouched for me. They cited reasons such as fear of gang retaliation due to being "outed" as gay or appearing disloyal by discussing gang business with non-affiliated individuals, thus also risking being shunned or physically harmed by their gangs. There was also concern that I was a police officer, which I return to shortly; some men were too busy or disinterested to participate; and others thought they did not fit the eligibility criteria. I found instances of this last point to be especially compelling. My fieldwork allowed me to meet far more than 53 eligible participants, but some of them insisted they were not eligible; this was because of how they conceptualized their criminal activity. For example, although I was present when the friend of a participant answered a call from an unhappy customer seeking to rectify an unfair prescription drug deal, he insisted he was not a drug seller; rather, he was a "haggler," a "negotiator," and someone who "does favors" for friends. While I would like to have interviewed him, he declined because he did not self-report involvement in any criminal activity or identify as a member of a gang. There were two other instances where, after explaining the study goals, I completed the screening questions with seemingly interested interviewees who then denied gang membership or criminal activity; thus, they were not interviewed either.

Despite these challenges, I obtained a sample of 53 gay gang- and crime-involved men of varying ages, ethnicities, and other pertinent characteristics. Table MA.1 presents information regarding the sample characteristics. In terms of demographics such as age, my sample is fairly similar to other ethnographic samples of gang members,[5] but due to my sampling strategy, may overrepresent men who are out and are willing to seek services.

TABLE MA.1. Demographics of Sample (n = 53)*

Mean age (Range: 18–28)	21.5
RACE/ETHNICITY AND MIGRATION	
Black/African American	77%
White	11%
Latino	2%
Biracial	9%
Born in a country/state other than Ohio	42%
Parents are immigrants	9%
Immigrated to U.S. with parents	4%
EMPLOYMENT STATUS	
Employed (legally or off the books)	45%
Unemployed	49%
Receiving SSI benefits (also unemployed)	6%
EDUCATION	
High school diploma/GED or some college	75%
In high school at time of interview	17%
Not enrolled; did not earn HS diploma or GED	8%
FATHERED CHILDREN	19%
HIV STATUS	
HIV-positive	11%
HIV-negative	87%
Unsure	2%
HISTORY OF CRIMINAL JUSTICE SYSTEM CONTACT	
Arrested	77%
Incarcerated (Range: 2 days–8 years)	55%
Foster care (Range: 3 months–13 years)	28%
GANG MEMBERSHIP	91%
Gang involved at time of interview: mean age	21.4
Gang joining: mean age	16.2
Mean length of time in gang, in years	4.0

*There were no meaningful distinctions between the full sample and the gang subsample.

Specifically, whether or not they are out to their gangs or families, my sample is comprised of men who are out to some degree, because they either associate with other gay men who were able to refer them to the study, or they have used services directed at the gay community, such as the Columbus drop-in youth center. As further illustration of this point, 52 of the 53 men in my study (or 98 percent) had been tested for HIV and knew whether they were HIV-positive or HIV-negative at the time of the interview. A recent Centers for Disease Control and Prevention study found that only 37 percent of men who have sex with men (MSM) ages 18 to 29 who were infected with HIV were aware of their HIV status.[6] The fact that so many participants knew their status also suggests a willingness to seek services. In these ways, I may not have reached the most marginalized men who fit my eligibility criteria. Indeed, there are likely many urban young gay men who are disconnected from services and are not out, and I hope this book also moves our conversation forward about those young men's lives.

INTERVIEWS

Keeping in mind that I wanted to gather rich data with a woefully understudied population, I chose to conduct in-depth interviews, which allow participants to speak for themselves without having artificial concepts or categories imposed on them.[7] I asked a series of screening questions to confirm eligibility before beginning each interview. Non-heterosexual identity and either gang membership or involvement in criminal activity, determined through self-nomination, made a man[8] eligible to participate.[9] I also opted to interview men 18 and older, partially for reasons related to protecting the privacy of minors, but also in recognition of identity formation processes: young adults are arguably better able to articulate identity formation over time.[10]

Interviews focused on participants' life histories, relationships, gay/bisexual and masculine identities, and experiences with gangs, crime, violence, and the criminal or juvenile justice systems. The interview instrument is unique to this study, but includes questions used in prior research that have been adapted or borrowed verbatim.[11] I also drew inspiration from my own lived experience as a queer person and the many conversations I have had over the years with other self-identified LGBTQ individuals about their lives.

I sought to keep the interview as close to a conversation as possible and tried to let the men structure their narratives in ways that made sense to them. My knowledge of gay culture, gang/criminal justice system argot, and Columbus's landmarks served me well, and helped me to explore meaningful concepts or experiences in my participants' lives as queer people. For example, I am aware that the "coming out" process—and the resultant "coming out" narrative—plays an important role in the construction of gay identity. Accordingly, I asked a number of follow-up questions to draw out these narratives, and to indicate I understood the importance of this process. As mentioned in the preface, shared knowledge and language helps to build rapport and provide a baseline understanding of concepts.[12] Participants were sometimes surprised when I used a slang term correctly, but were ultimately delighted with my appreciable mastery of gay slang and my willingness to learn new terms.

The men I spoke to chose to be interviewed in such locations as their homes, a private meeting room at a public library, a park, and my car. They were paid $15 for the interview and reimbursed for gas, bus, or parking expenses if they had to travel to the interview location, but usually I traveled to them.[13] Interviews lasted between 45 minutes and two hours and 45 minutes, but most were between one and two hours. They were audio recorded with consent, and were then transcribed. Virtually all transcriptions were done by me because interviews contained a substantial amount of gang/crime terminology, gay slang, central Ohio streets/schools/landmarks, and references to other participants (using numerous names to refer to each unique person), which proved difficult for an outside transcriber to accurately capture.[14]

I did not want anyone to face any negative repercussions for speaking to me, so I obtained a Certificate of Confidentiality from the National Institute of Health, a waiver of signed informed consent from my IRB, and utilized pseudonyms for participants' names, gang names, and others in their lives. The men came up with these code names, but the names sometimes had to be changed later when I realized they were too close to real names. At the start of the interview, I also gave interviewees a list of referrals for various LGBTQ-centered services, including counseling, suicide prevention, alcohol/drug treatment, and HIV/STD testing. Several men were very pleased to receive that list, as they suggested they needed these services.

Although interviews were one-on-one, many of them took place with the referring party or other participants, friends, or family members within earshot of the interview or in an adjoining room. Sometimes this was out of necessity, such as with the six interviews that took place in my car during the winter, because we could not find a suitable indoor location. Other times, it was simply because of the layout of the residence in which I was interviewing, or because people would come and go from it as they pleased. This was usually beyond my and the participant's control, especially when I interviewed them in locations other than their own homes. There were also a few occasions where they were very willing to let their friends listen so that these individuals could hear the questions and decide whether they wanted to complete their own interview. When I was not able to secure a quiet, private, low-traffic place, I was careful to let each participant know that we could reschedule for a time when no one else would hear us; no participant took this option. They sometimes suggested their friends "knew everything" anyway.

Interestingly, these exchanges with onlookers sometimes produced deeper data, as those folks who were listening helped to elaborate concepts without my prompting, fill in forgotten details, or challenge their friends' statements in ways I often would not.[15] I acknowledge that there may have been some performance happening, where they wanted to present themselves in a certain way in front of their friends. Although these interview environments may have prevented some participants from being fully honest, there were times when they revealed information that (audibly) surprised the other individuals present, which suggests candor. Revelations included the use of illicit drugs, selling sex, or opinions about hot-button political topics like gay marriage and abortion.

Because I had little guidance about gay gang members from the literature before beginning my study, I wanted to retain some inductivity in my data collection process. That is, I wanted to let themes emerge and be able to pursue these emergent themes whenever possible.[16] Interviews were transcribed and initially coded on an ongoing basis, which was concurrent with data collection. I used a basic word processing program (Microsoft Word) to code the data. As themes began to emerge, I needed additional information to best make sense of some themes. I created theoretical memos, or write-ups of my ideas about my codes,[17] that reflected my current thinking about the concepts. The memos also included ideas for how to gather the additional information that I thought would help flesh out the concepts. I then returned to the field with these ideas in mind to delve deeper into those themes during subsequent interviews and fieldwork. Sometimes I was able to go back and ask a participant about something he had mentioned during his interview that I wanted to understand better; in other cases, I could only collect additional information during subsequent interviews with new participants. Near the end of each interview, I also asked if there was a question I should have asked; I routinely began asking some of these "left out" questions of subsequent interviewees. I also tried to explore emergent themes in fieldwork, which I was often able to do.

FIELDWORK

In addition to conducting interviews, I also spent additional time[18] with just over half of my participants to better understand their lives. Conducting fieldwork allowed me to see how they interacted with friends, family, significant others, and, in some cases, their clients (people they sold drugs or sex to). I was able to witness firsthand how they constructed masculinity, and also to gain insight regarding their interview responses, or descriptions of their interactions with others. Not all participants opted to give me their phone number or email address, so I never spoke to some of them after the interview (since we were initially connected by a referral). Of those who did, I would call, text, or email periodically for updates on their health, living situation, or relationship status, but also to invite them to hang out or to follow up with them on referrals for new participants.

Due to the consistent contact, I temporarily became a character, even if peripheral, in some of my participants' lives. For example, almost one year after King was interviewed, he made sure to tell me that he was going to appear on an early-morning Columbus news segment. He was proud of his transition from "gangbanger" to upstanding citizen, as evidenced by his good works with a competitive youth sports team at his neighborhood recreation center. Three months after I interviewed Eric, we were still on such good terms that I attended his 25th birthday party, which was a relatively small gathering of friends. Once, after having gone about six weeks without hearing from me, Silas texted me and jokingly asked if I was "alive" and "still gay." As of mid-2013, I was still in semi-regular contact with several participants; as recent as late 2015, participants occasionally called or texted me to chat. Mentions, pictures, or videos of me have made appearances on participants' Twitter pages and Facebook walls, though these were all participant-initiated as I was too concerned with their confidentiality to initiate any public, online posts. Technology is rapidly becoming a useful method to recruit participants, stay in contact, and gather richer data.

There is much to do in Columbus, and accordingly, my fieldwork took me all over. There were many places the men liked to go, including pool halls, shopping malls, metropolitan parks, recreation centers, and bars. Perhaps most pertinent to my study, there were no less than 10 gay and lesbian clubs/bars to frequent, most of which were located in the Short North or in the arena/downtown districts in about a three-mile radius. These areas are recognized for their density of gay-owned establishments, some that sell goods and services, others that sell food and drink. Furthermore, several places in those districts were not specifically queer clubs, but had at least one night per week aimed at LGBTQ patrons. There was also the large Pride parade and festival, though many other festivals provided entertainment and places to socialize. Other popular festivals include the Community Festival, the Jazz and Rib Fest, Festival Latino, and the "Red, White, and Boom!" Fourth of July fireworks display. All of these occurred over the summer in one or more of the metro parks. These festivals, in addition to the gay clubs, provided spaces where groups of people could meet, but also develop rivalries or actually physically fight. Such instances became prominent moments in the collective memory and mythologies of the men in this study.

Unsurprisingly, and as I have discussed throughout the book, participants and I hung out and did typical things that young adults do, such as going on many social outings. We did "gay stuff" like frequenting several gay bars/clubs and other events that catered to queer people, such as the Columbus Pride Festival, but also bowling, parties, and even a visit to the Columbus Zoo. Very few of my participants had a car, so I always offered to drive and was usually asked to do so. I was also occasionally texted and asked simply to drive a participant somewhere, such as to get a haircut, pay a cell phone bill, or visit a boyfriend. If I was in town, I usually obliged. It was also common for me to drive participants somewhere after their interview, such as school or work. Once, on my way to a participant's home, I was even asked to pick up a bag of potatoes for him, as he said he "had a crock pot going." Perhaps the most exciting use of my car was when I took several participants to the vogue ball described in chapter 2.

A car was totally necessary in my fieldwork, and it is a good thing to have in Columbus. The city occupies over 220 square miles. Although it has an extensive bus system, some well-traveled routes still have busses that only run every 30–45 minutes, and there aren't any trains or light rails. My participants lived all over Columbus except for the far north and northwest sections, which are some of the safest and financially prosperous areas of the city. This is not to say that all lived in the most depressed urban areas at the time of the interview, but the vast majority had lived in high-poverty areas for at least a short period of their lives. Several moved every few months, sometimes completely across town, which further underscored the cross-neighborhood mobility of many participants. Summing up a residential history similar to those of a few other participants, Nate said, "I moved all over Columbus. I been on the North Side, the East Side, the South Side, I'm back on the West Side." The largest concentration of participants lived in eastern parts of the city. A recent study ranked Columbus as the 22nd most segregated city in the United States. Its Black/white dissimilarity score in 2010 was 59.9; a dissimilarity index score of 60.0 or above is considered very high segregation, as the index of dissimilarity measures the evenness with which two groups are distributed across a city.[19] The neighborhoods where these men lived generally mapped onto the neighborhoods identified by demographers as high-minority areas.

There was a stunning diversity of living conditions, from modern condominium apartment communities on the outskirts of town that they had saved up for and needed roommates to afford, to free-standing houses with broken doors, black streaks on the walls, and water that dribbled out of the faucets in a thin stream. One apartment where four of my participants lived had no furniture in the living room, several large holes in the walls, and was home to at least one maggot-looking bug that crawled on my leg during an interview, but they kept the lights and heat on, the fridge fully stocked, and it was the favorite hangout of all of their friends. A favorite, of course, except for the thriving gay club scene.

HERE'S "WHITE GIRL"

Another common question I get was how I negotiated being different from my participants in many noticeable ways. Although we were in the same general age category and occasionally were of the same race, often the only thing we had in common was our shared experience of growing up gay, which did indeed serve me well. Some participants specifically told me that they wouldn't have spoken to me were I not gay, and/or if my study goals did not include improving the lives of young LGBTQ people. They wanted their voices to be heard, without straight people misinterpreting their words or assigning their own meanings.[20] This truly helped us get on the same page about the study, but I would be remiss if I did not consider how my social location affected the rapport I developed and thus the data I was able to collect. Explorations of power, privilege, and positionality in research, as well as a commitment to social progress, are fully consistent with the ethics of feminist and queer research methods.[21] I strongly identify with these traditions.

Perhaps the most obvious and universal difference between me and the men in my study was my status as a woman. However, this undoubtedly interacted with my race and (perceived) class status to structure some of the ways participants interacted with me, and vice versa. They were sometimes nervous that their language would offend me when they discussed sexual behavior, used expletives, or used the word "nigga." For example, they would use expressions such as "Excuse me" or "Pardon my French" when they employed such language; some remarked that they didn't know if it was "allowed" or "okay." I always encouraged them to speak freely. When they were clearly hesitant and choosing their words carefully, my next question would be something extremely direct and would include words like "fuck" to communicate that any words they'd like to use were acceptable. Almost always they would follow suit, sometimes expressing relief I had used expletives first, which suggested that it was the cue they were looking for. Darius said, "Okay, now I can just talk like myself." I presume that their feelings of decorum arose not only from an interest in being polite and chivalrous, but may also reflect a cultural history of Black men being accused of sexual impropriety with white women to provide false justifications for brutality against them.[22] Indeed, participants were initially hesitant to be sexually explicit even when it was necessary to explain their involvement in sex work, but would freely discuss the "gory" details of their involvement in other crimes, as well as their own extensive victimization.

Despite being careful not to offend me with expletives, they did not hesitate to express misogynistic sentiments, such as Raphael saying that "current females" (women in this day and age) are selfish in relationships, and "just want their back rubbed, or their feet rubbed, or they want somethin' to eat." In contrast, he said, men were willing to perform those duties for their male partners. In one of his comments about "real men," Boog said, "You [a man] should be able to take it, we're tougher than women." And when Jeremy discussed how "a lotta gay people around me irritates me," he mentioned that "gay boys" are "worse than females." Participants usually didn't try to explain these comments away, though they did offer qualifiers: Raphael made sure to say it was "some" females who act that way, and Boog made a point to say that although women were weaker than men, they were "better than men" because women can "keep everything in a straight line."

One common challenge for women conducting research with male participants (and perhaps vice versa) is the potential for sexual advances and, in some cases, disturbing and pervasive sexual or gender harassment.[23] The fact that I am a gay woman who was interviewing gay men effectively neutralized those concerns. Even though some of the men in my study identified as bisexual and were actively sexually involved with women and with men, I never felt any sexual tension with participants. My sense is that, based on my own butchy gender presentation and queer study goals, they had no expectation that any sort of physical relationship would follow from my research endeavors. Despite this, it was still jarring whenever they called me attractive or complimented my appearance or personal style. I always accepted these comments graciously, but did wonder sometimes if the remarks were totally benign.

Although my biological sex differed from theirs, because my gender presentation is more traditionally masculine than many other women, participants often accepted me as "one of the guys." As was mentioned above, after some initial hesitation, they stopped censoring themselves around me, often before the interview was even halfway completed.

Sometimes, their comments suggested that they had temporarily forgotten I had grown up female, such as one man asking if I remembered certain things about the ways little boys would behave in the boys' bathroom.

Participants' increased rapport with me allowed them to speak candidly about their life experiences, which often included graphic depictions of their illegal activities, sexual behavior, or negative life experiences. During fieldwork especially, they would encourage me to share details of my personal life, such as who I was seeing romantically. Sometimes, due to my desensitization toward sexually explicit language, I found myself engaging in what amounted to misogynistic talk about women's bodies or their sexual prowess (instead of their personalities) that I would not have engaged in with other acquaintances. It is curious that these men largely were not objectifying women in their talk, but because the conversation shifted to me and my life, women became the ones who were objectified. As a feminist and social activist for women's and queer people's equality, I wasn't terribly proud of those moments, but did at least feel like I was engaging in some level of reciprocity with participants. If only for a moment, I understood the patriarchal bargain faced by the gang girls studied by criminologist Jody Miller: they could become "one of the guys," but perhaps at the expense of other girls, and only if they eschewed traditional feminine norms.[24] Regardless, the men in my study appreciated that I was candid with them and shared information about myself.

For the vast majority of my participants, my whiteness contrasted with their own racial or ethnic identity. It was another undeniable, physical reminder of our differences and my privilege. I sometimes heard them refer to me as "white girl," and understandably so, as I was the only one in their lives that I knew of. One time, when I returned Spiderman's call, he happened to be with another participant, Ricky, whom he wanted to pass the phone to. I heard Spiderman say, "It's Vanessa." There was a pause, followed by Spiderman whispering quietly, "White girl." It was then that Ricky picked up the phone, said hello, and told me about his new job. Only one time did I get testy about the way I was discussed: I overheard someone (not a participant) refer to me as "that white bitch" when coordinating rides, and I interjected into the conversation to say, "Yes, this white bitch is driving him." He laughed, put his arm around me, and apologized, which is far more than I anticipated or even wanted;

I was very accustomed to hearing "bitch" used, to the point where I actually started using it as well even after years of not doing so. It was just something about the combination, three words to describe me as other, that irritated me.

However, I truly was the "other," and there was no reason in the field to try to conceal or downplay things that were unavoidably present (like my female body or my whiteness), so instead I always tried to foster a space where they knew I welcomed their viewpoints and, if they wanted, could ask questions about my experience. I did my best to be receptive any time participants wanted to talk through dynamics of power with me. Sometimes their comments were fairly pointed, like talking about things I was doing that I wasn't being punished for that they supposed they might be. For example, Imani joked that the only reason a "car full of Negroes" didn't get stopped by police while speeding or doing illegal U-turns was because the driver was a white girl. Another time, Hurricane ad-libbed a conversation that he imagined taking place were a police officer to determine that I had THC in my system from being around marijuana smokers, exclaiming, "They [Black men] blew the smoke in your face, didn't they?!"

At one point, I actually did come into contact with police when I was lost on my way to an interview, but did not end up having any trouble because of it. Even though I had pulled over and parked illegally next to a vacant lot in a high-drug and -crime area while driving a car with out-of-state plates, the police officer who approached my window was courteous to me when I expressed that I was lost (read: knew I shouldn't be there) and just needed to get out my GPS (read: and am leaving right away). Escaping this suspicious scenario without even handing over my license stood in stark contrast to the ways participants described their interactions with police.

On this subject of police, some men suspected I was a police officer. I sometimes got advice on how to minimize participants' suspicions while in the field. Les, a transgender man who helped reintroduce me to Batman and Imani and explain to them why I needed their help with the study, gave me some fashion advice before my first outing to the hip hop night at a gay club (the same gay club that was a staging ground for violence). What follows is an excerpt from a text message conversation on June 24, 2010:

LES: What're you wearing tonite? Cuz if u get me n trouble I will b
  pissed

VP: Haha, whatever! Prob what I wore to Pride . . . Blue plaid shirt
  with khaki shorts. I am already gonna look a little dorky, so, who
  cares!

LES: Lmao omg[25] not the shorts. What else do you hav?

VP: Too preppy huh? What about a blue tshirt and plaid shorts? Or the
  blue plaid and dark pants? I can do pants no problem.

LES: Yeah plaid shorts would b awesome and whateva kind of shirt.

He later told me that people might think I was a cop if I continued to
wear khakis, so I never again wore them to an interview or to an outing
with participants. I am not quite sure what the connection was between
police and khaki shorts, but perhaps my intended audience associated
khakis with white men, whom they also associated with police.

On the subject of cross-racial perceptions, white participants sometimes communicated derogatory sentiments about people of color. Even
though in my fieldwork I saw them date and maintain close friendships
with people of diverse racial and ethnic backgrounds, some of their
comments suggested less than full acceptance. For example, Silas freely
admitted that he was scared of "large Black men"; I also heard several
white participants use the word "nigger" (which made me extremely
uncomfortable) or talk about someone or something who was "ghetto."
However, many participants of color were also ready to indict "ghetto"
people, ghetto gay people especially. That is, for all participants, someone who was "ghetto" engaged in a series of poor behaviors, but was not
necessarily a person of color. Though I became desensitized enough to
use "fag" and "bitch," I never used "nigga" with any participants, not
even to repeat verbatim something they said.

Although I made attempts at reciprocity and prioritized participants'
meanings, I was sometimes reminded of our relative positions in the
study. During the interview, several participants asked if they were "allowed" or if it was "okay" to do certain things, such as cuss, "get vulgar,"
answer the phone, or go to the bathroom. I felt uncomfortable giving
them directives when they had given up their time to talk to me (especially in their own homes), but because they were looking for reas-
surance, I always gave it. However, it was times like these where I was

acutely aware that participants might see the interviews as something I exclusively controlled. After all, I was the one with the agenda, digital recorder, paperwork, and cash.

This possession of cash meant that I was perceived to always have extra money. Sometimes, between interviews, referrals, and food/cigarettes, participants saw me handing out upward of $100 over the course of the day. They sometimes expected me to pay for things, which was fine, or would ask me for very small loans, which I had to carefully consider each time and make a decision based on the circumstances. I did mention several times during the course of my fieldwork that I had picked up a second job solely to pay for study expenses (which was fully true), but regardless, I still had more money than many of them did.

However, participants did give me or buy me items occasionally. They have bought me drinks when we have gone to bars/clubs, had me over for dinner, and Silas's boyfriend even gave me an early-model smart phone that he didn't use anymore because he thought I needed to make the shift to having Internet on-the-go. I ended up giving it back to him at a later date without using it, but greatly appreciated the gesture. I think many participants were unclear about what sort of resources I actually had, if my parents were putting me through school, and so on, because they would occasionally ask; alternately, they would be careful not to offend me if they did not know. This sort of occurrence didn't happen often, but one time, Max said, "Everybody doesn't have the life where, not sayin' this is you, but you know, there's a lotta people where your parents were stable enough to help you through school, to where they just paid for school." Regardless, participants respected the fact that I was furthering my education, and hoped they too would be able to do the same.

I admit that after all was said and done, I too was a bit surprised that I was able to attain a decently sized and diverse sample while living far away, and similarly being "far" from these men on some critical dimensions. But in fact, many participants were eager to share their experiences and opinions, and contrary to what the Craigslist poster assumed, a sizable number told me that they would have done the interview for free. On the subject of their outlook on and experiences of being gay in this world, they said they had been waiting to be asked. I know this for sure: we need to continue asking.

NOTES

INTRODUCTION

1 To protect confidentiality, all names provided here are pseudonyms.
2 I use this term primarily as an adjective to reference LGBTQ identity, but also very intentionally to communicate the word's contested history, association with people or acts outside of the mainstream, and possibilities for resistance. See Butler 1993; Brontsema 2004.
3 Ingraham 1994.
4 Collier 1998; Messerschmidt 1993.
5 E.g., Katz 1988; Miller 1998.
6 Panfil and Peterson 2015.
7 Decker, Bynum, and Weisel 1998; Wilson and Baker 2010.
8 Miller 1958.
9 Bérubé 2001, 246–247.
10 See Panfil 2014a for more detail regarding these arguments.
11 E.g., Hagedorn 1998; Totten 2000.
12 Drawing from Miller 2001, and Peterson, Miller, and Esbensen 2001.
13 Blumer 1969; Goffman 1959.
14 Goffman 1963; West and Zimmerman 1987.
15 Collins 2004.
16 Connell 2005; Connell and Messerschmidt 2005.
17 Often referred to as "localized hegemonic masculinity"; Majors and Billson 1993.
18 Anderson 1999.
19 Cobbina, Miller, and Brunson 2008, 687.
20 Bourgois 1995; Messerschmidt 1993.
21 Miller 2002.
22 Mahalik et al. 2003, 3.
23 Trebay 2000a.
24 Lewin 2009.
25 Crichlow 2004.
26 Cooper 2013.
27 Grindstaff 2006.
28 E.g., Comstock 1991; Herek and Berrill 1992; Island and Letellier 1991; Renzetti 1992.
29 E.g., Herek et al. 1997. See Panfil 2014a.

30 See Dunn 2012 for information on gay men's desires to fight back (physically or by receiving services to recover) and to resist further victimization.

31 Kosciw et al. 2010; Grossman et al. 2009.

32 E.g., Bontempo and D'Augelli 2002; Espelage et al. 2008. Also see Panfil 2014b.

33 Button, O'Connell, and Gealt 2012; Kann et al. 2011; Russell, Franz, and Driscoll 2001.

34 Panfil 2014a.

35 Miller 2002.

36 Totten 2000.

37 Johnson 2007. Bisexual gang-involved young women, as reported in Totten 2012, also engaged in gay-bashing incidents.

38 Though see Pettiway 1996 for in-depth narratives of five African American transgender women who detail their experiences growing up gay, transitioning to living as women, selling sex, using drugs, and resisting their marginalization.

39 E.g., Panfil 2014c; Woods 2014.

40 Queer Nation 1990.

41 See, for example: Ball 2016; Ball, Buist, and Woods 2014; Buist and Lenning 2016; Dwyer, Ball, and Crofts 2016; Peterson and Panfil 2014.

42 Best 2011, 910.

43 Snow and Anderson 1987, 1348.

44 McAdams 1993, 12.

45 Presser 2008.

46 Maruna 2001.

47 Aronson 1992.

48 Scott and Lyman 1968, 46.

49 Mills 1940.

50 Bandura et al. 1996.

51 Snow and Anderson 1987.

52 Copes, Hochstetler, and Williams 2008.

53 Jacinto et al. 2008.

54 Lamont and Molnár 2002.

55 Although some men told me during their interviews that they occasionally date or have sex with women and would identify as bisexual, they were still eligible to be interviewed, regardless of whether they identified as gay, bisexual, or as some other term that suggested sexual minority status. For parsimony moving forward, I refer to my participants as "gay" men, but understand the arguments against collapsing the fluidity of sexual identification into tidy categories for researchers' or readers' convenience (see, for example, Ball 2014; Woods 2014). However, collapsing "gay or bisexual" into simply "gay" was even done by participants: the bisexual participants reflexively referred to themselves as gay at least sometimes, and often they spoke of "gay men," "gay culture," "acting gay," etc. in ways that referred to the same-sex nature of those constructs. That is, they meant to mark themselves as something other than heterosexual.

56 I was inspired by questions in preexisting instruments that sought to measure gang sex composition, or the ratio of females to males in the gang. See, e.g., Esbensen 2003.

57 Occasionally, participants would list and discuss every member of his gang and his/her sexual orientation, so the percentages for smaller gangs are likely more accurate than others. I discuss other complications in estimating gang sexual orientation composition in chapter 5.

58 It is important to note that some descriptions of modern gangs describe them as "hybrid gangs" due to their mixed racial or ethnic makeup, their members' participation in multiple gangs or co-offending with rival gangs, and their unclear rules, symbols, or colors (Starbuck, Howell, and Lindquist 2001; though see Bolden 2014). I am not measuring those features in this book. Throughout, when I use the term "hybrid gangs," I am referring specifically to a gang with a mixed sexual orientation makeup, where heterosexuals are in the majority but GLB people make up one-quarter to nearly one-half of its members.

59 Richards 2014.

60 Hoewischer 2011, 48.

61 Resnick 2007.

62 CNN 2005.

63 Equality Ohio 2012.

64 GLSEN 2011.

65 National Gang Center 2009.

66 Spergel and Curry 1990.

67 Huff 1989.

68 Hallett 2011.

69 10TV News 2011.

70 Huff 1989; Miller 2001.

71 Panfil 2015.

72 Weerman et al. 2009, 20.

73 Ohio Revised Code § 2923.41.

74 Esbensen et al. 2001, 124.

75 Brotherton and Barrios 2004, 23.

CHAPTER 1. "WHY DO I HAVE TO HIDE IT?"

1 "Finna," as shorthand for "fixing to," is used like "going to."

2 Brooks 2000; Epstein 1997.

3 Anderson 1999; Matza and Sykes 1961.

4 Poteat and Espelage 2005; Smith and Smith 1998; Thurlow 2001.

5 Pascoe 2012.

6 Pharr 1997, 18.

7 Epstein 1997; McGuffey and Rich 1999; Pascoe 2012; Plummer 2001.

8 See D'Augelli, Grossman, and Starks 2006.

9 See, e.g., Bell, Weinberg, and Hammersmith 1981, from which more recent research draws. Troiden (1989) notes that once people identify as gay, lesbian, or bisexual, they reconceptualize gender-atypical behavior and feelings of difference as evidence that they were "always" gay.

10 Rosenfeld 2003; Yoshino 2002.

11 Troiden 1989.

12 E.g., Pascoe 2012.

13 See also Plummer 2001.

14 Griffin 2006; Ward 2005. For a discussion of homophobia, Black masculinity, and religious attendance, see Lemelle and Battle 2004.

15 Eighty percent of the gender-atypical gay or bisexual male youth in D'Augelli, Grossman, and Starks's (2006) study said their fathers had negative reactions to their gender atypicality.

16 See again Griffin 2006; Ward 2005; also Crichlow 2004.

17 Daley et al. 2008; McCready 2004.

18 Conerly 2001; Crichlow 2004.

19 See Lennox and Waites 2013. Interestingly, white Western religious organizations are playing pivotal roles in some African countries' criminalization of same-sex sexual conduct.

20 Rosenfeld 2003, 72.

CHAPTER 2. WHO'S THE FAG?

1 *Oxford English Dictionary* 2016.

2 Pascoe 2012, 81.

3 Chen 1998.

4 Brontsema 2004, 1.

5 Meaning to mark them as different, in order to create social distance from them.

6 See Mogul, Ritchie, and Whitlock 2011.

7 See, for example, Hennen 2008; Crichlow 2004.

8 For a discussion of how queer youth in rural areas negotiate visibility, see Gray 2009.

9 Ward 2015.

10 Herek, Gillis, and Cogan 2009, 33.

11 Ross and Rosser 1996.

12 Hamilton and Mahalik 2009.

13 Bruce, Ramirez-Valles, and Campbell 2008; Jerome and Halkitis 2009.

14 Rowen and Malcolm 2002.

15 Troiden 1989. For transgender identity formation, see Beemyn and Rankin 2011.

16 Allen and Oleson 1999; Rowen and Malcolm 2002.

17 Ross and Rosser 1996.

18 Herek, Gillis, and Cogan 2009.

19 See, for example, nohomophobes.com.

20 Yoshino 2002, 772; emphases in original.

21 *Paris Is Burning* 1990.

22 Goffman (1976) would argue that that any presentation of gender is a dramatization of the culture's idealization of masculinity or femininity, though such portrayals in vogue balls are exaggerated. See also Butler 1993; West and Zimmerman 1987.

23 For a discussion of the effects of my race and gender in the field, see the Methods Appendix.

24 Kitsuse 1980, 9.

CHAPTER 3. GAY GANGS BECOMING "KNOWN"

1 One man was a current member of a gay gang and a former member of a straight gang.

2 E.g., Lauger 2012.

3 Johnson 2007.

4 Panfil 2014b.

5 Brotherton and Barrios 2004; Decker and Curry 2000; Maxson and Whitlock 2002; Peterson, Taylor, and Esbensen 2004; Thornberry et al. 2003.

6 Weisel (2002) discusses organizational shifts of gangs and the groups that become them.

7 See also Thrasher 1927/2000.

8 To "throw shade" does not usually entail an object being thrown. "Shade" is an insider term meaning disrespect or fakeness; someone who engages in these behaviors is "throwing shade" or is being "shady."

9 Including its leader, ATL's gang was made up entirely of males, but he refers to his "gay mother" (the leader) as "she/her." I retain the feminine pronoun because it is the only pronoun he used with reference to this person. In general, it was not uncommon for research participants to use female pronouns to describe males, and they would sometimes clarify that they were describing a biological woman by using phrases such as "she's a real girl."

10 Only one of the all-gay gangs, cliques, crews, sets, etc. described by participants was missing a criterion set forth in both the Eurogang Program of Research's and the state of Ohio's definitions of a gang (see the Introduction for these definitions). Although Nate answered "yes" to the gang-screening question and described his former group as a "clique" (as many of the other gay gangs' members did), it is questionable whether his group's identity included involvement in illegal activity, based on his descriptions of their activities, all of which were legal. He may have avoided telling me about their illegal activities, or was using "clique" solely as synonym for a friendship group; regardless, he did answer affirmatively to a question with the word "gang" in it.

11 Sometimes I did feel a bit odd seeing participants trade money for drugs or arrange transactions, but it was not my job to police them. Fieldwork often means that we are let into the most private moments in research participants' lives. The only times I felt true concern was when romantic partners roughhoused with each other, and it seemed far more like a fistfight than play.

12 Just as illegal activities do in other gangs, even though the popular imagination would have us believe otherwise. For an example, see Ward 2013.

13 Reiss 1961.

14 Though see Weisberg 1985 for an exception.

15 Totten 2000; Totten 2012.

16 There is a bit of ambiguity regarding whether or not it is fully accurate to call the B.o.B. (and perhaps other "gay gangs") an all-gay gang, even though that is how the gang's members describe it. When study participants met certain individuals in the B.o.B. or grew up with them, everyone identified as gay and may still reflexively refer to themselves as gay, but some may also be on the transgender spectrum. That is, no current member seemed to be engaging in a full social and biological transition from male to female, but some may be contemplating a transition or taking the first steps. Furthermore, participants occasionally expressed confusion about someone's gender identity. For example, when commenting on a "transgender" member of the B.o.B. who beat up his little sister, Jeremiah called this person by male pronouns and remarked, "Even though you think you're a girl, you're still a boy." Or, when discussing the B.o.B., some of whose members dressed up in women's clothes to sell sex or to perform in the ballroom scene, Boss referred to their gang as a "trannies-by-night, boys-by-day type of thing," so it was unclear if these individuals identified as female. Strictly speaking, a transgender woman who is attracted to men would be considered heterosexual (GLAAD 2014), but transgender individuals may prefer to still identify as gay, to reflect their previous experiences and connection to the gay community.

17 Although this word can connote fun and parties, staying at a friend's house was necessary for some because of their unreliable sleeping or living arrangements (see also Ward 2013).

18 Intragang fights also occur in straight gangs. Former gang member and gang scholar Robert Durán (2013, 170) notes, "I had just as many fights with my own gang as I had with rivals."

19 Becoming "known" is a motivation for other groups to engage in behavior that can help create a public identity, such as gang violence (Lauger 2012) and graffiti writing (Snyder 2011).

20 Mullins, Wright, and Jacobs 2004; see also Griffiths, Yule, and Gartner 2011.

21 Drawing from Esbensen 2003.

22 Panfil 2015.

23 Weston 1997; Plummer 1995; Nelson 2013.

24 See, for example, Miller 2001.

25 Weston 1997; see also Plummer 1995.

26 Mendoza-Denton 1996, 56.

CHAPTER 4. "IN THE GAME"

1 The top-rated definition in the Urban Dictionary for "that nigga," posted by a user named "Suburban Thug," is as follows (verbatim): "That Nigga is a proper

title which refers to a man who is usually black. Often very sexy, respectable, performs well sexually, and well liked and respected by all by all. He is an OG in alot of ways but not like an ignorant hoodrat. That Nigga while civilized can whoop yo ass. That Nigga often has some sophistication. People dont fuck with That Nigga."

2 Hu and Pastor 2014; Wilson and Baker 2010.

3 Decker, Bynum, and Weisel 1998.

4 Miller 1958.

5 Totten 2000; Totten 2012.

6 See Panfil and Peterson 2015.

7 See, for example, Miller 2001; Peterson, Miller, and Esbensen 2001.

8 Klein and Maxson 2006.

9 Decker and Curry 2000; Maxson and Whitlock 2002; Peterson, Taylor, and Esbensen 2004; Thornberry et al. 2003.

10 Durán 2013; Vigil 1988. See also Crichlow 2014.

11 Brotherton and Barrios 2004.

12 Lien 2001; Miller 2001; Zatz and Portillos 2000.

13 For a review, see Klein and Maxson 2006.

14 See also van Gemert 2001; Decker 1996.

15 For examples of this in Columbus's gangs, see Huff 1989; Miller 2001. For a discussion of gang proliferation, including homegrown gangs and the less common case of gang migration, see Klein and Maxson 2006.

16 Decker 1996; Hagedorn 1988; Joe-Laidler and Hunt 1997; Miller 2001; Padilla 1992; Vigil 1988.

17 For a review, see Klein and Maxson 2006.

18 E.g., Klein 1995; Ward 2013.

19 Fleisher 1998; Joe and Chesney-Lind 1995; Wortley and Tanner 2006.

20 Battin et al. 1998; Esbensen and Huizinga 1993; Esbensen et al. 2010; Thornberry et al. 2003.

21 For a detailed description of these practices (and others) as performances of gang identity, see Garot 2010.

22 Decker 1996, 259.

23 Bjerregaard 2010; Decker 2000; Esbensen and Winfree 1998.

24 Hagedorn 1994; Padilla 1992; Taylor 1990. See also chapter 7 of this book.

25 Sánchez-Jankowski 1991, 101.

26 Esbensen and Huizinga 1993; Peterson, Taylor, and Esbensen 2004; Taylor et al. 2007; Thornberry et al. 2003.

27 Bourgois 1995; Jacobs 2000; Wright and Decker 1997.

28 Decker 1996; Decker and Van Winkle 1996; Lauger 2012.

29 See also, for example: Miller 1998; Peterson, Taylor, and Esbensen 2004; Taylor et al. 2007; Thornberry et al. 2003.

30 Rios 2011, 55.

31 Miller 2001; Miller and Brunson 2000.

32 Because both Brad's and M6's respective gangs were based primarily in prison (not public/"street" oriented) and had members of varying ages, they would fit the state of Ohio's definition of gangs, but not the Eurogang Program of Research's definition of gangs; see the Introduction for these definitions.

33 Peterson, Miller, and Esbensen 2001; Peterson and Carson 2012; Weerman 2012.

34 Miller 2001; Miller and Brunson 2000.

35 Miller 2001.

36 Kanter 1977.

37 Blalock 1967.

38 Miller 2001; Peterson, Miller, and Esbensen 2001; Peterson and Carson 2012.

39 Miller 2001.

40 Totten 2000.

41 The talk show was *Rolonda*, hosted by Rolonda Watts; the other existing scholarship is Totten 2000 and Totten 2012; and the documentary is *Homeboy*.

CHAPTER 5. HYBRID GANGS AND THOSE THAT COULD HAVE BEEN

1 See also Thrasher 1927/2000; Weisel 2002.

2 D.C. was in a straight gang and also joined by way of a sexual relationship, but he was not out to his gang and they did not know about the relationship.

3 Fleisher and Krienert 2004; Joe and Chesney-Lind 1995; Miller 2001; Zatz and Portillos 2000.

4 Durán 2013; Miller 2001; Schalet, Hunt, and Joe-Laidler 2003; Decker and Van Winkle 1996.

5 In contrast, Lauger (2012) discusses how some gang members gain status by constructing their gangs as "real" or "pure" vis-à-vis "fake" or "imitation" gangs.

6 Blau 1977.

7 Miller 2001; Peterson, Miller, and Esbensen 2001; Peterson and Carson 2012; see also Blalock 1967.

8 Gates 2011.

9 Panfil and Peterson 2015.

10 See Ward 2015 for an extensive discussion of straight men who engage in sex with other men.

11 Ibid.

CHAPTER 6. "NOT A FAG"

1 Connell 2005; Mahalik et al. 2003; Messerschmidt 1993.

2 Anderson 1999; Majors and Billson 1993.

3 Bandura et al. 1996; Matza 1964.

4 Messerschmidt 2000.

5 Anderson 1999; Ferguson 2000; Rios 2011.

6 Hochstetler, Copes, and Williams 2010; Katz 1988; Sykes and Matza 1957.

7 Presser 2003.

8 Matza and Sykes 1961.

9 See the "Summary of Participant Characteristics and Experiences" Appendix for an individualized breakdown.

10 Cobbina, Miller, and Brunson 2008; Roy 2004.

11 Campbell, Bibel, and Muncer 1985. See Garot 2010 for similar examples.

12 Sykes and Matza 1957.

13 Wells and Horney 2002.

14 Several other participants suggested that the most publicly homophobic men are the ones who try to pursue them sexually in private, similar to claims discussed in chapter 5. In those scenarios, the anti-gay harassment was exponentially more offensive, as it was used to cover up the harasser's own same-sex sexual interests.

15 Bandura 1973.

16 Kosciw et al. 2010.

17 Anderson 1999; Ferguson 2000; Rios 2011.

18 Grossman et al. 2009.

19 Herrenkohl et al. 2000.

20 See Panfil 2014b for this exchange.

21 Ferguson 2000; Rios 2011.

22 See Miller 2008 for examples of teacher non-intervention in serious instances of sexual harassment in schools, and a discussion of the conditions that structure non-intervention.

23 Anderson 1999, 10. Though see Stewart, Schreck, and Simons 2006, as well as Garot 2010, for empirical evidence to the contrary.

24 Messerschmidt 2000, 13.

25 For additional information regarding how school-based homophobic bullying and harassment contributed to participants' decisions to fight back in school and/ or join gangs, see Panfil 2014b.

26 Sociologist Curtis Jackson-Jacobs's (2014, 175) comparison of fights to athletic contests is illustrative: "The idea is not simply to injure, but to overcome the opponent's active resistance, and to do so by creative feats of athleticism under pressure."

27 Herek 2009.

28 See Panfil 2014c for this argument in further detail.

29 Totten 2000.

CHAPTER 7. "TIRED OF BEING STEREOTYPED"

1 Fagan and Freeman 1999.

2 Bourgois 1995; Fader 2013; Hagedorn 1994; Valentine 1978.

3 Jeffrey and MacDonald 2006; Rosen and Venkatesh 2008; Valentine 1978; Wright and Decker 1994; Wright and Decker 1997.

4 Rosen and Venkatesh 2008.

5 Ibid.

6 Jeffrey and MacDonald 2006.

7 Fagan and Freeman 1999.

8 Jeffrey and MacDonald 2006; Wright and Decker 1994; Wright and Decker 1997.
9 Valentine 1978.
10 Venkatesh 2008, 201.
11 Hagedorn 1994, 209.
12 Connell and Messerschmidt 2005.
13 Anderson 1999; Majors and Billson 1993.
14 Admittedly, there is some slippage here, as the boundary maintenance techniques they used to distance themselves from certain activities may muddle whether or not they were involved. The boundaries regarding transactional sex can be blurred anyway. For example, Batman denied that he had ever sold sex, but did say that were he to travel to engage in sex with someone, he welcomed receiving gas money from them. When asked whether there was a monetary transaction if they came to him and he incurred no travel expenses, he said no. Jordan also accepted gas money from casual partners for sex, but said that if not for the money offered, he probably wouldn't travel to have sex with someone.
15 See the "Summary of Participant Characteristics and Experiences" Appendix for an individualized breakdown.
16 Interestingly, Trebay (2000b) suggested that historically, some vogue houses have specialized in certain crimes that include shoplifting or credit card fraud.
17 Crystal meth ("tina") was also associated with gay men, but not discussed as much as powder cocaine.
18 Kaye 2007.
19 Kaye 2003.
20 Morse et al. 1991, 535.
21 Bimbi 2007.
22 See, for example, Fendrich et al. 2010.
23 See Mogul, Ritchie, and Whitlock 2011 for more detail.
24 West 1993.
25 Wilson 1996. Crutchfield (2014) provides an in-depth analysis of labor markets and the relationships between unemployment and crime.
26 Pager 2003.
27 See Fader 2013 for a discussion of the civics and personality tests that also face applicants.
28 American Bar Association 2013.
29 Brunson 2007; Carr, Napolitano, and Keating 2007.
30 Jeffrey and MacDonald 2006; Rosen and Venkatesh 2008; Wright and Decker 1994; Wright and Decker 1997.
31 Fagan and Freeman 1999.
32 Ohio Department of Commerce 2011.
33 Jacinto et al. 2008, 432–433.
34 E.g., Maruna 2001.
35 Hagedorn 1994.
36 Sánchez-Jankowski 1991.

37 See also Luckenbill 1986.

38 For empirical evidence, see Logan 2010.

39 See, for example, Parsons, Koken, and Bimbi 2007.

40 Juan, the other participant to do so, said he used condoms when he thought a client might be HIV-positive, but otherwise, after four or five encounters, he started to establish trust with them and would not use protection if they requested not to.

41 Morrison and Whitehead 2007, 209.

42 Anderson 1978, 214–215.

CONCLUSION

1 Conti 2015.

2 Ibid.

3 As evidenced by the growing number of collections or books on the topic, including: Ball 2016; Ball, Buist, and Woods 2014; Buist and Lenning 2016; Dwyer, Ball, and Crofts 2016; Peterson and Panfil 2014.

4 Panfil and Miller 2014.

5 Panfil 2014a.

6 Brotherton 2015. See also Crichlow 2014.

7 Brotherton 2008, 55.

METHODS APPENDIX

1 Lofland et al. 2006.

2 E.g., Fleisher 1998.

3 Heckathorn 1997.

4 Through summer 2012, I continued to conduct occasional fieldwork and seek updates, but not as regularly as during the two-year period prior.

5 My sample is different than many self-report gang samples, but is consistent with other ethnographic studies and law enforcement statistics. Self-report studies have consistently shown the peak ages of gang participation to be 14 and 15; also, a majority of youth cycle in and out of gangs within one year (Esbensen and Winfree 1998; Klein and Maxson 2006; Thornberry et al. 2003). In contrast, samples from ethnographic studies, perhaps due to the fact that they are naturalistic and do not necessarily utilize age-limited samples, show greater variation in age at gang joining, as well substantially longer periods of time in gangs (see, for example, Decker and Van Winkle 1996; Hagedorn 1988). National law enforcement statistics suggest that two-thirds of gang members are adults. Additionally, larger cities and suburban counties (which are more likely than smaller cities to have long-standing gang problems) report greater percentages of adult gang members than juvenile gang members (National Gang Center 2009). Also, because of my study criteria, the average age of my sample would never be below 18. Chapters 3, 4, and 5 contain further detail regarding participants' ages at gang joining, length of time in gangs, and differences across gang types. Relatedly, in some cases, the age of gang joining or length of time spent in the gang had to be estimated due

to slight inconsistencies or ambiguities. Often, I was able to identify these during the interview and talk through the participant's timeline with him to provide a best estimate; however, I did not immediately recognize the inconsistency in every case. I also did not always probe to find out exactly how old he was when a particular event happened, or was not always successful when I did (and instead accepted responses of a grade level or estimates such as "a couple of years ago" and then tried to work backward). For those that required a decision after the interview, I made these by reviewing each participant's narrative in its entirety and comparing his gang involvement to the ages of other life events we had discussed.

6 Centers for Disease Control and Prevention 2010.

7 Becker 1967; Taylor and Bogdan 1998; Wright and Bennett 1990.

8 It is also appropriate to mention that several participants were beginning to explore living as women or considering identifying as transgender. However, each said that their gender was male at the beginning of the interview, self-reflexively referred to themselves as a "man," a "dude," or a "boy" repeatedly throughout the interview, and self-identified as gay, with attractions to males. Because of the parameters of this book, I am not able to extensively explore their evolving gender identities and transitions.

9 The experiences of lesbian or bisexual female gang members are equally as important as gay male gang members; however, I did not have any existing connections to (let alone rapport with) lesbian gang members at the time I began data collection. Based on empirical evidence that young women's experiences in gangs differ from young men's experiences (e.g., Miller and Brunson 2000; Panfil and Peterson 2015), as well as my study's goals of exploring masculine and gay identities, a study of lesbian/bisexual gang members' experiences would likely require a different instrument, at the very least. I do plan to pursue these lines of inquiry in the future.

10 The intermediary period between childhood and adulthood is wrought with transitions and identity crises, one of which is the formation of sexual identity (e.g., Troiden 1989). It would have been ineffective to ask questions about gay identity formation and coming out processes of someone for whom these experiences were just beginning. Additionally, identity construction in adolescence can, and often does, change. Thus, by interviewing young adults whose identity development is further along, I was able to explore social identities that are salient to them, and which will likely shape their behaviors for some time. This is not to say that adults and/or individuals who have identified as gay for years will identify as gay for the rest of their lives. I acknowledge that sexual identity is fluid, and identity construction is an ongoing interactive process that changes with time and experience. To this end, several participants mused that they would eventually marry women for social reasons, but were not confident that they would be happy or could remain sexually faithful to one woman.

11 See Panfil 2013 for the interview instrument and the attribution of the questions.

12 For specific examples, especially as they relate to bridging differences in demographic characteristics, see Panfil 2015. See also Holstein and Gubrium 1995.

13 I also paid $15 for each referral, but only if the referring party arranged the interview, went to the interview location with me, and the would-be participant was eligible for the interview. I paid to honor the referring party's time and trouble, as well as his reputation, which he put on the line to vouch for me.

14 Although the interviews were transcribed verbatim, I have removed repeated words, filler phrases such as "you know," and non-lexical vocables such as "uhh" from the quotes presented in this book unless they were relevant to the quote's content (communicating hesitancy, for example).

15 For more information, see Panfil 2015.

16 Glaser and Strauss 1967; Charmaz 2006.

17 Lofland et al. 2006.

18 Over 225 hours in total.

19 Logan and Stults 2011.

20 See Panfil 2015.

21 Harding and Norberg 2005; Panfil and Miller 2015; Sprague 2005.

22 Collins 2004; Messerschmidt 1997.

23 E.g., Presser 2006.

24 Miller 2001.

25 "Lmao omg" means "Laughing my ass off, oh my God."

REFERENCES

10TV News. 2011, July 11. "Police Sweep through Park, Arresting Alleged Gang Members." www.10tv.com.

Allen, David J., and Terry Oleson. 1999. "Shame and Internalized Homophobia in Gay Men." *Journal of Homosexuality* 37(3): 33–43.

American Bar Association. 2013. "Ohio." *ABA National Inventory of Collateral Consequences of Conviction.* www.abacollateralconsequences.org/map.

Anderson, Elijah. 1978. *A Place on the Corner.* Chicago: University of Chicago Press.

Anderson, Elijah. 1999. *Code of the Street: Decency, Violence, and the Moral Life of the Inner City.* New York: W. W. Norton & Co.

Aronson, Elliot. 1992. "The Return of the Repressed: Dissonance Theory Makes a Comeback." *Psychological Inquiry* 3(4): 303–311.

Ball, Matthew. 2014. "What's Queer about Queer Criminology?" In *Handbook of LGBT Communities, Crime, and Justice*, edited by Dana Peterson and Vanessa R. Panfil, 531–555. New York: Springer.

Ball, Matthew. 2016. *Criminology and Queer Theory: Dangerous Bedfellows?* London: Palgrave Macmillan.

Ball, Matthew, Carrie L. Buist, and Jordan Blair Woods. 2014. "Introduction to the Special Issue on Queer/ing Criminology: New Directions and Frameworks." *Critical Criminology* 22(1): 1–4.

Bandura, Albert. 1973. *Aggression: A Social Learning Analysis.* Englewood Cliffs, NJ: Prentice-Hall.

Bandura, Albert, Claudio Barbaranelli, Gian Vittorio Caprara, and Concetta Pastorelli. 1996. "Mechanisms of Moral Disengagement in the Exercise of Moral Agency." *Journal of Personality and Social Psychology* 71(2): 364–374.

Battin, Sara R., Karl G. Hill, Robert D. Abbott, Richard F. Catalano, and J. David Hawkins. 1998. "The Contribution of Gang Membership to Delinquency beyond Delinquent Friends." *Criminology* 36(1): 93–116.

Becker, Howard S. 1967. "Whose Side Are We On?" *Social Problems* 14(3): 239–247.

Beemyn, Genny, and Susan Rankin. 2011. *The Lives of Transgender People.* New York: Columbia University Press.

Bell, Alan Paul, Martin S. Weinberg, and Sue Kiefer Hammersmith. 1981. *Sexual Preference: Its Development in Men and Women.* Bloomington: Indiana University Press.

Bérubé, Allen. 2001. "How Gay Stays White and What Kind of White It Stays." In *The Making and Unmaking of Whiteness*, edited by Birgit Brander Rasmussen, Eric

Klinenberg, Irene J. Nexica, and Matt Wray, 234–265. Durham, NC: Duke University Press.

Best, Amy L. 2011. "Youth Identity Formation: Contemporary Identity Work." *Sociology Compass* 5(10): 908–922.

Bimbi, David S. 2007. "Male Prostitution: Pathology, Paradigms and Progress in Research." *Journal of Homosexuality* 53(1/2): 7–35.

Bjerregaard, Beth. 2010. "Gang Membership and Drug Involvement: Untangling the Complex Relationship." *Crime & Delinquency* 56(1): 3–34.

Blalock, Hubert M. 1967. *Toward a Theory of Minority-Group Relations*. New York: John Wiley & Sons.

Blau, Peter M. 1977. *Inequality and Heterogeneity: A Primitive Theory of Social Structure*. New York: Free Press.

Blumer, Herbert. 1969. *Symbolic Interactionism: Perspective and Method*. Berkeley: University of California Press.

Bolden, Christian L. 2014. "Friendly Foes: Hybrid Gangs or Social Networking." *Group Processes & Intergroup Relations* 17(6): 730–749.

Bontempo, Daniel E., and Anthony R. D'Augelli. 2002. "Effects of At-School Victimization and Sexual Orientation on Lesbian, Gay, or Bisexual Youths' Health Risk Behavior." *Journal of Adolescent Health* 30(5): 364–374.

Bourgois, Philippe. 1995. *In Search of Respect: Selling Crack in El Barrio*. Cambridge, UK: Cambridge University Press.

Brontsema, Robin. 2004. "A Queer Revolution: Reconceptualizing the Debate over Linguistic Reclamation." *Colorado Research in Linguistics* 17(1): 1–17.

Brooks, Franklin L. 2000. "Beneath Contempt: The Mistreatment of Non-Traditional/ Gender Atypical Boys." *Journal of Gay & Lesbian Social Services* 12(1/2): 107–115.

Brotherton, David C. 2008. "Beyond Social Reproduction: Bringing Resistance Back in Gang Theory." *Theoretical Criminology* 12(1): 55–77.

Brotherton, David C. 2015. *Youth Street Gangs: A Critical Appraisal*. London: Routledge.

Brotherton, David C., and Luis Barrios. 2004. *The Almighty Latin King and Queen Nation: Street Politics and the Transformation of a New York City Gang*. New York: Columbia University Press.

Bruce, Douglas, Jesus Ramirez-Valles, and Richard T. Campbell. 2008. "Stigmatization, Substance Use, and Sexual Risk Behavior among Latino Gay and Bisexual Men and Transgender Persons." *Journal of Drug Issues* 38(1): 235–260.

Brunson, Rod K. 2007. "'Police Don't Like Black People': African-American Young Men's Accumulated Police Experiences." *Criminology & Public Policy* 6(1): 71–101.

Buist, Carrie L., and Emily Lenning. 2016. *Queer Criminology*. London: Routledge.

Butler, Judith. 1993. "Critically Queer." *GLQ: A Journal of Lesbian and Gay Studies* 1: 17–32.

Button, Deeanna M., Daniel J. O'Connell, and Roberta Gealt. 2012. "Sexual Minority Youth Victimization and Social Support: The Intersection of Sexuality, Gender, Race, and Victimization." *Journal of Homosexuality* 59(1): 18–43.

Campbell, Anne, Daniel Bibel, and Steven Muncer. 1985. "Predicting Our Own Aggression: Person, Subculture, or Situation?" *British Journal of Social Psychology* 24(3): 169–180.

Carr, Patrick J., Laura Napolitano, and Jessica Keating. 2007. "We Never Call the Cops and Here Is Why: A Qualitative Examination of Legal Cynicism in Three Philadelphia Neighborhoods." *Criminology* 42(2): 445–480.

Centers for Disease Control and Prevention. 2010. "Prevalence and Awareness of HIV Infection among Men Who Have Sex with Men: 21 Cities, United States, 2008." *Morbidity and Mortality Weekly Report* 59(37): 1201–1207.

Charmaz, Kathy. 2006. *Constructing Grounded Theory: A Practical Guide through Qualitative Analysis*. Thousand Oaks, CA: Sage Publications.

Chen, Melinda Yuen-Ching. 1998. "'I Am an Animal!' Lexical Reappropriation, Performativity, and Queer." In *Engendering Communication: Proceedings of the Fifth Berkeley Women and Language Conference*, edited by Suzanne Wertheim, Ashlee C. Bailey, and Monica Corston-Oliver, 129–140. Berkeley, CA.

CNN. 2005. "Ohio Issue 1: County Results." *America Votes 2004*. www.cnn.com.

Cobbina, Jennifer E., Jody Miller, and Rod K. Brunson. 2008. "Gender, Neighborhood Danger, and Risk-Avoidance Strategies among Urban African-American Youths." *Criminology* 46 (3): 673–709.

Collier, Richard. 1998. *Masculinities, Crime, and Criminology*. London: Sage.

Collins, Patricia Hill. 2004. *Black Sexual Politics: African Americans, Gender, and the New Racism*. New York: Routledge.

Comstock, Gary David. 1991. *Violence against Lesbians and Gay Men*. New York: Columbia University Press.

Conerly, Gregory. 2001. "Are You Black First or Are You Queer?" In *The Greatest Taboo: Homosexuality in Black Communities*, edited by Delroy Constantine-Simms, 7–23. Los Angeles: Alyson.

Connell, R. W. 2005. *Masculinities* (2nd ed.). Berkeley: University of California Press.

Connell, R. W., and James W. Messerschmidt. 2005. "Hegemonic Masculinity: Rethinking the Concept." *Gender & Society* 19(6): 829–859.

Conti, Allie. 2015, March 5. "'Check It' Is a New Documentary about America's Only All-Gay Gang." *Vice*. www.vice.com.

Cooper, Andrew. 2013. *Changing Gay Male Identities*. London: Routledge.

Copes, Heith, Andy Hochstetler, and J. Patrick Williams. 2008. "'We Weren't Like No Regular Dope Fiends': Negotiating Hustler and Crackhead Identities." *Social Problems* 55(2): 254–270.

Crichlow, Wesley. 2004. *Buller Men and Batty Bwoys: Hidden Men in Toronto and Halifax Black Communities*. Toronto: University of Toronto Press.

Crichlow, Wesley. 2014. "Weaponization and Prisonization of Toronto's Black Male Youth." *International Journal of Crime, Justice and Social Democracy* 3(3): 113–131.

Crutchfield, Robert D. 2014. *Get a Job: Labor Markets, Economic Opportunity, and Crime*. New York: New York University Press.

D'Augelli, Anthony R., Arnold H. Grossman, and Michael T. Starks. 2006. "Childhood Gender Atypicality, Victimization, and PTSD among Lesbian, Gay, and Bisexual Youth." *Journal of Interpersonal Violence* 21(11): 1462–1482.

Daley, Andrea, Steven Solomon, Peter A. Newman, and Faye Mishna. 2008. "Traversing the Margins: Intersectionalities in the Bullying of Lesbian, Gay, Bisexual and Transgender Youth." *Journal of Gay & Lesbian Social Services* 19(3/4): 9–29.

Decker, Scott H. 1996. "Collective and Normative Features of Gang Violence." *Justice Quarterly* 13(2): 243–264.

Decker, Scott H. 2000. "Legitimating Drug Use: A Note on the Impact of Gang Membership and Drug Sales on the Use of Illicit Drugs." *Justice Quarterly* 17(2): 393–410.

Decker, Scott H., Tim Bynum, and Deborah Weisel. 1998. "A Tale of Two Cities: Gangs as Organized Crime Groups." *Justice Quarterly* 15(3): 395–425.

Decker, Scott H., and G. David Curry. 2000. "Addressing Key Features of Gang Membership: Measuring the Involvement of Young Members." *Journal of Criminal Justice* 28(6): 473–482.

Decker, Scott H., and Barrik Van Winkle. 1996. *Life in the Gang: Family, Friends, and Violence*. Cambridge, UK: Cambridge University Press.

Dunn, Peter. 2012. "Men as Victims: 'Victim' Identities, Gay Identities, and Masculinities." *Journal of Interpersonal Violence* 27(17): 3442–3467.

Durán, Robert J. 2013. *Gang Life in Two Cities: An Insider's Journey*. New York: Columbia University Press.

Dwyer, Angela, Matthew Ball, and Thomas Crofts, eds. 2016. *Queering Criminology*. London: Palgrave Macmillan.

Epstein, Debbie. 1997. "'Boyz' Own Stories: Masculinities and Sexualities in Schools." *Gender and Education* 9(1): 105–115.

Equality Ohio. 2012. *Lobby Day 2012*. www.equalityohio.org.

Esbensen, Finn-Aage. 2003. *Evaluation of the Gang Resistance Education and Training (G.R.E.A.T.) Program in the United States, 1995–1999* (2nd ICPSR ver.). Ann Arbor, MI: Inter-University Consortium for Political and Social Research.

Esbensen, Finn-Aage, and David Huizinga. 1993. "Gangs, Drugs, and Delinquency in a Survey of Urban Youth." *Criminology* 31(4): 565–589.

Esbensen, Finn-Aage, Dana Peterson, Terrance J. Taylor, and Adrienne Freng. 2010. *Youth Violence: Sex and Race Differences in Offending, Victimization, and Gang Membership*. Philadelphia: Temple University Press.

Esbensen, Finn-Aage, and L. Thomas Winfree. 1998. "Race and Gender Differences between Gang and Nongang Youths: Results from a Multisite Survey." *Justice Quarterly* 15(3): 505–526.

Esbensen, Finn-Aage, L. Thomas Winfree, Jr., Ni He, and Terrance J. Taylor. 2001. "Youth Gangs and Definitional Issues: When Is a Gang a Gang, and Why Does It Matter?" *Crime and Delinquency* 47(1): 105–130.

Espelage, Dorothy L., Steven R. Aragon, Michelle Birkett, and Brian W. Koenig. 2008. "Homophobic Teasing, Psychological Outcomes, and Sexual Orientation among

High School Students: What Influence Do Parents and Schools Have?" *School Psychology Review* 37(2): 202–216.

Fader, Jamie J. 2013. *Falling Back: Incarceration and Transitions to Adulthood among Urban Youth*. New Brunswick, NJ: Rutgers University Press.

Fagan, Jeffrey, and Richard B. Freeman. 1999. "Crime and Work." *Crime & Justice: A Review of Research* 25: 225–290.

Fendrich, Michael, Mary Ellen Mackesy-Amiti, Timothy P. Johnson, and Lance M. Pollack. 2010. "Sexual Risk Behavior and Drug Use in Two Chicago Samples of Men Who Have Sex with Men: 1997 vs. 2002." *Journal of Urban Health* 87(3): 452–466.

Ferguson, Ann Arnett. 2000. *Bad Boys: Public Schools in the Making of Black Masculinity*. Ann Arbor: University of Michigan Press.

Fleisher, Mark S. 1998. *Dead End Kids: Gang Girls and the Boys They Know*. Madison: University of Wisconsin Press.

Fleisher, Mark S., and Jessie L. Krienert. 2004. "Life Course Events, Social Networks, and the Emergence of Violence among Female Gang Members." *Journal of Community Psychology* 32(5): 607–622.

Garot, Robert. 2010. *Who You Claim: Performing Gang Identity in School and on the Streets*. New York: New York University Press.

Gates, Gary J. 2011. *How Many People Are Lesbian, Gay, Bisexual, or Transgender?* Los Angeles: Williams Institute. williamsinstitute.law.ucla.edu.

GLAAD. 2014. *Media Reference Guide* (9th ed.). www.glaad.org.

Glaser, Barney G., and Anselm L. Strauss. 1967. *The Discovery of Grounded Theory: Strategies for Qualitative Research*. Chicago: Aldine.

GLSEN. 2011. *School Climate in Ohio* (Research Brief). New York: GLSEN.

Goffman, Erving. 1959. *The Presentation of Self in Everyday Life*. Garden City, NY: Doubleday.

Goffman, Erving. 1963. *Stigma: Notes on the Management of Spoiled Identity*. New York: Simon and Schuster.

Goffman, Erving. 1976. "Gender Display." *Studies in the Anthropology of Visual Communication* 3: 69–77.

Gray, Mary L. 2009. *Out in the Country: Youth, Media, and Queer Visibility in Rural America*. New York: New York University Press.

Griffin, Horace L. 2006. *Their Own Receive Them Not: African American Lesbians and Gays in Black Churches*. Cleveland, OH: Pilgrim Press.

Griffiths, Elizabeth, Carolyn Yule, and Rosemary Gartner. 2011. "Fighting over Trivial Things: Explaining the Issue of Contention in Violent Altercations." *Criminology* 49(1): 61–94.

Grindstaff, David Allen. 2006. *Rhetorical Secrets: Mapping Gay Identity and Queer Resistance in Contemporary America*. Tuscaloosa: University of Alabama Press.

Grossman, Arnold H., Adam P. Haney, Perry Edwards, Edward J. Alessi, Maya Ardon, and Tamika Jarrett Howell. 2009. "Lesbian, Gay, Bisexual and Transgender Youth Talk about Experiencing and Coping with School Violence: A Qualitative Study." *Journal of LGBT Youth* 6(1): 24–46.

Hagedorn, John M. 1988. *People and Folks: Gangs, Crime and the Underclass in a Rust-belt City*. Chicago: Lake View.

Hagedorn, John M. 1994. "Homeboys, Dope Fiends, Legits, and New Jacks." *Criminology* 32(2): 197–219.

Hagedorn, John M. 1998. "Frat Boys, Bossmen, Studs, and Gentlemen: A Typology of Gang Masculinities." In *Masculinities and Violence*, edited by Lee H. Bowker, 152–167. Thousand Oaks, CA: Sage.

Hallett, Joe. 2011, January 1. "Q & A: Mayor Michael B. Coleman." *Columbus Dispatch*: A1, A4.

Hamilton, Christopher J., and James R. Mahalik. 2009. "Minority Stress, Masculinity, and Social Norms Predicting Gay Men's Health Risk Behaviors." *Journal of Counseling Psychology* 56(1): 132–141.

Harding, Sandra, and Kathryn Norberg. 2005. "New Feminist Approaches to Social Science Methodologies: An Introduction." *Signs: Journal of Women in Culture and Society* 30 (4): 2009–2015.

Heckathorn, Douglas D. 1997. "Respondent-Driven Sampling: A New Approach to the Study of Hidden Populations." *Social Problems* 44(2): 174–199.

Hennen, Peter. 2008. *Faeries, Bears, and Leathermen: Men in Community Queering the Masculine*. Chicago: University of Chicago Press.

Herek, Gregory M. 2009. "Hate Crimes and Stigma-Related Experiences among Sexual Minority Adults in the United States: Prevalence Estimates from a National Probability Sample. *Journal of Interpersonal Violence* 24(1): 54–74.

Herek, Gregory M., and Kevin T. Berrill, eds. 1992. *Hate Crimes: Confronting Violence Against Lesbians and Gay Men*. Newbury Park, CA: Sage.

Herek, Gregory M., J. Roy Gillis, and Jeanine C. Cogan. 2009. "Internalized Stigma among Sexual Minority Adults: Insights from a Social Psychological Perspective." *Journal of Counseling Psychology* 56(1): 32–43.

Herek, Gregory M., J. Roy Gillis, Jeanine C. Cogan, and Eric K. Glunt. 1997. "Hate Crime Victimization among Lesbian, Gay, and Bisexual Adults: Prevalence, Psychological Correlates, and Methodological Issues." *Journal of Interpersonal Violence* 12(2): 195–215.

Herrenkohl, Todd I., Eugene Maguin, Karl G. Hill, J. David Hawkins, Robert D. Abbott, and Richard F. Catalano. 2000. "Developmental Risk Factors for Youth Violence." *Journal of Adolescent Health* 26(3): 176–186.

Hochstetler, Andy, Heith Copes, and J. Patrick Williams. 2010. "'That's Not Who I Am': How Offenders Commit Violent Acts and Reject Authentically Violent Selves." *Justice Quarterly* 27(4): 492–516.

Hoewischer, Travis. 2011, June. "Why Is Columbus So Gay?" *614 Magazine* 27: 48–54.

Holstein, James A., and Jaber F. Gubrium. 1995. *The Active Interview*. Thousand Oaks, CA: Sage.

Homeboy. 2011. Directed by Dino Dinco. United States: Homeboy Films. Motion Picture.

Hu, Winnie, and Kate Pastor. 2014, February 20. "14-Year Term for Leader in Bronx Antigay Attack." *New York Times*. www.nytimes.com.

Huff, C. Ronald. 1989. "Youth Gangs and Public Policy." *Crime & Delinquency* 35(4): 524–537.

Ingraham, Chrys. 1994. "The Heterosexual Imaginary: Feminist Sociology and Theories of Gender." *Sociological Theory* 12(2): 203–219.

Island, David, and Patrick Letellier. 1991. *Men Who Beat the Men Who Love Them: Battered Gay Men and Domestic Violence*. Binghamton, NY: Harrington Park Press.

Jacinto, Camille, Micheline Duterte, Paloma Sales, and Sheigla Murphy. 2008. "'I'm Not a Real Dealer': The Identity Process of Ecstasy Sellers." *Journal of Drug Issues* 38(2): 419–444.

Jackson-Jacobs, Curtis. 2014. "Competitive Violence and the Micro-Politics of the Fight Label." *Sociological Review* 62(2): 166–186.

Jacobs, Bruce A. 2000. *Robbing Drug Dealers: Violence beyond the Law*. New York: Aldine.

Jeffrey, Leslie Ann, and Gayle MacDonald. 2006. "'It's the Money, Honey': The Economy of Sex Work in the Maritimes." *Canadian Review of Sociology* 43(3): 313–327.

Jerome, Roy C., and Perry N. Halkitis. 2009. "Stigmatization, Stress, and the Search for Belonging in Black Men Who Have Sex With Men Who Use Methamphetamine." *Journal of Black Psychology* 35(3): 343–365.

Joe, Karen A., and Meda Chesney-Lind. 1995. "'Just Every Mother's Angel': An Analysis of Gender and Ethnic Variations in Youth Gang Membership." *Gender & Society* 9(4): 408–431.

Joe-Laidler, Karen A., and Geoffrey Hunt. 1997. "Violence and Social Organization in Female Gangs." *Social Justice* 24(4): 148–169.

Johnson, Dominique. 2007. "Taking Over the School: Student Gangs as a Strategy for Dealing with Homophobic Bullying in an Urban Public School District." *Journal of Gay & Lesbian Social Services* 19(3/4): 87–104.

Kann, Laura, Emily O'Malley Olsen, Tim McManus, Steve Kinchen, David Chyen, William A. Harris, and Howell Wechsler. 2011. *Sexual Identity, Sex of Sexual Contacts, and Health-Risk Behaviors among Students in Grades 9–12: Youth Risk Behavior Surveillance, Selected Sites, United States, 2001–2009*. Atlanta, GA: U.S. Centers for Disease Control and Prevention.

Kanter, Rosabeth Moss. 1977. "Some Effects of Proportions on Group Life: Skewed Sex Ratios and Responses to Token Women." *American Journal of Sociology* 82(5): 965–990.

Katz, Jack. 1988. *Seductions of Crime: Moral and Sensual Attractions in Doing Evil*. New York: Basic Books.

Kaye, Kerwin. 2003. "Male Prostitution in the Twentieth Century: Pseudohomosexuals, Hoodlum Homosexuals, and Exploited Teens." *Journal of Homosexuality* 46(1): 1–77.

Kaye, Kerwin. 2007. "Sex and the Unspoken in Male Street Prostitution." *Journal of Homosexuality* 53(1/2): 37–73.

Kitsuse, John I. 1980. "Coming Out All Over: Deviants and the Politics of Social Problems." *Social Problems* 28(1): 1–13.

Klein, Malcolm W. 1995. *The American Street Gang: Its Nature, Prevalence, and Control.* Oxford: Oxford University Press.

Klein, Malcolm W., and Cheryl L. Maxson. 2006. *Street Gang Patterns and Policies.* New York: Oxford University Press.

Kosciw, Joseph G., Emily A. Greytak, Elizabeth M. Diaz, and Mark J. Bartkiewicz. 2010. *The 2009 National School Climate Survey: The Experiences of Lesbian, Gay, Bisexual and Transgender Youth in Our Nation's Schools.* New York: GLSEN.

Lamont, Michèle, and Virág Molnár. 2002. "The Study of Boundaries in the Social Sciences." *Annual Review of Sociology* 28: 167–195.

Lauger, Timothy R. 2012. *Real Gangstas: Legitimacy, Reputation, and Violence in the Intergang Environment.* New Brunswick, NJ: Rutgers University Press.

Lemelle, Anthony J., Jr., and Juan Battle. 2004. "Black Masculinity Matters in Attitudes toward Gay Males." *Journal of Homosexuality* 47(1): 39–51.

Lennox, Corinne, and Matthew Waites, eds. 2013. *Human Rights, Sexual Orientation and Gender Identity in the Commonwealth: Struggles for Decriminalisation and Change.* London: Human Rights Consortium, Institute of Commonwealth Studies.

Lewin, Ellen. 2009. *Gay Fatherhood: Narratives of Family and Citizenship in America.* Chicago: University of Chicago Press.

Lien, Inger-Lise. 2001. "The Concept of Honor, Conflict and Violent Behavior among Youths in Oslo." In *The Eurogang Paradox: Street Gangs and Youth Groups in the U.S. and Europe,* edited by Malcolm W. Klein, Hans-Jürgen Kerner, Cheryl L. Maxson, and Elmar G. M. Weitekamp, 165–174. Dordrecht, Germany: Kluwer Academic Publishers.

Lofland, John, David Snow, Leon Anderson, and Lyn H. Lofland. 2006. *Analyzing Social Settings: A Guide to Qualitative Observation and Analysis* (4th ed.). Belmont, CA: Wadsworth/Thomson.

Logan, John R., and Brian J. Stults. 2011. *The Persistence of Segregation in the Metropolis: New Findings from the 2010 Census.* Census Brief prepared for Project US2010. www.brown.edu.

Logan, Trevon D. 2010. "Personal Characteristics, Sexual Behaviors, and Male Sex Work: A Quantitative Approach." *American Sociological Review* 75(5): 679–704.

Luckenbill, David F. 1986. "Deviant Career Mobility: The Case of Male Prostitutes." *Social Problems* 33(4): 283–296.

Mahalik, James R., Benjamin D. Locke, Larry H. Ludlow, Matthew A. Diemer, Ryan P. J. Scott, Michael Gottfried, and Gary Freitas. 2003. "Development of the Conformity to Masculine Norms Inventory." *Psychology of Men and Masculinity* 4(1): 3–25.

Majors, Richard, and Janet Mancini Billson. 1993. *Cool Pose: The Dilemmas of Black Manhood in America.* New York: Touchstone.

Maruna, Shadd. 2001. *Making Good: How Convicts Reform and Rebuild Their Lives.* Washington, DC: American Psychological Association.

Matza, David. 1964. *Delinquency and Drift.* New York: Wiley and Sons.

Matza, David, and Gresham M. Sykes. 1961. "Juvenile Delinquency and Subterranean Values." *American Sociological Review* 26(5): 712–719.

Maxson, Cheryl, and Monica L. Whitlock. 2002. "Joining the Gang: Gender Differences in Risk Factors for Gang Membership." In *Gangs in America* (3rd ed.), edited by C. Ronald Huff, 19–36. Thousand Oaks, CA: Sage Publications.

McAdams, Dan P. 1993. *The Stories We Live By: Personal Myths and the Making of the Self.* New York: Guilford Press.

McCready, Lance Trevor. 2004. "Some Challenges Facing Queer Youth Programs in Urban High Schools: Racial Segregation and De-Normalizing Whiteness." *Journal of Gay & Lesbian Issues in Education* 1(3): 37–51.

McGuffey, C. Shawn, and B. Lindsay Rich. 1999. "Playing in the Gender Transgression Zone: Race, Class, and Hegemonic Masculinity in Middle Childhood." *Gender & Society* 13(5): 608–627.

Mendoza-Denton, Norma. 1996. "'Muy Macha': Gender and Ideology in Gang-Girls' Discourse about Makeup." *Ethnos* 61(1/2): 47–63.

Messerschmidt, James W. 1993. *Masculinities and Crime: Critique and Reconceptualization of Theory.* Lanham, MD: Rowman & Littlefield.

Messerschmidt, James W. 1997. *Crime as Structured Action: Gender, Race, Class, and Crime in the Making.* Thousand Oaks, CA: Sage Publications.

Messerschmidt, James W. 2000. *Nine Lives: Adolescent Masculinities, the Body, and Violence.* Boulder, CO: Westview.

Miller, Jody. 1998. "Up It Up: Gender and the Accomplishment of Street Robbery." *Criminology* 36(1): 37–66.

Miller, Jody. 2001. *One of the Guys: Girls, Gangs, and Gender.* New York: Oxford University Press.

Miller, Jody. 2002. "The Strengths and Limits of 'Doing Gender' for Understanding Street Crime." *Theoretical Criminology* 6(4): 433–460.

Miller, Jody. 2008. *Getting Played: African-American Girls, Urban Inequality, and Gendered Violence.* New York: New York University Press.

Miller, Jody, and Rod K. Brunson. 2000. "Gender Dynamics in Youth Gangs: A Comparison of Males' and Females' Accounts." *Justice Quarterly* 17(3): 419–448.

Miller, Walter B. 1958. "Lower Class Culture as a Generating Milieu of Gang Delinquency." *Journal of Social Issues* 14(3): 5–19.

Mills, C. Wright. 1940. "Situated Actions and Vocabularies of Motive." *American Sociological Review* 5(6): 904–913.

Mogul, Joey L., Andrea J. Ritchie, and Kay Whitlock. 2011. *Queer (In)Justice: The Criminalization of LGBT People in the United States.* Boston: Beacon Press.

Morrison, Todd G., and Bruce W. Whitehead. 2007. "'Nobody's Ever Going to Make a Fag *Pretty Woman*': Stigma Awareness and the Putative Effects of Stigma among a Sample of Canadian Male Sex Workers." *Journal of Homosexuality* 53(1): 201–217.

Morse, Edward V., Patricia M. Simon, Howard J. Osofsky, Paul M. Balson, and H. Richard Gaumer. 1991. "The Male Street Prostitute: A Vector for Transmission of HIV Infection into the Heterosexual World." *Social Science & Medicine* 32(5): 535–539.

Mullins, Christopher W., Richard Wright, and Bruce A. Jacobs. 2004. "Gender, Streetlife and Criminal Retaliation." *Criminology* 42(4): 911–940.

National Gang Center. 2009. *National Youth Gang Center Survey Analysis*. www.nationalgangcenter.gov.

Nelson, Margaret K. 2013. "Fictive Kin, Families We Choose, and Voluntary Kin: What Does the Discourse Tell Us?" *Journal of Family Theory & Review* 5(4): 259–281.

Ohio Department of Commerce. 2011. "2011 Minimum Wage." Retrieved from www. mainsourcebank.com.

Ohio Revised Code. 2007. *Criminal Gang Definitions*. § 2923.41.

Oxford English Dictionary. 2016. "Faggot." www.oed.com.

Padilla, Felix M. 1992. *The Gang as an American Enterprise*. New Brunswick, NJ: Rutgers University Press.

Pager, Devah. 2003. "The Mark of a Criminal Record." *American Journal of Sociology* 108(5): 937–975.

Panfil, Vanessa R. 2013. *Socially Situated Identities of Gay Gang- and Crime-Involved Men*. Doctoral Dissertation, State University of New York at Albany.

Panfil, Vanessa R. 2014a. "Better Left Unsaid? The Role of Agency in Queer Criminological Research." *Critical Criminology* 22(1): 99–111.

Panfil, Vanessa R. 2014b. "Gay Gang- and Crime-Involved Men's Experiences with Homophobic Bullying and Harassment in Schools." *Journal of Crime and Justice* 37(1): 79–103.

Panfil, Vanessa R. 2014c. "'I Will Fight You Like I'm Straight': Gay Gang- and Crime-Involved Men's Participation in Violence." In *Handbook of LGBT Communities, Crime, and Justice*, edited by Dana Peterson and Vanessa R. Panfil, 121–145. New York: Springer.

Panfil, Vanessa R. 2015. "Queer Anomalies? Overcoming Assumptions in Criminological Research with Gay Men." In *Qualitative Research in Criminology (Advances in Criminological Theory, Vol. 20)*, edited by Jody Miller and Wilson R. Palacios, 169–189. New Brunswick, NJ: Transaction Publishers.

Panfil, Vanessa R., and Jody Miller. 2014. "Beyond the Straight and Narrow: The Import of Queer Criminology for Criminology and Criminal Justice." *Criminologist* 39(4): 1–8.

Panfil, Vanessa R., and Jody Miller. 2015. "Feminist and Queer Perspectives on Qualitative Methods." In *Routledge Handbook of Qualitative Criminology*, edited by Heith Copes and J. Mitchell Miller, 32–48. New York: Routledge.

Panfil, Vanessa R., and Dana Peterson. 2015. "Gender, Sexuality, and Gangs: Re-Envisioning Diversity." In *The Handbook of Gangs*, edited by Scott H. Decker and David C. Pyrooz, 208–234. West Sussex, UK: John Wiley & Sons.

Paris Is Burning. 1990. Directed by Jennie Livingston. United States: Off White Productions. Motion Picture.

Parsons, Jeffrey T., Juline A. Koken, and David S. Bimbi. 2007. "Looking beyond HIV: Eliciting Individual and Community Needs of Male Internet Escorts." *Journal of Homosexuality* 53(1/2): 219–240.

Pascoe, C. J. 2012. *Dude, You're a Fag: Masculinity and Sexuality in High School*. Berkeley: University of California Press.

Peterson, Dana, and Dena C. Carson. 2012. "The Sex Composition of Groups and Youths' Delinquency: A Comparison of Gang and Nongang Peer Groups." In *Youth Gangs in International Perspective: Tales from the Eurogang Program of Research*, edited by Finn-Aage Esbensen and Cheryl L. Maxson, 189–210. New York: Springer.

Peterson, Dana, Jody Miller, and Finn-Aage Esbensen. 2001. "The Impact of Sex Composition on Gangs and Gang Member Delinquency." *Criminology* 39(2): 411–440.

Peterson, Dana, and Vanessa R. Panfil, eds. 2014. *Handbook of LGBT Communities, Crime, and Justice*. New York: Springer.

Peterson, Dana, Terrance J. Taylor, and Finn-Aage Esbensen. 2004. "Gang Membership and Violent Victimization." *Justice Quarterly* 21(4): 793–815.

Pettiway, Leon E. 1996. *Honey, Honey, Miss Thang: Being Black, Gay, and on the Streets*. Philadelphia: Temple University Press.

Pharr, Suzanne. 1997. *Homophobia: A Weapon of Sexism* (expanded ed.). Berkeley, CA: Chardon Press.

Plummer, David C. 2001. "The Quest for Modern Manhood: Masculine Stereotypes, Peer Culture and the Social Significance of Homophobia." *Journal of Adolescence* 24(1): 15–23.

Plummer, Ken. 1995. *Telling Sexual Stories: Power, Change and Social Worlds*. London: Routledge.

Poteat, V. Paul, and Dorothy L. Espelage. 2005. "Exploring the Relation between Bullying and Homophobic Verbal Content: The Homophobic Content Agent Target (HCAT) Scale." *Violence and Victims* 20(5): 513–528.

Presser, Lois. 2003. "Remorse and Neutralization among Violent Male Offenders." *Justice Quarterly* 20(4): 801–825.

Presser, Lois. 2006. "'I'll Come Back and Stalk You': Contradictions of Advocacy and Research for Women Criminologists." *Women & Criminal Justice* 17(4): 19–36.

Presser, Lois. 2008. *Been a Heavy Life: Stories of Violent Men*. Urbana: University of Illinois Press.

Queer Nation. 1990. *History Is a Weapon: The Queer Nation Manifesto*. www.history isaweapon.com.

Reiss, Albert. J., Jr. 1961. "The Social Integration of Queers and Peers." *Social Problems* 9(2): 102–120.

Renzetti, Claire M. 1992. *Violent Betrayal: Partner Abuse in Lesbian Relationships*. Newbury Park, CA: Sage.

Resnick, Eric. 2007, May 27. "The Second Lobby Day Focuses on Specific Items." *Gay People's Chronicle*. www.gaypeopleschronicle.com.

Richards, Jennifer Smith. 2014, May 22. "Columbus' Population Keeps Rising." *Columbus Dispatch*. www.dispatch.com.

Rios, Victor M. 2011. *Punished: Policing the Lives of Black and Latino Boys*. New York: New York University Press.

Rosen, Eva, and Sudhir Alladi Venkatesh. 2008. "A 'Perversion' of Choice: Sex Work Offers *Just Enough* in Chicago's Urban Ghetto." *Journal of Contemporary Ethnography* 37(4): 417–441.

Rosenfeld, Dana. 2003. *The Changing of the Guard: Lesbian and Gay Elders, Identity, and Social Change*. Philadelphia: Temple University Press.

Ross, Michael W., and B. R. Simon Rosser. 1996. "Measurement and Correlates of Internalized Homophobia: A Factor Analytic Study." *Journal of Clinical Psychology* 52(1): 15–21.

Rowen, Christopher J., and James P. Malcolm. 2002. "Correlates of Internalized Homophobia and Homosexual Identity Formation in a Sample of Gay Men." *Journal of Homosexuality* 43(2): 77–92.

Roy, Kevin. 2004. "Three-Block Fathers: Spatial Perceptions and Kin-Work in Low-Income African American Neighborhoods." *Social Problems* 51(4): 528–548.

Russell, Stephen T., Brian T. Franz, and Anne K. Driscoll. 2001. "Same-Sex Romantic Attraction and Experiences of Violence in Adolescence." *American Journal of Public Health* 91(6): 903–906.

Sánchez-Jankowski, Martín. 1991. *Islands in the Street: Gangs and American Urban Society*. Berkeley: University of California Press.

Schalet, Amy, Geoffrey Hunt, and Karen Joe-Laidler. 2003. "Respectability and Autonomy: The Articulation and Meaning of Sexuality among the Girls in the Gang." *Journal of Contemporary Ethnography* 32(1): 108–143.

Scott, Marvin B., and Stanford M. Lyman. 1968. "Accounts." *American Sociological Review* 33(1): 46–62.

Smith, George W., and Dorothy E. Smith. 1998. "The Ideology of 'Fag': The School Experience of Gay Students." *Sociological Quarterly* 39(2): 309–335.

Snow, David A., and Leon Anderson. 1987. "Identity Work among the Homeless: The Verbal Construction and Avowal of Personal Identities." *American Journal of Sociology* 92(6): 1336–1371.

Snyder, Gregory J. 2011. *Graffiti Lives: Beyond the Tag in New York's Urban Underground*. New York: New York University Press.

Spergel, Irving A., and G. David Curry. 1990. "Strategies and Perceived Agency Effectiveness in Dealing with the Youth Gang Problem." In *Gangs in America*, edited by C. Ronald Huff, 288–309. Newbury Park, CA: Sage.

Sprague, Joey. 2005. *Feminist Methodologies for Critical Researchers: Bridging Differences*. Walnut Creek, CA: AltaMira Press.

Starbuck, David, James C. Howell, and Donna J. Lindquist. 2001. "Hybrid and Other Modern Gangs." *Juvenile Justice Bulletin*. Washington, DC: U.S. Department of Justice.

Stewart, Eric A., Christopher J. Schreck, and Ronald L. Simons. 2006. "'I Ain't Gonna Let No One Disrespect Me': Does the Code of the Street Reduce or Increase Violent Victimization among African American Adolescents?" *Journal of Research in Crime and Delinquency* 43(4): 427–458.

Sykes, Gresham M., and David Matza. 1957. "Techniques of Neutralization: A Theory of Delinquency." *American Sociological Review* 22(6): 664–670.

Taylor, Carl S. 1990. *Dangerous Society*. East Lansing: Michigan State University Press.

Taylor, Steven J., and Robert Bogdan. 1998. *Introduction to Qualitative Research Methods* (3rd ed.). New York: John Wiley & Sons.

Taylor, Terrance J., Dana Peterson, Finn-Aage Esbensen, and Adrienne Freng. 2007. "Gang Membership as a Risk Factor for Adolescent Violent Victimization." *Journal of Research in Crime and Delinquency* 44(4): 351–380.

Thornberry, Terence P., Marvin D. Krohn, Alan J. Lizotte, Carolyn A. Smith, and Kimberly Tobin. 2003. *Gangs and Delinquency in Developmental Perspective*. Cambridge, UK: Cambridge University Press.

Thrasher, Frederic M. 1927/2000. *The Gang: A Study of 1,313 Gangs in Chicago*. Chicago: New Chicago School Press.

Thurlow, Crispin. 2001. "Naming the 'Outsider Within': Homophobic Pejoratives and the Verbal Abuse of Lesbian, Gay and Bisexual High-School Pupils." *Journal of Adolescence* 24(1): 25–38.

Totten, Mark D. 2000. *Guys, Gangs, and Girlfriend Abuse*. Peterborough, ON: Broadview.

Totten, Mark. 2012. "Gays in the Gang." *Journal of Gang Research* 19(2): 1–24.

Trebay, Guy. 2000a, February 1. "Homo Thugz Blow Up the Spot: A Gay Hip-Hop Scene Rises in the Bronx." *Village Voice*. www.villagevoice.com.

Trebay, Guy. 2000b, January 11. "Legends of the Ball: Paris Is Still Burning." *Village Voice*. www.villagevoice.com.

Troiden, Richard R. 1989. "The Formation of Homosexual Identities." *Journal of Homosexuality* 17(1/2): 43–73.

Valentine, Bettylou. 1978. *Hustling and Other Hard Work: Life Styles in the Ghetto*. New York: Free Press.

van Gemert, Frank. 2001. "Crips in Orange: Gangs and Groups in the Netherlands." In *The Eurogang Paradox: Street Gangs and Youth Groups in the U.S. and Europe*, edited by Malcolm W. Klein, Hans-Jürgen Kerner, Cheryl L. Maxson, and Elmar G. M. Weitekamp, 145–152. Dordrecht, Germany: Kluwer Academic Publishers.

Venkatesh, Sudhir. 2008. "Reply to Critics." *Qualitative Sociology* 31(2): 199–202.

Vigil, James Diego. 1988. *Barrio Gangs: Street Life and Identity in Southern California*. Austin: University of Texas Press.

Ward, Elijah G. 2005. "Homophobia, Hypermasculinity and the US Black Church." *Culture, Health & Sexuality* 7(5): 493–504.

Ward, Jane. 2015. *Not Gay: Sex between Straight White Men*. New York: New York University Press.

Ward, T. W. 2013. *Gangsters without Borders: An Ethnography of a Salvadoran Street Gang*. New York: Oxford University Press.

Weerman, Frank M. 2012. "Are the Correlates and Effects of Gang Membership Sex-Specific? Troublesome Youth Groups and Delinquency among Dutch Girls." In

Youth Gangs in International Perspective: Tales from the Eurogang Program of Research, edited by Finn-Aage Esbensen and Cheryl L. Maxson, 271–289. New York: Springer.

Weerman, Frank M., Cheryl L. Maxson, Finn-Aage Esbensen, Judith Aldridge, Juanjo Medina, and Frank van Gemert. 2009. *Eurogang Program Manual: Background, Development, and Use of the Eurogang Instruments in Multi-Site, Multi-Method Comparative Research*. Eurogang Program. www.umsl.edu.

Weisberg, D. Kelly. 1985. *Children of the Night: A Study of Adolescent Prostitution*. Lexington, MA: Lexington.

Weisel, Deborah Lamm. 2002. *Contemporary Gangs: An Organizational Analysis*. New York: LBF Scholarly Publishing.

Wells, William, and Julie Horney. 2002. "Weapon Effects and Individual Intent to Do Harm: Influences on the Escalation of Violence." *Criminology* 40(2): 265–296.

West, Candace, and Don H. Zimmerman. 1987. "Doing Gender." *Gender & Society* 1(2): 125–151.

West, Cornel. 1993. *Race Matters*. Boston: Beacon Press.

Weston, Kath. 1997. *Families We Choose: Lesbians, Gays, Kinship*. New York: Columbia University Press.

Wilson, Michael, and Al Baker. 2010, October 8. "Lured into a Trap, Then Tortured for Being Gay." *New York Times*. www.nytimes.com.

Wilson, William Julius. 1996. *When Work Disappears: The World of the New Urban Poor*. New York: Knopf.

Woods, Jordan Blair. 2014. "'Queering Criminology': Overview of the State of the Field." In *Handbook of LGBT Communities, Crime, and Justice*, edited by Dana Peterson and Vanessa R. Panfil, 15–41. New York: Springer.

Wortley, Scot, and Julian Tanner. 2006. "Immigration, Social Disadvantage, and Urban Youth Gangs: Results of a Toronto-Area Survey." *Canadian Journal of Urban Research* 15(2): 18–37.

Wright, Richard, and Trevor Bennett. 1990. "Exploring the Offender's Perspective: Observing and Interviewing Criminals." In *Measurement Issues in Criminology*, edited by Kimberly L. Kempf, 138–151. New York: Springer-Verlag.

Wright, Richard T., and Scott H. Decker. 1994. *Burglars on the Job: Streetlife and Residential Break-ins*. Boston: Northeastern University Press.

Wright, Richard T., and Scott H. Decker. 1997. *Armed Robbers in Action: Stickups and Street Culture*. Boston: Northeastern University Press.

Yoshino, Kenji. 2002. "Covering." *Yale Law Journal* 111(4): 769–939.

Zatz, Marjorie S., and Edward L. Portillos. 2000. "Voices from the Barrio: Chicano/a Gangs, Families, and Communities." *Criminology* 38(2): 369–402.

INDEX

"acting gay," 11, 52–54, 55–56, 102, 172, 189, 254n55
agency, of gay men, 7–9, 229
American Dream, 198
Anderson, Elijah, 5–6, 187, 223
anti-equality movement, 229
anti-gay epithets. *See* fag/faggot; punk; queer/LGBTQ; sissy
anti-gay harassment: as motive for fighting, 70, 87–88, 106, 165–166; avoidance of, 55, 78, 169–174; by closeted men, 88, 149, 153–155, 157, 261n14; upon gang leaving, 128, 225, 231. *See also* anti-gay epithets; bullying in schools; fighting back
anti-violence task forces of Columbus, 236

Backpage, 217
Bandura, Albert, 183
banjee, 90; banjee realness, 65
Barrios, Luis, 16
"being a man," questions about, 13
Bérubé, Allen, 4
Best, Amy, 10
bias crime victimization, literature on, 4, 9, 52; likelihood of, 192
bisexuality, of study participants, 2, 7, 12, 31, 33, 34, 58, 82, 109, 124–125, 135, 147, 159, 248, 254n55
Black Gay Chat, 217
Black Lives Matter movement, 231
Blalock, Hubert, 134, 146
Blau, Peter, 146

boundaries: between acceptable and unacceptable behavior for gay men, 5, 49–59, 62, 69–70, 191, 196–197, 226, 232; between acceptable and unacceptable illicit work, 196–197, 211–222, 226; between gangs and other group types, 103, 142, 230; between straight and gay gangs, 139; in neighborhoods, 118, 170–171; theoretical and disciplinary, 17, 193, 227–229, 230, 232
boundary maintenance: as concept, 10–11, 222–223; to create social distance, 11, 155, 222–223, 256n5, 262n14; in meaning systems, 11–12, 16–17, 226
Boys of Bang, aka the B.o.B. (gay gang), as family, 103; characteristics of, 74–75; formation of, 77–78; possible transgender members of, 258n16; rivalry with the Royal Family, 89; reputation for violence, 74, 89–94, 101
Brontsema, Robin, 51
Brotherton, David, 16, 230
bullying in schools: based on LGBTQ identity, xi, 4, 8–9, 78, 168, 185–188, 261n25; teacher non-intervention in, 185, 186–187, 188. *See also* fighting back: building a reputation for

Certificate of Confidentiality, 242
Check It: documentary, 225; gang of same name, 225
chosen families, 105; gang get-together as family reunions, 83; gay or hybrid gangs as, 82, 98–107, 143, 231

ABOUT THE AUTHOR

Vanessa R. Panfil is Assistant Professor in the Department of Sociology and Criminal Justice at Old Dominion University. She is the co-editor of the *Handbook of LGBT Communities, Crime, and Justice*.

CPSIA information can be obtained
at www.ICGtesting.com
Printed in the USA
LVOW03*2315130218
566521LV00001B/2/P